Around the Roof of the World

Portrait of Nina Shoumatoff. (*Charcoal drawing by Mstislav Dobujinsky.*)

Around the Roof
of the World

Edited by
NICHOLAS AND NINA SHOUMATOFF

Ann Arbor

THE UNIVERSITY OF MICHIGAN PRESS

Copyright © by the University of Michigan 1996
All rights reserved
Published in the United States of America by
The University of Michigan Press
Manufactured in the United States of America
⊗ Printed on acid-free paper

1999   1998   1997   1996   4   3   2   1

A CIP catalog record for this book is available from the British Library.

Library of Congress Cataloging-in-Publication Data

Around the roof of the world / edited by Nicholas and Nina Shoumatoff.
    p. cm.
  Includes bibliographical references and index.
  ISBN 0-472-10741-0 (hc : alk. paper)
  1. Asia, Central—Description and travel.   I. Shoumatoff,
Nicholas.   II. Shoumatoff, Nina.
DS327.8.A76   1996
958—dc20   96-24435
                                                                  CIP

To Nina, a lovely mountain muse, whose laughter graced the heights of Central Asia, in her love for the wordless poetry of its nature and people's lives.

For the Khan of This
Yurt from his 1ST
wife ....
for my husband -
Nicholas- to remind you
of all the beauties we
have seen together,
Nina -

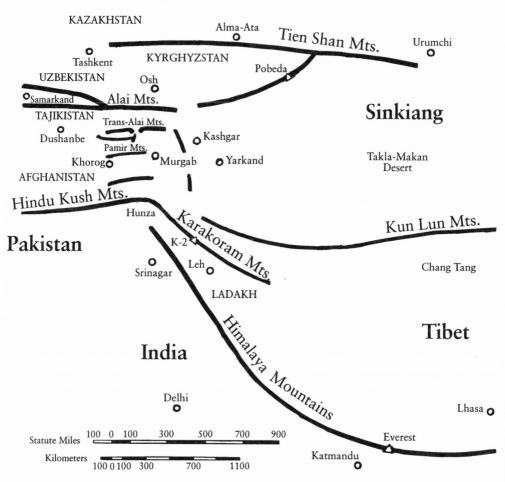

Great Steppes

KAZAKHSTAN

Alma-Ata

Tien Shan Mts.

Urumchi

Tashkent

KYRGHYZSTAN

UZBEKISTAN

Osh

Pobeda

Samarkand

Alai Mts.

Sinkiang

TAJIKISTAN

Trans-Alai Mts.

Dushanbe

Kashgar

Takla-Makan
Desert

Pamir Mts.

Khorog

Murgab

Yarkand

AFGHANISTAN

Hindu Kush Mts.

Hunza

Kun Lun Mts.

Pakistan

K-2

Karakoram Mts.

Srinagar

Leh

Chang Tang

LADAKH

Tibet

India

Himalaya Mountains

Delhi

Lhasa

Statute Miles 100 0 100   300   500   700   900

Kilometers

Everest

100 0 100   300   700   1100

Katmandu

Major mountain ranges and towns of Central Asia

Preface

The global significance of Asia's immense interior is reemerging. We offer a diversified panorama of that region but with little concern for its current politics or economics. Our interest is in its more fundamental elements of nature and ancient cultures, especially in its remarkable uplands. It is an awesomely attractive land of adventure.

From Russia, the United States and Austria, eight eminent explorers, personally known to us, have contributed twenty of the twenty-three chapters in this book. To them we are especially thankful for their assistance, friendship and inspiration. Their names are Andrey Avinoff, Alexandre Iacovleff, Edward Murray, Heinrich Harrer, John Clark, Vladimir Ratzek, Okmir Agakhanyantz and Anatoly Ovtchinnikov. The first two of these, both outstanding artists, have also contributed to the illustrations. On the second of our expeditions to Central Asia, we attended International Mountaineering Camps, one in the Kyrghyz and two in the Tajik parts of the high Pamir, all three under the technical direction of Dr. Ovtchinnikov. On the five occasions when we met Dr. Agakhanyantz in various parts of the former USSR and through frequent correspondence, he has helped us greatly with our book.

In the pleasant company of our neighbor Patricia Keesee of Mount Kisco, New York, and Robert Hebb of the New York Botanical Garden, our first Central Asian expedition was a walking tour through the mountains of the Kazakh, Kyrghyz, Uzbek and Tajik republics. To our many hosts in the unmourned former USSR and elsewhere in the course of this work, we express our thanks for their warm hospitality. We include shorter passages from two intrepid women explorers—Fanny Bullock Workman and Alexandra David-Neel—and from other personalities associated with Central Asia. Sixteen of the chapters are translated by us from the Russian or French and were not previously available in English. Talented and extensive editorial assistance during development of the manuscript was given to us by Zoric Shoumatoff Ward, Henry Williams and Benjamin Clark. Colin Day, director of the University of Michigan Press, made possible the publication of our book through his enthusiastic encouragement and in his role as its editor. To all of those mentioned, we are deeply grateful.

We most gratefully acknowledge the generous grant received from the Carnegie Museum of Natural History toward the publication of this book. The permissions from the following are also gratefully acknowledged: from the University of Pittsburgh, to include the text and drawings by Dr. Andrey Avinoff; from the National Geographic Society to include the text by Dr. Edward S. Murray; from Professor Heinrich Harrer and The Putnam Publishing Group to include the text by Professor Harrer; from HarperCollins Publishers to include the text by Dr. John Clark; and from Professor Okmir E. Agakhanyantz, Professor Dr. Anatoly G. Ovtchinnikov, and the family of Gold Medalist of the Russian Geographical Society Vladimir Y. Ratzek, to include their respective texts. We are also thankful to Mr. and Mrs. Benjamin S. Clark for making available the text and artwork by Alexandre Iacovleff.

A Note on the Text

Chapters 2 through 21 are by the contributors identified in the preface, in the table of contents and in the chapter headings, from sources in the bibliography, and with chapter titles generally differing from those in the cited sources. Chapters 2, 4, 5 and 6 are from English originals, while chapters 3, 18 and 20 are translated from the French and the other thirteen contributed chapters are translated from the Russian. These translations have not been published previously and are all by Nicholas and Nina Shoumatoff. Chapters 2, 3, 18 and 20 are the complete cited articles, while the other sixteen contributed chapters are selections from the indicated sources. All other parts of the text, including chapters 1, 22 and 23, the numbered notes for each chapter and the introductory notes for the contributed chapters, are the work of Nicholas and Nina Shoumatoff and have not been published previously. The illustrations are by Nicholas and Nina Shoumatoff except as otherwise noted.

Contents

Illustrations

CHAPTER 1

The Central Asian World

Nicholas and Nina Shoumatoff

The interior of Asia is the land of six, mainly east-west ranges, all of which exceed 24,000 feet (7,315 m) and tower over any other mountains on earth. From the west the Hindu Kush and from the east the Himalayas, Karakoram, Kun Lun and Tien Shan, listed from south to north, all converge into the Pamir, whose name in Persian means the "roof of the world." From the ramparts of these extraordinary highlands, the steppes for which the region is famous reach over immense plains to the Siberian taiga. More than once, great waves of nomadic horsemen thundered across those prairies and conquered most of the civilized world. As herdsmen of horses, sheep and yaks on low and high pastures, their descendants still dwell in portable *yurts* following ways of life that are thousands of years old.

This region includes the sources of the great Indus, Brahmaputra, Ganges, Mekong, Yangtze and Yellow Rivers. Mostly, however, it is drained by lakes and seas that have no outlet, by the Caspian Sea and the Aral Sea, which is fed by the westward-flowing Amu Darya (Oxus) and Syr Darya Rivers. It is a land of striking beauty and contrasts in its landscapes, flora and fauna but with awesome underlying forces that often wreak destructive violence in the form of earthquakes, mudflows and landslides. They result from movements of the earth's crust, specifically the northward drift of the Indian subcontinent, propelled by currents in the magma deep below. These forces not only lifted and continue to lift the mountains and the Tibetan Plateau out of what was once the Tethys Sea but also keep their immense masses from sinking back down (Schroder 1989; Molnar 1989).

The region is also known as Central Asia, but its precise definition varies among scholars. Krader (1971) limits the term to the five republics of the erstwhile Russian Turkestan, but the Royal Geographical Society (1987) applies it mainly to western China, Tibet and Mongolia. The latter usage is customary among Russians, who called their Turkestan Middle Asia (Agakhanyantz 1965–66). Hambly (1969) includes both of these areas but strictly within political frontiers excluding those parts of Afghanistan, Pakistan and India reaching north of the Hindu Kush and Himalaya. Physically rather than politically, one could start at the south slopes of these two ranges. For us, Central Asia thus stretches for 3,000 miles (5,000 km), from the Great Wall of China to the shores of the Caspian Sea, and for 1,500 miles (2,500 km) from the mountains of Sikkim and Bhutan to the forests of Siberia.

Throughout Central Asia, winters are cold, summers warm and rainfall or snowfall sparse. The formidable southern ranges intercept the region's rainfall and thereby gave birth to the huge deserts of the Gobi, the Takla Makan and those of the black and red sands to the west. On the slopes of the southern Himalayas, which are exposed to the monsoons, the annual precipitation may reach 200 inches (5 m), while north of the Trans-Himalaya (Kailas) range and in most of Tibet it is only 8 inches (.2 m). This combination of deserts and mountain barriers has obstructed the ways in which the region has been affected by the surrounding civilizations of Iran, India, China and Russia. Conversely, the outer world's knowledge of Central Asia's complex history is mostly confined to scholars (Grousset 1970; Hambly 1969; Krader 1971) except for episodes associated with the names of four great conquerors. Centuries later, the legacies and legends of these men still influence the Eurasian world.

1. Alexander the Great, during his brief life (B.C. 356–323), led his Greek warriors on a blitzkrieg through Southwest Asia, which was followed by Hellenization of the land. In parts of what became Afghanistan and Turkestan, the Graeco-Bactrian Kingdom endured until the first century A.D. Greek cultural influence formerly extended even into China (Jouguet 1926). From these fabled Greeks, an illustrious lineage is claimed by blue-eyed people who are scattered throughout the region. The local version of Alexander's name is often used geographically, for example, in the town of Iskander and the lake of Iskanderkul in Turkestan. This was the setting for Kipling's story "The Man Who Would Be

King." When Alexander invaded Samarkand, then known as Marakanda, he stayed a year and is said to have exclaimed: "Everything I have ever heard about the beauty of Marakanda is true, except that it is more beautiful than anything I could have imagined."

2. Reversing this military movement, Attila, "the Scourge of God" (A.D. 406?–453), led his Huns on murderous sweeps through eastern and western Europe almost to the Atlantic Ocean, precipitating the downfall of imperial Rome. The Huns, who gave Hungary its name, are generally believed to have been Turks. Their name is thought to derive from the Chinese Hiung-nu, which goes back to 2000 B.C., but this "was probably a generic term applied to Turkic, Mongol and perhaps Tungus peoples" (Wheeler 1963). Linking the history and saga of east and west, the Nibelung Strasse at Melk on the Danube in Austria commemorates the place where Attila is said to have married Brunhild, that is, the Burgundian queen of the original legend not the Wagnerian Valkyrie Brunnhilde.

3. A much larger and more enduring conquest of Asia and eastern Europe was achieved by the Mongol Genghiz Khan (Jenghiz or Chingiz, 1162–1227) and his successors. The name of the Mongols derives from their word *mong,* which means "brave." They were highly sophisticated, well-equipped, mounted warriors who developed an effective system of long-range communication and government but who destroyed many of the cities they conquered, even the beauty of Samarkand. The human stream that they set in motion throughout Central Asia consisted mainly of Turkic nomads who were subdued by the Mongols and carried along with them. The dreaded Turko-Mongol hordes, led by Mongol chieftains, conquered the immense central belt of Eurasia from the Pacific through Budapest and eastern Poland. They ruled Russia for more than two centuries and China for eighty years, where their great Kublai Khan was visited by Marco Polo and became a Tibetan Buddhist.

4. Timur (1336?–1405), a Turkicized Mongol prince who claimed descent from Genghiz Khan and is commonly known as Tamerlane, was a devout Muslim who led his Turkic warriors on almost equally extensive conquests from Kashgar (Kashi) in western China to Damascus, Baghdad and the Caucasus. He set up his

capital at Samarkand, which he and his heirs rebuilt to unprecedented architectural and intellectual magnificence inspired, however, more by the cosmopolitan culture of Persia than by pastoral
Turko-Mongol ways. Lord Curzon, the viceroy of British India,
visited Samarkand and was impressed by its central square, the
Registan, flanked by three *medressas,* or universities, which he
called cathedrals, whose soaring facades are elaborately encrusted
with multicolored tiles. He pronounced the Registan to be "the
noblest public square in the world." Tamerlane's descendant
Babur (Baber or Babar, 1483–1530) founded the Mogul (Timurid)
dynasty of India, the legacies of which include the Taj Mahal of
Shah Jehan (1592–1666).

Later, especially in the eighteenth and nineteenth centuries, the British and Russian Empires subdued large areas of Southern and Central
Asia, respectively, with competitive contact at the highlands in what
Kipling called the Great Game. This contest was largely settled by the
Anglo-Russian Border Commission of 1895, which established the present boundaries of Afghanistan with a buffer zone in the Wakhan panhan-
dle to insulate the two empires from each other. The British then invaded
Lhasa and, after the thirteenth Dalai Lama fled to Mongolia, forced his
government to sign the Anglo-Tibetan Treaty of 1904, which foreclosed
Russian aspirations there (Younghusband 1905; Rayfield 1976). This was
ratified by the Anglo-Russian Treaty of 1907.

In many ways and in the minds of many people throughout the
world, Tibet (Xizang) represents the essence of Central Asia. The Tibetan
people, who are ethnically related to the Mongolians, have various local
names, such as the Khampa of eastern Tibet, which is known to them as
Kham, while Bhodpa is the general term for the people of Tibet as a whole,
which is known to them as Bhod. The latter is the source of the name of
the Bhotias, who are Tibetan people of Nepal, Sikkim and Bhutan. In
addition, the Tibetans include the Sherpas of eastern Nepal, the Ladakhis
of Kashmir and related people in the surrounding provinces in China.
Situated between the Himalayan and Kun Lun crests and extending for
1,000 miles (1,600 km) east to west, the Tibetan Plateau has an average
altitude well over 4,000 meters (13,100 ft.) and is the world's most massive upland of that height. Because of the bleakness of its northern por-

tion, which is known as the Chang Tang, the country was unattractive to the great Mongol and Turkic conquerors and was little affected by them.

However, it has a long history of military engagements with lesser Mongol, Chinese, Gurkha and British invaders. Significant Chinese armed forces entered it in 634, 1720, 1750, 1792, 1910, 1950 and 1959. These actions and the ensuing treaties, especially the 1951 Treaty of Peking, have led to international recognition of Chinese suzerainty over Tibet. The United Nations General Assembly passed resolutions of 1959, 1961 and 1965 protesting Chinese violations of Tibetan human rights, and supporting their right to self-determination. In 1960 the International Commission of Jurists in Geneva found China guilty of genocide conducted against the Tibetans. These protests had little effect on the Chinese.

Tibet's religious history is also long and complex (Snellgrove and Richardson 1968). Buddhism became established there in the seventh and eighth centuries, especially after the arrival of the Indian Tantric teacher Padma Sambhava, who is venerated by the Red Hat sect, the country's oldest. The Yellow Hat, or reform, sect was founded in the fourteenth century, and in 1641, under the fifth Dalai Lama, it gained complete spiritual and temporal dominion over the Tibetan people. Their religion is widely known as Tibetan Buddhism, which is a major branch of Buddhism. A lama is a teacher, more than an ordinary monk, while *dalai* is a Mongolian word meaning "ocean." Tibet was the world's last theocracy until 1959, when the fourteenth Dalai Lama was forced to escape to India. His charm, integrity and insistence on the use of peaceful means in the cause of his religion and his country won the admiration and affection of the world, and in 1989 he was awarded the Nobel prize for peace. He has also contributed greatly to the worldwide strength and stature of Tibetan religion and culture. Lhasa, the capital, is still the main goal for Buddhist pilgrims from Tibet and Mongolia, like Mecca is for Muslims.

In the southern Himalayas, a peripheral part of Central Asia, the Hindu tribes of Garwhal, Kumaon, Himachal, Nepal, Sikkim and Bhutan are ancient denizens of the Asian mountain world. Some of them migrated there during the Muslim conquests of India, first by the Arabs, then by the Turks (1000–1526) and finally by the Turkic Timurids (1526–1707). Many Himalayan peaks are named for Hindu deities, and the region includes important Hindu shrines such as the source of the Ganges and the Amarnath Cave. The northern tip of India, though its precise boundary is still in dispute, is the point of convergence for the three great cultures of Asia: Islamic, Hindu and Buddhist.

The dissolution of the British Empire in 1947 was accompanied by the partition of the Indian subcontinent and the emergence of India and Pakistan as new sovereign nations, both of which reach into Central Asia even north of the Himalayan crest. Similarly, when the USSR came to an end in 1991, the old Russian empire in Central Asia collapsed and was replaced by Kyrghyzstan, Kazakhstan, Uzbekistan, Turkmenistan and Tajikistan as infant independent countries. Before World War I, after being liberated from various khans such as those of Bukhara and Kokand, they became loosely mixed as undifferentiated parts of Russian Turkestan, except for northern Kazakhstan, which had been a part of Siberia. In the wake of the war, with its ensuing civil strife, the region briefly enjoyed independence. It was after its reconquest by the USSR that these countries were first separated from each other approximately according to their present boundaries. Their establishment as Soviet Socialist republics was completed only in 1936, with frontiers intertwined like a jigsaw puzzle in a futile attempt to separate the ethnic groups. The fertile Ferghana Valley, which is known as the jewel of Central Asia, is carved up by complex boundaries among Uzbeks, Kyrghyz and Tajiks, including islands of the latter completely surrounded by Kyrghyz and Uzbek lands.

Since long before the Christian era, the eastern part of Central Asia has been occupied by peoples of what was commonly called Mongolian stock, which includes the original Turks, while the western part was previously inhabited by Indo-Europeans, mostly Scythians in the north and Sogdians, an Iranian group, in the south. More than a thousand years ago, the Scythians and Sogdians were gradually replaced or assimilated by Turks and Mongols migrating from the east in search of new pastures for their flocks. The birthplace of the Turks was in the northeast part of the Mongolian Plateau, near that of the Mongols (Liddell Hart, 1963). The Turks, whose name has been associated with the Chinese term Tu-Kiu, were first identified as "the nomad people who in the 6th century A.D. founded an empire stretching from Mongolia to the Black Sea" (Wheeler 1963). In the seventh century they submitted to the suzerainty of the T'ang Chinese, who thus extended their sway over Central Asia. The death of Genghiz Khan in 1227 was followed by widespread Islamization of Central Asia's Turks, who then virtually absorbed the Mongols outside of Mongolia except for the Kalmuks of western China and the Volga region. In Turkish their name, Kalmak, means "to survive."

Of the present ethnic groups, the Kyrghyz, Kazakhs, Uzbeks and Uighurs are closest to the early Turks. Of these the Kyrghyz (Qirqiz) have by far the oldest identity, having been mentioned in Han dynasty Chinese annals of the first century B.C. From A.D. 840 to 924 they ruled Mongolia, after which time they retired to the region between Lake Baikal and the Yenisei River in Siberia, where they remained until the twelfth century. After that they moved to the formidable ramparts of the Tien Shan and northern Pamir, which are now in Kyrghyzstan. There they were bypassed by the conquering nomads of Genghiz Khan and Tamerlane. The name of the Kyrghyz is Turkic for "forty maidens," who were their legendary ancestors.

Physically, Kazakhstan is by far the largest of the former Soviet Central Asian republics, stretching from near the Volga to the western tip of Mongolia. It is mostly flat, with only a small spur of the Tien Shan in its southeast, near its capital of Almaty. The steppes are the true homeland of the Kazakhs, where they continue to be primarily nomadic herders. Their identity under their present name is relatively recent, dating only from the thirteenth-century Mongol conquests, during which they became part of the Kipchak (Qipchak) khanate better known as the Golden Horde, which was named after the golden tent of Batu, a grandson of Genghiz Khan. The Kazakhs are said to have acquired their name, which in Turkish means "homeless" or "outlaw," because they were fugitives from the khans of Bukhara and Khiva. Later they were divided into three clans, the Little, Middle and Great Hordes, each headed by a descendant of Genghiz Khan, whereby they were organized into a hereditary aristocracy. In the middle of the eighteenth century, Russians and Ukrainians from the north began to settle both rural and urban areas of Central Asia, especially in Kazakhstan where they soon outnumbered the Kazakhs.

The Kazakhs and Kyrghyz belong to the Kipchak (Qipchak) northwest group of Turks, along with the Kara-Kalpaks (black hats) of western Uzbekistan and the Tatars of the Volga region, who are the main descendants of the Golden Horde. During the struggles for grazing grounds, the Kazakhs were constantly abducting Kalmuk women and thereby acquired a more Mongolian appearance than other Turks possess. The Russians used an erroneous and confusing nomenclature for the Kazakhs and Kyrghyz, which persisted until 1926. According to Chantal Lemercier-Quelquejay (1969), the Kyrghyz were "formerly known as Kara-Kirghiz [black Kyrghyz] to distinguish them from the Kazakhs, who were then known as Kirghiz" (148): black because, unlike the Kazakhs, they allegedly lacked a noble class, but the Kazakhs also called them Ak-kalpak (white hats). Krader (1971) explains that, in the 1926 census, "Kirgiz (Kirgiz-Kazakhs) of 1897 were classified as Kazakhs; Kara-Kirgiz were now classified as Kirgiz" (182); and Kirgiz "was the name used by XIX century Kazakh intellectuals" (63). The nineteenth-century Russians called Kazakhs Kyrghyz to distinguish them from the Cossacks, a hybrid Russian-Tatar group of the western steppes. We trust that all this is now perfectly clear.

Of the two remaining major Turkic groups in what was once Soviet Central Asia, the Uzbeks and the Turkomans, the latter are closest, both geographically and ethnically, in their homeland of Turkmenistan, to the western Turks of Turkey and Azerbaijan, resembling Indo-Europeans more than Mongolians. The Uzbeks, like the Kazakhs, are of relatively recent ethnic identity, deriving their name from Uzbeg Khan, a fourteenth-century leader of the Golden Horde. They became the region's ruling tribe, having migrated from what is now Kazakhstan. Uzbeks have a rich blend of Turkic and Iranian heredity. In the 1926 census of the USSR, the Sarts and Uzbek-Sarts, who were of Iranian stock, were reclassified as Uzbeks (Krader 1971). In the last years of the USSR, the population of Uzbekistan exceeded twenty million. Of these people, 69 percent were called Uzbeks and 11 percent Russians, and the rest were classified as belonging to various nationalities, including Koreans and Central Asian Jews.

The history of their present homeland, however, is much older than that of the Uzbeks themselves. Under the T'ang dynasty in the seventh century A.D., when the Chinese ruled almost all of Central Asia, they established a western administrative center at Tashkent, which they called Uni. They were followed by the Arabs, who left a more indelible imprint on most of Central Asia, not ethnically but culturally, after spreading the Islamic religion, which still dominates the region except in Buddhist Tibet and Mongolia. Turkic languages were mostly written in Arabic script until the Soviet era, when the populace was forced to shift to Cyrillic letters. In the eleventh century, reflecting the mixture of its population, the name of Tashkent was changed from the Sogdian Shash to its present linguistic hybrid, in which *tash* is a Turkic word for stone and *kent* is an Iranian word for city, like *kand* in Samarkand. *Tash* refers to red granite from the nearby Tien Shan foothills, which was used extensively in its construction rather than the dried mud bricks used in most Asian towns. Tashkent, the largest city of Central Asia, was the capital of Russian Turkestan and is now the capital of Uzbekistan.

Tajikistan is the only one of the five former Soviet republics in Central Asia that is still inhabited primarily by people of Iranian stock. The Tajiks since ancient times have been sedentary agricultural farmers rather than nomadic herdsmen. They are the main representatives of the original Iranians who inhabited Central Asia before the Turkic migrations, and their language is Iranian rather than Turkic. However, about twice as many Tajiks live in Afghanistan as in Tajikistan. This split between the two major groups of Tajiks resulted when the Anglo-Russian Border Commission of 1895 established the Amu Darya (Oxus River) as Afghanistan's northern frontier.

The Tajiks of both countries are "pale-skinned hirsute Europiform Pamirians with light hair (10% blonde) and eyes (15% blue)" (Trevor 1963). Those with fair complexions are more prevalent in parts of the Pamir uplands, where they claim descent from the Greek warriors who held out in the mountains after their Bactrian Kingdom fell. Each of the Pamir valleys has its own Iranian language so that the mountain Tajiks of adjacent valleys must communicate in lowland Tajik. In the Yagnob Valley of northern Tajikistan, people still speak a language closely related to ancient Sogdian. Lowland Tajiks, like the Turkic peoples, are orthodox Sunni Muslims, but mountain Tajiks are Ismaili Shiites, headed by their imam, the Aga Khan, and earlier by "The Old Man of the Mountains" who terrorized the Crusaders.

The Uighurs, whose identity dates from a horde of the tenth and eleventh centuries, are the major Turkic group of Sinkiang (Xinjiang) in western China. Unlike other Central Asian Turks, of whom the Kazakhs and Kyrghyz are minorities in Sinkiang, the Uighurs are traditionally settled agriculturalists, like the Tajiks, rather than pastoral nomads. A major part of Sinkiang is occupied by the vast Takla Makan Desert in the Tarim Basin, which is even less hospitable for all forms of life than is the still larger Gobi Desert in Mongolia. Much of Sinkiang is separated from Tibet by the towering Kun Lun range, but west of Tibet its frontiers lead into Ladakh, Kashmir, Pakistan, Afghanistan and the former Soviet republics. West of the Takla Makan, the oasis towns of Kashgar (Kashi) and Yarkant (Shache) lie on trade routes that extend over the Karakoram range into Ladakh and Hunza.

Southward, across the 18,290-foot (5,575 m) Karakoram Pass from

Sinkiang, the isolated land of Ladakh was formerly part of Tibet and is often called Western Tibet or Little Tibet. Its majority is Tibetan Buddhist, but it includes a substantial Muslim minority. It was separated from Tibet in 1841 through conquest by the maharajah of Kashmir and Jammu, and since then it has been part of Kashmir. West of Ladakh, the main part of Kashmir, with its Muslim majority, presents an apparently insoluble problem in its resistance to administration by India and in the lack of an agreed-upon boundary between India and Pakistan dating from the partition between them in 1947. Farther west, in Pakistan, the mountainous districts of Gilgit, Hunza and Chitral are, like Ladakh, north of the Himalayan crest, so that, by our definition, they are parts of Central Asia. The people of Hunza, like the mountain Tajiks of the Pamir, are Ismaili Muslims of Iranian stock.

In Turkestan, both Russian and Soviet authorities had more respect for indigenous Central Asian cultures than did the Chinese in Sinkiang and Tibet, though the Soviets reduced the number of active mosques from twenty thousand to three hundred. Their program of liberation from Islamic taboos, which have always been weaker among the nomads, was approved by many, especially the women, who publicly burned their veils at Samarkand in 1927. With the collapse of Soviet power, the Islamic religion in Central Asia has flourished again, but the decades of Soviet secular education have, up to now, provided a buffer in most areas against the repressive forms of Islamic fundamentalism.

An unfortunate exception has occurred in Tajikistan. Being closer, both ethnically and geographically, to the militant Muslims of Afghanistan and Iran, it has suffered murderous regional, religious and ideological conflicts between the lowland and highland Tajiks, especially between those of the Kulyab and Garm Districts, and also between Islamic fanatics and the formerly dominant agnostic communists. For the present, the latter have prevailed with the aid of Russian troops who are nominally there to help Tajikistan guard its border with Afghanistan, which has been the main source of the militant Islamic threat. However, the fighting continues, especially near the frontier.

Other areas of Central Asia have likewise endured traumatic violence in recent years. After the Soviets withdrew from Afghanistan in 1990, factions of the "holy warriors" (*mujahedin*) and other Islamic fundamentalists have fought each other in and around its capital, Kabul. The decades-old violence between Hindus and Muslims has intensified in Kashmir and northern India, even on glaciers with disputed borders at elevations up to 6,000 meters (20,000 ft.). The Central Asian peoples have also suffered by violating their own environment. In Hunza, Nepal and elsewhere throughout the southern tier of the region, both nature and culture are threatened by the cutting of trees, shrubs and leaves for fuel and fodder, causing widespread deforestation and erosion (Clark 1956; Bishop and Bishop 1971). The Soviets, in their eagerness to modernize Central Asia, introduced industry, mining and cotton monoculture. The latter, through its great demand for irrigation, has disastrously dried up the Aral Sea (Agakhanyantz 1988; Keller 1988).

Whatever may be the results of these traumas, the natural treasures of Central Asia still survive in most of the mountainous areas. Its cultural legacies are also alive in large parts of the region, in its homes, bazaars, folk arts, rituals, pastoral hegiras, sporting events, architectural monuments and legends of an eventful past. They have outlasted the inroads of previous conquests and civilizations and may even survive the present ones. Such are the foundations upon which the future could evolve in this old and gigantic land.

This book moves across Central Asia broadly, from south to north and from west to east, from the great mountains to the great steppes and from Samarkand to Lhasa. Its narratives, in addition to our own, have come to us through direct links of companionship, hospitality and kinship. We begin with Andrey Avinoff, who for nineteen years was director of the Carnegie Museum of Natural History, presenting in chapter 2 his intrepid exploration of the Himalayan world of the lamas in what was formerly Western Tibet. Alexandre Iacovleff, who was the charismatic chief instructor at the Boston Fine Arts Museum School, writes in chapter 3 of the remarkable Citroën expedition from Beirut over the mountains to Beijing, of which he was the gifted ethnographer. In chapter 4, Edward Murray of Iowa, a prominent research physician, describes his unprecedented summer with Kyrghyz and Mongol nomads. Heinrich Harrer, noted for the first ascent of the Eiger north face, tells us in chapter 5 of his harrowing and triumphant experiences in Tibet. In chapter 6, John Clark, a geologist at Chicago's Field Museum, reviews his two years of enlightened work with the people of remote Himalayan Hunza.

Vladimir Ratzek, legendary scholar-mountaineer and lifelong resident of Central Asia, gives voice to the hearts of Turkestan, Tien Shan and Pamir in chapters 7, 8 and 9. The many-talented geobotanist Okmir Agakhanyantz, veteran of more than thirty years in the Pamir, offers enticing glimpses in chapters 10 through 15 of his fieldwork and the lives of the local people. In chapters 6 through 21, Anatoly Ovtchinnikov, the authoritative but modest Moscow metallurgist who is known as the "iron man" of Soviet mountaineering describes achievements that challenge human limits at literally the apex of the Pamir, Tien Shan and Himalaya. Sixteen of these twenty narratives were not previously available in English.

After a brief sketch in chapter 22 of our expeditions to Turkestan and the Pamir, we conclude in chapter 23 with a frank debate on the spirituality for which the highlands of Asia are famous. This is based on insights from women and men who are prominently associated with Central Asia, including appropriate elements of humor even from the present Dalai Lama himself. Our panorama thus expands from the natural and human into the numinous dimensions, a triad that spans the diapason of Central Asia's mountain world.

CHAPTER 2

A Trip to Western Tibet

Andrey Avinoff, 1931

Andrey Avinoff (1884–1949) was born at Tulchin in what was then southwestern Russia. After graduating from the University of Moscow in 1905, he served in an impressive array of official posts in both the Old and New Worlds,[1] but his life's ruling passions remained in his entomological research and his own creative art.[2] In 1893, his family moved for two years to Tashkent, then the capital of Turkestan, where his father was stationed as a general in the Russian army. They fled from the summer heat to a military camp in the western Tien Shan mountains, where the young Avinoff fell victim to a permanent infatuation with Central Asia. In 1912, on the journey described in this chapter, he traveled almost 3,200 kilometers (2,000 mi.) on horses and yaks, meandering through north-western India, the Himalayas and the Karakorams between Kashmir and Kashgar. As we learned on later travels with him, almost everything was an occasion for laughter, which this narrative shows also applied to his highest Central Asian adventures.[3]

Nineteen years ago [in 1912], I made a journey in the western Himalayas, Ladakh and Chinese Turkestan, over the southeastern slope of the Roof of the World. At that time I was studying the distribution of the butterflies in the temperate and northern section of the Old World and was anxious to obtain for my collection some representatives of the winged population of the Asiatic mountains, which I had hitherto missed.

We started on our voyage, M. Mamaieff (an enthusiastic young sportsman) and I, on a steamer of the Nord-Deutsches Lloyd. The typical scenery of Ceylon, the grand old cities of India—Madras, Agra, Delhi and Benares—were an enchanting succession of unforgettable impressions.

The grandiose panorama of the main range of the Himalayas, as seen from Darjeeling, was a foretaste of the mountain world in which we were to stay for months to come. Through the courtesy of the government of the viceroy, I received the necessary permission to visit less accessible sections in the land of the maharajah of Kashmir. A captain of the British army volunteered to accompany us—presumably not without the authorization of his superiors—on a part of our itinerary. He relinquished us, apparently, only when he was fully convinced that we were nothing more than harmless naturalists, entirely innocuous to the security of the Indian frontier—for in those days Anglo-Indians lived in no little distrust of the "Empire of the North."

We left the railroad at Rawalpindi, where A. Jacobson (an entomologist with wide experience in Asiatic exploration) was waiting for us, having arrived via Bombay, and we proceeded together to the capital of Kashmir in primitive native vehicles called *dongas*. A terrific storm accompanied by a torrential rain, one of those equinoctial tempests at the breaking of the monsoon, wrought havoc on the road winding along the river Sind and compelled us to continue the crossing over the ridge with the assistance of some seventy coolies. It was during this episode that the captain displayed his administrative ingenuity—in hiring men to carry our luggage. Through a sweeping piece of strategy on the part of our military escort, we entrusted our packages and *yakhtans* to a detachment of porters, and enjoyed the slower pace. It gave us an opportunity not only to enrich our entomological booty but also to learn more about this picturesque stretch of land, which brought us finally to the Happy Valley.

The view of the meandering Jhelum River—a favorite pattern on certain ancient Kashmir shawls, which portray it as conventionally flowing on the background of an astounding millefleur design—was an enrapturing landscape. An alley of white poplars running for a stretch of many miles brought us to the gates of Srinagar, the city made famous by Lalla Rookh, and the sojourn of Shah Jehan, most romantic and visionary of all the Great Moghuls, and his beloved wife, immortalized in the Taj. Srinagar bears the aspect of an oriental Venice, with numerous canals, many bridges, commodious houseboats and colorful aquatic festivities.

It was the time of rose blossoms; the air was laden with the sweet and heavy scent of attar, as a truly Kashmirian background for the sparkling song of the bulbul, the nightingale. In the dense shade of the sycamores surrounding the ancient Chena-bag we could not refrain from an experiment in moth hunting, which brought us many thrills.

Yak caravan entering Ladakh at Zoji-la. (*Pen and ink drawing by A. Avinoff.*)

Several days were busily spent in preparation for the trip to Ladakh. A few interviews for arranging the details of our itinerary, the hiring of servants (including the inevitable tiffin coolie, whose main duty is to serve luncheon) and the acquisition of the necessary equipment for traveling and hunting, consumed considerable time.

The day before our departure from Srinagar, as we felt free to relax after a period of strenuous work, we decided to pay a visit to one of the merchants who had been incessantly besieging us during the whole week. It was a most worthwhile experience, not so much for the importance of our purchases as for the variety of things we saw. The store was located in an old wooden house on the banks of the river Jhelum, with an ornate carved balcony facing the snowy range of Pir Panjal. We settled leisurely on comfortable sofas of carved wood with an involved tracery of foliage providing the desired resilience, and while sipping green tea and nibbling assorted spicy tidbits we embarked on an unhurried inspection of a bewildering array of beautiful merchandise. Boxes of sandalwood, with fantastic dragons and intricate patterns of *chenar* leaves, were followed by a display of lacquer work on papier maché (in the old Persian manner, with conventional roses and bulbuls), embroideries and *pachmina*, a fabric woven of the finest wool of special goats. By imperceptible steps we were led to objects of increasing beauty and prices. As long as the valuation was within our buying power we made some sundry purchases, but the figures grew in a lively crescendo until we reached the assortment of ancient Kashmir shawls. Our host proved to be as much a born poet and disinterested lover of beautiful things as a shrewd trader. Toward the end of our visit his commercial instincts subsided and he was glad to display his riches without any hope of selling. We had reached a placid stage of platonic contemplation. As the crowning number there emerged a shawl of surpassing splendor, with the celebrated Jhelum motif curling and swinging over a magic carpet of the most delicate floral decoration, interspersed with fanciful birds. A whole generation of craftsmen was said to have been engaged in the production of this unique masterpiece. Thus we spent an afternoon that seemed to waft us to the land of the Thousand and One Nights, and so took our leave of Srinagar.

We made the first leg of our journey to the mountains in a houseboat rowed by a family of Kashmiri, who provided both the motive power and a diversified musical entertainment of quaint songs. Having reached Ganderbal, we hired a caravan of horses. The foothills of the Himalayas were all in blossom. The slopes were spangled with a gorgeous variety of irises,

The Lamayuru monastery, Ladakh. (*Pen and ink drawing by A. Avinoff.*)

ranging from tender pastel hues of lavender and mauve to deep tones of brilliant violet and royal purple. As we ascended along a path, frequently crossing rapid mountain streams, the scenery gradually acquired a more alpine character. We entered into the balmy zone of fir trees and made a halt at Sonomarg, an elevated valley with meadows and birch forests surrounded by snow-capped hills crisply cut against the cloudless sky. A stay of a few days at this favorite camp on the way to Ladakh brought some excellent entomological trophies. We met here another party of travelers, Dr. and Mrs. Bullock Workman from Philadelphia, who were on their way to explore the greatest known massif of glaciers, the mighty system of Karakoram. Although the pass ahead, over the main chain of the Himalayas, is not over 12,000 feet, nevertheless Zoji-la is considered a rather treacherous passage on account of the deep snow, which is likely to give way under the weight of the pack animals. For safety's sake one has to start early, before dawn, so as to cross the pass when the snow is still solid. Zoji-la is, in fact, not so much a pass as a footstep leading onto the tableland of Western Tibet, since there is scarcely any appreciable descent beyond it. Here the nature of the land was changed completely. All forests were gone, leaving no vestige of trees whatever. For two of our party [Avinoff and Jacobson], who had previously been on the Pamirs, the landscape appeared decidedly like the characteristic scenery of the Roof of the World. And so, after a few days of march over this desolate and dreary country, we entered into the land of the lamas.

The inhabitants of Ladakh are nominally Buddhists, although the teaching of the Gautama has undergone an almost unrecognizable alteration. The pantheon of gods and demigods worshipped in India has been amplified by magic rites and ceremonies borrowed from the ancient Bon religion. This form of shamanism, tempered by Hindu and Buddhist influences, is more prevalent among the red lamas than among the yellow ones. The two divisions of lamaism represent different degrees in the blending of Buddhist teaching with beliefs in sorcery and demons. The majority of the Ladakhi adhere to the red sect, more remote from the tenets of the Enlightened One.

One of the largest and most revered lamaseries in Ladakh is that of Lamayuru. It has the weird aspect of an enchanted city of hobgoblins, with grotesque chasms, overhanging structures of various colors, many caves honeycombing the rocks, numerous *chortens*—religious monuments symbolizing the five elements of nature—and winding walls of stones bearing the sacramental inscription engraved: "Om mani padme

The Indus River not far from Leh. (*Pen and ink drawing by A. Avinoff.*)

hum," which signifies "O treasure in the lotus flower." Nothing can excel Lamayuru as a most bizarre, outlandish place, fit to be an abode of gnomes and magicians of the Arthur Rackham style. But there is nothing malign about the monastic population of this fairyland stronghold. The monks, like all the Ladakhi, are kindly, sociable, cheerful people. They live in a labyrinth of cells, which converge in a central temple adorned with a statue of a thousand-handed deity. To make the image still more fantastic, the idol is surmounted by a many-headed superstructure of wild and fearful countenances. A profusion of painted banners around the walls depict in gaudy colors and confused patterns the mythology of the rulers of the lamaistic hall. The monks displayed with genial willingness and real delight the gruesome paraphernalia of the so-called devil dance. Strange looking masks of fantastic birds, skulls and infernal beings, festooned with beads fashioned out of human bones, seemed to provide for our obliging hosts a source of undisguised and contagious merriment. The caricaturesque element in the attributes of their cult was, apparently, keenly enjoyed by the jolly congregation.

On our way to Leh we encountered several other monasteries, although none was so imposing as Lamayuru. The number of populous lamaseries in Ladakh made one wonder at the existence of a sufficient excess of male population to explain the prevailing custom of polyandry, since native women not infrequently have three or four husbands.

During the last days of the march, before we arrived at the capital of Ladakh, we followed the course of the Indus, which rolls its turbulent yellow waters between mottled sandstone banks. An exceptional length of *padme* walls heralded the existence of an important center. Presently we perceived the city itself, surmounted by an oasis of vegetation brought to life by an elaborate system of irrigation. On a commanding point rose the citadel of the erstwhile royal palace. Ladakh no longer forms a part of actual Tibet since it was added to the domains of the maharajah of Kashmir. The ancient dynasty was deposed and the former king lives as a private individual in a city over which his ancestors long ruled. We had occasion to see him through the courtesy of an obliging Moravian missionary who became interested in us as fellow naturalists. The deposed potentate is a rather striking figure, with his widely crossed eyes—which defect is said to be intentionally cultivated. The king, as I was told, is supposed scarcely to deign to look with both eyes on any ordinary mortal he addresses. His son, as well, was already quite proficient in subtending a sizable angle in his binocular gaze.

Headman of Tanamik, Ladakh. (*Watercolor by A. Avinoff.*)

Meditating Buddhist monk, Tanamik, Ladakh. (*Watercolor by A. Avinoff.*)

A Ladakhi woman in a jeweled headdress. (*Watercolor by A. Avinoff.*)

A Himalayan panorama above Zoji-la. (*Watercolor by A. Avinoff.*)

Avinoff's horse-caravan camp in Ladakh (beside a glacier-topped mountain). (*Watercolor by A. Avinoff.*)

Dawn on Kursong pass, Karakorams. (*Watercolor by A. Avinoff.*)

A Buddhist chorten at Gya, Karakorams. (*Watercolor by A. Avinoff.*)

Gur Emir, Tamerlane's tomb in Samarkand. (*Watercolor by A. Avinoff.*)

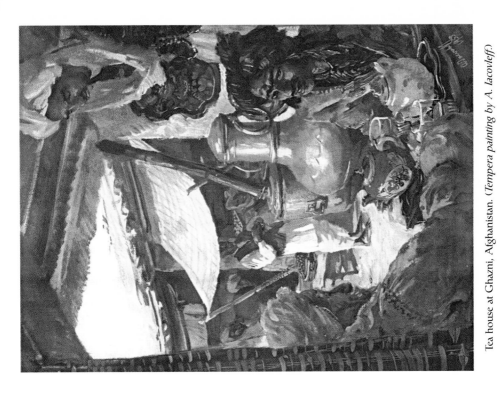

Tea house at Ghazni, Afghanistan. (*Tempera painting by A. Iacovleff.*)

Group of Afghans with their steeds. (*Tempera painting by A. Iacovleff.*)

Aged Kyrghyz man at Peyik, Sinkiang. (*Crayon drawing by A. Iacovleff.*)

Sir Muhamed Nazim Khan, mir of Hunza, K.C.I.E. (Knight Commander of the Indian Empire). (*Crayon drawing by A. Iacovleff.*)

The guide Khumbo at Urumchi, Sinkiang. (*Crayon drawing by A. Iacovleff.*)

Old Mongol woman at Hsi-Hsu-Ming, China. (*Crayon drawing by A. Iacovleff.*)

Mongol herdsmen of Tibetan-type horses. (*Tempera painting by A. Iacovleff.*)

Chinese Turkestan women, Aksu, Sinkiang. (*Tempera painting by A. Iacovleff.*)

The former king of Ladakh, showing his cultivated monocular gaze. (*Pen and ink drawing by A. Avinoff.*)

In response to the presentation of a beautiful cup of jade, I recipro-
cated by offering to his ex-majesty a flashlight, which was accepted as
something on the borderline of the miraculous. I may mention in passing
that I departed from Leh before the battery was exhausted!

Our most profitable entomological hunting was accomplished during
a trip to the southeast of Ladakh, along the frontier of Tibet proper, in a
region called Rupshu. It is a land of high elevation, with many passes
attaining the altitude of 17,500 feet. Here we caught some of the choicest
forms of butterflies, including species and races entirely new to science.
The most extraordinary of our finds, subsequently described by me, was
Parnassius maharaja, which has never been found since, although explorers have repeatedly visited these territories—in some cases for the
specific purpose of collecting butterflies. At a point about 15,000 feet high
we saw a small group of shabby clay shacks, the highest year-round settlement. At greater altitudes the sparse population stays in temporary tents.
The Tibetans keep large herds of yaks, which are customarily used for
riding on this arid plateau and the steep mountain slopes. We had a few
yaks as our mounts for a period of some two weeks, having grown to be
fond of these husky, grunting creatures for their exceptionally reliable
surefootedness on dangerous inclines. Another typical feature of Rupshu
is the number of flocks of sheep, which serve for transporting specially
constructed bags of salt—the main object of trade in western Tibet. Several lakes with water of high salinity add a peculiar character to the
tableland. It was here that we saw the first wild asses, called *kiangs.* They
proved to be an inquisitive lot of animals, always prone to approach the
caravan and to run along with it for hours—at a distance, however, which
insured a swift retreat in case they sensed danger from such proximity.

The most difficult part of our trip was in the north of Ladakh, over
several passes, including the Karakoram, leading to Chinese Turkestan.
For that purpose we acquired a caravan of twenty-two horses. Six of the
passes were over 17,000 feet in altitude, the most formidable being Sasser-
la, with a steep and slippery glacier where we barely escaped losing two
horses that rolled down the ice. Only in one place did we strike a valley,
which made a pleasant contrast to the rugged severity of the adjacent
mountains. It was the vale of Nubra, called the Garden of Ladakh by a
rather generous stretch of optimistic allowance. There could be no doubt
that we were approaching the most difficult portion of our itinerary; the
fact was well attested by countless skeletons of horses, and occasional
camels, which had succumbed to the hardships of the land. The rarified air

Pamir butterflies named by Avinoff, *Parnassius autocrator* female and male, and
Karanasa decolorata iskander. (Pen and ink drawing by A. Avinoff.)

reduced our progress to a very slow and intermittent pace. The highest spot of the whole journey, on the Karakoram Pass, brought us to an altitude of 18,600 feet. Yet, nevertheless, at this elevation we managed to catch certain butterflies—in fact, some of the most desirable kind, known to inhabit only the highest zones of Central Asia. Topographically the pass is not difficult, since there is a gradual ascent to the top, but animals and men were equally sensitive to the lack of oxygen, which made us gasp for air at the least acceleration of movement. Under these circumstances our efforts to catch butterflies were successful only at the cost of considerable physical exertion. Jacobson and I became so absorbed in trying to procure some specimens we saw flying around that we found ourselves left behind; and then, to make matters worse, we were caught by a sudden blizzard, which obliterated all tracks of the main party. Rambling at random and beginning to feel somewhat uncomfortable—with our horses obviously sharing our anxiety—we suddenly heard in the growing darkness of night some faint voices calling us from afar. The happy reunion was appropriately celebrated with curried rice of an exceptionally hot variety, and every befitting accessory of a timely feast. It goes without saying that the big game hunting of Mamaieff throughout the trip was on the level of all expectations. He bagged several representatives of the genus *Ovis*, first cousin to the celebrated sheep of Marco Polo, inhabiting the Pamir; he obtained some ibexes, antelopes and a number of remarkable birds. Being equipped only with a net, I nevertheless almost succeeded in catching by the tail an uncommonly tame specimen of a huge mountain partridge but brought to the camp only a few feathers as a scarcely satisfactory trophy. But my properly armed companion killed on the same day a beautiful specimen of the coveted bird.

Shortly all the vicissitudes of mountain climbing were over. After crossing the paths of many earlier travelers, including that of the illustrious Venetian of the thirteenth century, we began our descent into the plain of Chinese Turkestan. The first authorities we met embarrassed us by requesting a Chinese passport, which we did not possess, as originally we had scarcely hoped to return to Russia through Turkestan. Resorting to a few innocent ruses, we managed to placate the insistent officials, and soon we were in the region where the Russian name meant a great deal. Finally we obtained the necessary documents in Kashgar, upon the request of the Russian consul. The remaining portion of the trip was without any entomological excitement, but we were recompensed by many unusual and amusing experiences, especially during receptions by Chinese dignitaries. On one occasion we had to endure a four-hour dinner of sixty courses composed of the most unexpected and variegated ingredients, constituting a fair revision of the Linnaean Systema Naturae. Some intriguing dried vermiform invertebrates, dipped in a bright indigo-blue sauce, made a dish that proved more memorable than appetizing.

The last lap of travel brought us from the torrid plains of the Tarim to the eastern part of the Pamir. Soon we arrived at Osh, a small city of Russian Turkestan on the railroad track. It made us feel with poignant sadness that the unique experience was over and that we were back in the world called civilized. Our memories still lingered with the majestic grandeur of the highest mountains of the globe, the hospitable and friendly people we had invariably encountered throughout the trip, the happy episodes of butterfly hunting—all of which now recede into a past that seems almost unreal, with all that was the Russia of those days.

CHAPTER 3

The Trans-Asia Expedition

Alexandre Iacovleff, 1934

Alexandre Iacovleff (1887–1938), the son of a Russian naval officer, was born in St. Petersburg where he studied at the Academy of Fine Arts. In 1913, the academy sent him on a four-year traveling fellowship to the Mediterranean and Far East.[1] After the collapse of Russia's monarchy, Iacovleff (as he spelled his name) stayed in the Orient for three years, then arrived in Paris and became a French citizen. He was the artist and ethnographer on two expeditions led by Georges Marie Haardt for which André Citroën, the automobile manufacturer, provided financing and tractor-tread vehicles.[2] On the second of these, "La Croisière Jaune," the expedition left the Mediterranean with seven such vehicles in early April 1931 and arrived in February 1932 at the East China Sea, a distance of 7,470 miles (12,030 km). It was said to be the first continuous overland journey between these two seas since the days of Marco Polo, whose route the expedition followed most of the way.[3] This chapter is Iacovleff's account of it, in his role as an artist, from his album of fifty Asian paintings and drawings reproduced in color in which he provides an incisive and elegant record of the trans-Asian journey.[4]

A campfire reunited us under the vault of the equatorial sky, with the Southern Cross at the bottom like a signature. The uncertain light seemed to weave a barricade of darkness around our traveling hearth, invoking that atmosphere of indefinable intimacy that is special to overnight camps. After the days of struggle against the swamps of Niassaland and Mozambique, we were almost at the end of the Croisière Noire, our expedition spanning Africa from north to south. Where will our next wanderings take us?

One could read this question in the expressions of my companions in adventure, who had become accustomed to the nomadic life. The imagination, with childlike eagerness, was already calling for new sensations and ventures. We knew that the idea of future expeditions was germinating in the mind of our leader, Georges-Marie Haardt. It was a secret desire, brooded over during the long months that followed the return of the Citroën Mission to Central Asia. But hardly had the exhibitions, books and films been completed when the restless spirit regained the momentum of a quest for new activity.

It was of little importance on which day the word *Asia* was pronounced for the first time. Had not all the unknowns of a sealed continent imposed themselves independently on our anxious search for the mystery? And today, the scientific and sporting exploit, the Croisière Jaune, which is our voyage across all of Asia from west to east, acquires, for the close friends of the leader, the character of a march toward destiny. Marked by fate, Georges-Marie Haardt will be pushed to deploy a ferocious energy in the struggle against all obstacles and, guided by his generous instinct, he will march toward the goal and toward the ultimate sacrifice.

Burdened by complex responsibilities at the very threshold of the effort that he undertakes, he sustains for months a fierce and patient battle to overcome the adverse forces that are opposed even to the idea of our departure. Nevertheless, the work is organized thanks to the support of M. André Citroën and to the powerful organization of his factories: workshop studies, trials on the limestone plateau of the Massif Central and in the deserts of southern Tunis, reconnaissance of the routes, and missions to store provisions along the way.

Meanwhile, the opposition grows louder. It comes from unexpected sources and seems capable of annihilating all the results we have already achieved. But this only strengthens our eagerness for the battle. Our activity intensifies, and our efforts become more feverish when the day approaches on which we are to leave Paris. It is a day whose emotional impact is hardly noticed amid the banal preoccupations of our departure.

After the last details are arranged, the morning finally arrives when, still rather awkwardly, each one of us hoists himself into his seat and takes the place that is to be his workstation. The vehicles shine with new paint, the trucks still display bright colors, and the tawny leather is soft to the touch.

The rose-colored dunes were outlined against a lightly white-capped sea, which is like a stretch of lapis lazuli, and the chain of the Levant rises—a friendly row of hills tinged with mauve—creating the first obstacle to stimulate the still-fresh energy of the voyagers.

Flying the "Golden Scarab," the emblem of our leader, the head car starts to move, the column gets under way toward the rising sun, and our caterpillar treads bite into their first slopes. From afar, the azure of the Mediterranean is still visible between the mountains, and then with a sudden turn it vanishes, like a sail furled by a friendly hand.

The moment of departure already belongs to the past. Like a monstrous chain whose links follow each other in a sinuous crawl, the caravan is on its way. Our vehicles in action, in the multiple details of their mechanisms, seem full of surprises and endowed with a new life. Had not we ourselves, directed by our chief, studied them at such great length and even adjusted each of their components?

The period of acclimatization lays down the conditions of life and work that will govern daily contacts during our long months together. Soon the rhythm of daily existence and travel will become routine and will dominate our personal habits and energies, welding them into a unified effort for our common purpose. The experience of some and the goodwill of others will, however, permit each one to respond to the needs of his own activity, creating the necessary environment for his particular work.

The constant movement of the convoy, whose stops are not determined by the eloquence of the picturesque, forces me to rely on the faithfulness of my memory in making studies of the landscape. Sketches drawn in a notebook, held at arm's length to dampen the jolts of the vehicle traveling over virgin territory, serve me as a point of departure.

These sketches are covered with identifying notes resembling zebra stripes or geographical maps made by the awkward hand of a child. They do not always provide me with the means to complete my studies, made in haste during the brief time when the tents are being set up for our little temporary village. Referring to them later, some of these notes become hieroglyphics for which the key has been lost. Still, with the aid of special marks, the memory often makes it possible to materialize certain visions already forgotten, which surge back, thanks to the passage of time, free from any element of chance.

Our first contact with human habitation in western Asia is deeply disconcerting. Being at the crossroads of three continents, it is the domain of perpetual and ancient migrations. The centuries have disrupted and modified the ethnic races, which carry the mark of military invasions. Old customs have become mixed up. Islam has left its stamp upon it. Now the

Western influence arrives as the leveler of this humanity, through the uniformity of clothing styles and a neutralizing mercantile attitude. It takes time, with constant observation and patient accumulation of numerous anthropological samples, to discern the profound racial differences that do not stand out at first sight.

And then, it is not always easy to obtain models. Among the local people, superstition, religion and suspicion make recruiting a delicate task. Meanwhile, persons of the upper classes often refuse to pose if they learn that people of lower extraction have already had their portraits drawn. For this reason, I sometimes have to delay the study of humbler mortals, so as not to give offense to some governor or general of whom one needs to make a noble effigy for a diplomatic purpose. Once the first drawing is finished, however, it is easy to make a choice from among the assistants, who by then are spurred by vanity and by the curiosity of spectators.

These difficulties are less intense in the regions influenced by Chinese culture, with its prodigious development of artistic and popular imagery. In China, both for the common people and for the elite, a painter is the embodiment of a lettered person. In the Far East, it is unquestionably a title of nobility. For the Chinese, a portrait casts an incomparable spell. It decorates the walls of palaces as well as hovels, even in the most remote regions, where photographs, enlargements, paintings and even silk embroideries immortalize the features of living persons and ancestors who occupy a place of honor.

This cult of the portrait was sometimes very useful for us as a talking point with local potentates. A delicate discussion becomes easier in the peaceful atmosphere created by the act of posing. An opportune gift of his likeness sweetens the attitude of such a *tao-tai* (prefect) and makes it easier to obtain his signature on a *hu-chao* (passport).

This work had, furthermore, an advantage in introducing me to certain personages in surroundings that revealed their individual personalities. When I was making the portrait of General Ma-Chao-Ou, the tao-tai of Kashgar, I remember that his son was present throughout the session, a child of eight years with a cranium in the form of a tower, like the one seen in traditional images of Lao Tse. After the murder of his older son by political enemies, the general never let this only remaining offspring out of his sight, and watched him with the eye of a bird of prey, glistening with a mystical and maternal tenderness.

When Marshal King, the president of Sinkiang, presented to me his face, with its wax-and-dust color of an opium addict, in the carefully studied pose of a military man such as one sees in Western newspaper photos, I made the drawing flanked by two executioner-type bodyguards with their hands on their Mausers and their cutlasses sheathed in scarlet leather shoulder straps. These precautions were not surprising in the marshal, whose experience had been enriched by becoming president via the assassination of his predecessor.

Old General Tchou, former governor of Hami, posed for me in an enormous room crammed with the noisy crowd of a wedding banquet. The strident sounds of an orchestra accompanied a theatrical performance taking place in the enclosed courtyard. Huge vases placed in the corners of the room allowed the joyous guests to relieve their digestive systems before returning to the continuing merriment at its height. A powerful aroma of opium (which explained the beatific and detached appearance of the general) competed with that of the local distilled spirits.

Finally, Mr. Tchen, commissioner of foreign affairs for Sinkiang, received me with an exuberant display of amiability. He inquired, with emphatic compliments, about my preference with regard to his costume. Having learned that I found him very elegant in his superb Chinese tunic, made of heavy brocaded satin, and flat cap with a coral sphere on top, he disappeared and returned shortly with a melon-shaped hat in his hand, dressed in a European-type outfit combining civilian and military styles, created by the great man of the Chinese Revolution and known as a Sun Yat Tsen national suit. I did not think that this absurd accoutrement flattered Mr. Tchen while he posed for me, but what a precious compensation it must have been for him to feel that he had succeeded in making it unpleasant for me.

The antique face of Asia is revealed in its many facets by the ruins that are the landmarks of its immense spaces and by the centuries of its history. Cultures superimposed and entangled. Influences and penetrations. Flux and reflux of migrations from a thousand years ago. The entire length of our journey borrows the itineraries of conquering armies and ancient caravan routes, which also are the conduits for the great mystical ideas of the past.

Alexander the Great, Darius, Mahomet, Genghiz Khan, the monk Hsuan-Tsang and the Venetian Marco Polo have left their traces there, both material and spiritual. The site of a famous battle enclosed by the contour of the horizon, a mountain that diverts an ancient route marked by a thousand-year-old milestone, grandiose ruins or even a simple burial mound are all witnesses that evoke, in the astoundingly precipitous terrain, a vision of natives and the movement of peoples. The whole epic of Alexander reemerges into a disturbing reality in the course of our journey. We live through it again right up to the center of the continent. The Hellenistic influence on the arts extends all the way to the Pacific. Its monuments rise along our route like grandiose sentinels, witnesses to the glories that have vanished.

Cruel scars often remind us of the fury of the conquests under the standard of the Prophet. It was thus, brutally mutilated by the sacred fanaticism of Islam, that we saw for the first time the serene effigy of the Buddha. In the valley of Bamian, the statue stands erect, immense, but in spite of its dimensions incomparably human. It is integral with the great rock mass of the cliff, which itself is excavated into a thousand cells permeated with mysterious life. It is a monumental page from an occult book, sculpted into the mountain.

A few fragments of mural paintings keep alive the Hellenistic inspiration through which it expresses a delicate charm. The finest of these, as much in the ease and mastery of their execution as in the freedom of their conception, are grouped in the vault above the head of the Great Buddha. Curious to analyze more deeply the spirit of this art and to preserve a few documents of these paintings of which, unfortunately, the years have not abstained from erasing the traces, I devote myself to the role of a copyist. Perched on an unstable deck chair on the colossal cranium, one must pass long hours of work, with one's head tilted back, to decipher the supple lines, so full of life, on a surface eroded by the weather and pitted by the rifle shots of Muhammadan fanatics.

Farther on, in Chinese Turkestan, there were other remarkable archaeological sites, but since all artistic and scientific work was at that time officially forbidden it was impossible for me to preserve anything other than a memory. It was only at Bazaklik, near Turfan, before paintings of great interest where the Hellenistic, Hindu and Sassanian influences were often dominated by the Chinese art of that period, that I was again able to take up my brushes. At that time, in December, a new technical obstacle was placed before me by a formidable enemy: the cold. Having adopted, from experience on my previous journeys, an ancient paint formula that the Italians call tempera, I always mixed my paints according to the colors needed but with a rapid rate of drying, which encouraged hasty work and facilitated putting my studies immediately into a carton. In the grottoes of Bazaklik, when the colors were diluted normally with water, they unfortunately froze quickly at that low temperature.

One had to contend with this inconvenience in addition to having one's hands become stiff at the joints, while setting up, with the aid of one of our faithful mechanics, a canvas palette heated by a gasoline stove. At the end of the day, enriched by my harvest, I was so impoverished in calories that I envisaged with joy, for the benefit of my circulation, the travel on foot over the several kilometers that separated the grottoes from our encampment in the village of Mourtouk.

In contrast, an unusual work environment always made one feel warm in the daily contact with those around me, in the intimate atmosphere of the mission in which each one could unconsciously get away from one's efforts, giving disinterested and almost fraternal expression to one's particular talents. At Urumtschi and at Suchow, where the expedition was immobilized, I passed the long evenings making portraits, those of my travel companions. They already filled the pages of my notebook in the form of sketches and caricatures. A game of cards replaced the routine, and by illustrating the menus I made my contribution to the Christmas Eve supper, held under a tree that was decorated with mechanical parts representing the traditional toys.

How often, in our ridiculous fur outfits, we gathered to watch near the vehicles, whose motors had to be frequently started to maintain their temperature. In long and intimate conversations, we either relived our old memories of Africa or sketched out the program of our future work around a fire of brush or dried dung, betraying the weariness that could be read on all our faces in the flickering light of the flames. These were the elements of a painting conceived in the course of those glacial nights.

Thus, the days of work alternated with days of struggle with nature or with the lagging confidence of the men. Willpower and patience ended in conquering the distance, kilometer by kilometer, and under the blond sun of the Chinese winter the expedition approached its goal.

Triumphant receptions. They give us, at first, the illusion that our task is finished, with an appearance of security acquired at the cost of long effort. Why does the joy of our success alternate with an indefinable melancholy? Was it because of contact with civilization rediscovered? Had reaching the goal erased in us the awareness of success? Strange uncertainties floated in the air.

One evening, when we were traveling by sea toward Indochina,

Haardt came into my cabin. He had decided to rest a few days in Hong Kong to get rid of the grippe that had refused to leave him since we left Peking. He would take the next boat to rejoin us at Hanoi. We were making our way through the fog, and at regular intervals the siren sent out its mournful call, when Haardt turned around as he was leaving through my door, and said:

"It's a gloomy night, isn't it, Iaco? It is like that night in Paris when together we saw that play, *Au Grand Large.*"

I can still hear the voice of that remarkable man, that friend, whose words would be his farewell to me. His death a few days later smote the entire expedition a brutal and unexpected blow.

Having been tied down in the course of our trip in accumulating numerous documents, now that the voyage was over I had another task: to assemble the results obtained through work in the studio. It seemed to me that my cartons and field notebooks were bulging with a disconcerting variety, which I had to condense and select from in accordance with a general concept of the whole. Each element of interest had to be developed as a function of a proper relationship that would give its true expression to such a long voyage. I had to pass through a stage of making preliminary outlines, which would define the character of each painting as well as the general spirit of my exposition. Human types whose features I had recorded in drawings made on the spot; reconstruction of the surroundings familiar to them; interpretation through successive images of the immense extent of our journey, which would likewise evoke the varied phases of our nomadic life; and finally the sense of measureless space, whose enormity seemed to make one faint—such was the thrust of my activity in homage to the memory of the friend whom I had lost.

As a partial expression of the collective effort that should consecrate the national significance of the achievement by our departed chief, my work was filled with a sentiment shared by all of our companions. Mr. Louis Audouin-Dubreuil, our assistant leader, put it into words in the preface of the catalog of my exhibition.

> In the course of the Asian campaign, which was studied at such great length by the inspired organizer who paid for that dream with his life, we lived for one year in four geographical seasons: spring in Persia, summer in the Himalaya, autumn in Turkestan and winter in China.
>
> Nothing will better serve the memory of our great leader and friend

than the dedicated and persevering realization of the projects he conceived but which death did not allow him to follow through to their end.

In the ceaseless, profound expression of a past that belongs to us, but that was his work, it is now up to us to materialize the creative thought of a man who has already entered into legend.

CHAPTER 4

With the Nomads of Central Asia

Edward Murray, 1936

Edward Stevenson Murray (1909–85) was born in Cedar Rapids, Iowa. After graduating in 1930 from Coe College in Cedar Rapids, he joined the faculty of Robert College, an American institution in Istanbul. Several of his students were from Central Asia, and it was in response to their invitation that he undertook an extended journey to that part of the world. In the autumn of 1934, he arrived at Kuldja (Xinyuan), a bustling former Silk Route town in northwest Sinkiang (Xinjiang), populated by various groups of Muslims, Buddhists and carousing Russians. The following June, he set off alone on horseback to spend the summer on the upper pastures of the Tekes Valley, a fabled "plateau paradise" at the feet of the highest Tien Shan peaks. There he would be a guest in the yurt of the highest chieftain of the Kyrghyz, who was a cousin by marriage of the Tatar students from Istanbul and Kuldja and was also responsible for the administration of the nearby Kalmuk Mongols. This chapter is Murray's perceptive account of a remarkable experience in which he shared the lives of the Central Asian nomads in a prolonged and intimate way, something few, if any, other Americans or Europeans have done.[1]

Beyond Bukhara and Samarkand lies Tashkent, and from Tashkent eastward stretches an ancient silk caravan route to Cathay. It winds across steppes, mountains and the Sino-Russian boundary until it runs past the glamorous Central Asian metropolis of Kuldja (or Ningyuan) in Sinkiang, whose bazaar is a riot of color and whose community is an amazing mixture of tongues. Here, in the winter, old-style Russians in gay troikas race to and from all-night parties, solemn processions of Mongol lamas parade through the streets on horseback, and long-robed Chinese and

Turkic merchants shout and gesticulate in the crowded marketplace. In summer lumbering oxcarts replace racing troikas, and from the streets, which have become dust ponds, clouds of fine sand swirl aloft to hover over the city like a pall. Then life in Kuldja becomes unbearable, and the populace, by horse, wagon and on foot, packs off for the mountains.

And so it was that, after spending seven winter and spring months in Kuldja, I found myself in mid-June two days by horse south of the city, half lost in the mountains and searching for the famous Tekes Valley. My trail was winding up the bottom of a deep ravine. The steep slopes were bare of trees but covered with an unbelievably rank growth of grass and weeds. This vegetation formed walls on the narrow trail. Suddenly a horseman emerged from the undergrowth onto the trail in front of me. I recognized him as a Kalmuk, a nomad from one of the Central Asian tribes of Mongols; his dark skin, high cheekbones and brimless, domed, felt hat made that certain. We rode up the trail for a short distance without speaking. It is a fine point of their social etiquette, so I always let the natives make the advances.

"Where are you going?" His expression was decidedly unfriendly.

"To the Tekes Valley," I replied.

"What is your business in the Tekes?"

"I visit Sayan Beg, the chieftain of the Kyrghyz."

The man swung his horse around, his face a complete transformation. Where before there had been sullen distrust, there was now smiling friendliness.

"This trail does not lead to the Tekes," he explained. "If you follow it you will be lost in the mountains." Then he gave me elaborate directions for retracing my steps and picking up the right trail. "And carry greetings from the Kalmuks to the chief of the highland Kyrghyz," he called after me as we parted.

I rode off on a trail that led over a series of hogbacks until suddenly I came out on the crest of the last ridge. At my feet lay the goal I had been aiming at for three years—the Tekes, valley of valleys, the nomad paradise of Central Asia. My eyes sought the opposite valley wall, above which the foothills of the Celestial Mountains leveled off to a great plain, which stretched away to meet the snow line. On that undulating plateau were those famed highlands I had come to see. Even in distant Istanbul we had heard tales of how the nomads migrate to these Tekes highlands, bringing with them their herds to spend the summer, drinking the famous mare's milk, feasting on mutton, sporting, loving and marrying. Far across the valley I made out a scattering of brown huts. It must be the winter quarters of Sayan Beg.

"So you are a real American," exclaimed Sayan Beg, the Kyrghyz chieftain. I had to explain to him my coming to the Tekes. His Tatar cousins had been my students at Roberts College in Istanbul. They had captured my fancy with tales of their home city, Kuldja, and the Tekes Valley. They had given me a warm invitation to visit them. Sayan Beg was strangely cast for a nomad chieftain, small, thin-boned and delicate, yet he had unbounded nervous energy and a regal manner, coupled with a quick, decisive way of uttering commands. Tribal headquarters was soon crowded with Kyrghyz. During a lull in my cross-examination by the circle of nomads, I questioned the chief about the different peoples living in the valley.

"There are two main races here in the Tekes, nomadic Turks and Mongols," he told me. "We Turks are represented by the Kyrghyz and Kazakhs, two great tribes whose customs, language and religion (Muhammadan Sunni) are almost identical. The Kalmuks, or Mongols, in the other end of the valley have lived here for centuries with their Tibetan religion, Mongolian language and unspeakable customs. The Chinese have found that they cannot rule us, so they have decided to let us rule ourselves. However, the Chinese, feeling the need for more centralized control, have given our family nominal jurisdiction over the whole valley. The scheme works admirably. While I am busy with tribal business, Ala Beg (Chief Ala) will be your guide and companion." Sayan Beg nodded toward a smiling young Kyrghyz of about twenty-five years who wore his white felt hat at a rakish angle and was fitted out in a corduroy coat, thick woolen riding breeches, homemade Russian knee boots and a sash of black homespun wound around his waist.

"Our tribal business here at the headquarters is finished," announced Sayan Beg one morning. "We leave for the highland pastures before sundown." He would gather a group of valley officials and visit the highland pastures to see that there was peace among the tribesmen. The day was magnificently clear—a rather unusual occurrence in the Tekes, where clouds commonly hover over the Tien Shan so that few and fleeting are the glimpses one gets of its towering peaks. Just once did I catch sight of the majestic 23,622-foot Khan Tengri. Within a quarter of an hour a brilliant day may change into a torrent of rain and hail or a driving windstorm. But it is this very rain that makes the Tekes unique in Central Asia—a verdant paradise in the hub of a large expanse of semidesert.

We were not the only ones on the trail. It was the last of June, and the hot weather on the valley floor was rapidly drying up the grass, sending the nomads up to fresher pastures. Servants and others too poor to own or keep horses ride oxback. Each caravan consisted of from three to a dozen cattle on which had been piled the dismantled yurts and their contents. Women on horseback were herding the pack animals along the trail.

For several hours the horses had been straining up the steep path. The warm air of the lowlands was giving way to upland air that made one tingle. Suddenly we came out on the highland plateau. It was far and above my wildest fancy. It was superb—mile after mile of rolling pastureland, knee-deep succulent grass, sharp ravines appearing like notches cut out of the highlands, irregular patches of tall pines running down the sides of the ravines. Here was grass to pasture millions. Dotting the plateau were little colonies of yurts—three or four in a group, with horses and sheep milling about them.

The nomads have evolved the yurt, a home that is easily transportable, commodious, cool in summer and warm in winter. The yurts vary in size from the one-man variety to a chieftain's yurt thirty to thirty-five feet in diameter. The structure consists of a collapsible trelliswork about three feet tall, which is set up in a circle, leaving an opening for the door frame. Next, arched poles resembling ribs of a huge umbrella are lashed all around to the top of the latticework, and the curved ribs, instead of meeting above in an apex, are socketed into a wooden ring about a yard across. The roof of arched poles is covered with large pieces of felt about a quarter-inch thick. In winter the trellis wall is covered on the outside with felt, but in warm weather it is simply screened with reed matting.

The open ring at the top lets light and air into the yurt and allows for the escape of smoke. A flap of felt can be drawn back and forth over the aperture by ropes; thus, the draft can be regulated or in rain the interior made watertight. To the right of the door as you enter is a reed matting enclosure, which serves as a storeroom for milk and cream and also affords the women a cramped bit of privacy. The family possessions are ranged along the back wall, set up off the ground on a low wooden platform. Here are the metalworked trunks that contain the family heirlooms of embroideries and gold and silver trinkets; around and on top of the trunks are piled gay-colored comforters.

"There is our destination," cried Ala Beg, pointing to a group of yurts at the head of a deep ravine. Our highland host came smiling to greet us as we galloped up abreast. We dismounted, threw our reins to the servants, and were soon inside the yurt, guzzling bowl after bowl of mare's milk. I soon discovered that kumiss is mildly intoxicating. When I got up to go out I found myself somewhat unsteady, and all from pure mare's milk a day old. First kumiss, then tea, then mutton; such is the order of a Tekes feast. We had arrived at sundown, and it was well on toward the setting of the quarter moon before we had disposed of the last of the sheep, licked our fingers and cleaned our knives. An old shepherd came in with a two-string lute; he warbled away in a high-pitched voice, a weird falsetto in which most of the Turkic songs are sung. We slept in a semicircle with our feet toward the smoldering fire, the host and his wife at the head end, Sayan Beg and myself next, while the rest of the party were graded in rank down to Ahmed, the servant, at the tail end.

Morning found us up at daybreak. A young Kyrghyz took me down the ravine to show me his gaming eagle and a small *illik* (Tien Shan roe deer) it had caught the day before. In the Tekes, hunting with falcons and eagles is traditional sport. There are gay hunting days when the men go off on horseback, the hooded birds fettered to the hunter's leather-protected arm. In addition to small game and illik, there are ibex, *Ovis poli,* bears, snow leopards, wolves and foxes.

The scene around the yurts in the encampment was typically nomadic: the men were sprawled on the grass, conversing; the women were toiling at household duties. In nomadic life, the woman does almost all the hard work. She must keep the fire and prepare the food, except for feasts, when the men cook the meat in special deference to and honor of their guests. She weaves carpets and ribbons, winds ropes and yarns, milks, and tends the flocks, children and household. It is the woman who catches, saddles and bridles the horse and brings it to her liege lord. In moving, the woman again bears the brunt of the labor; it is she who must pitch and strike the yurts, pack the goods on the oxen and drive them to the next camping ground.

Toward midday, as we were drinking kumiss inside the yurt, we heard a pounding of hoofs outside; it was the mares arriving for milking time. Ordinarily, the mares are docile and permit themselves to be milked; if one is obstreperous, the foal is first allowed to suckle a while and the milker takes its place. The mare's milk is put into a large sack, made of a sheep's skin or more often a colt's skin, in which there is still some sour milk with the fermentative bacteria left from the day before. The milk remains in the skin for about twenty-four hours, and intermittently the old women churn it with a dasher. Nerime, the old mother of our host, explained that they churn it from ten to a dozen times a day for five or ten minutes each time. The milk separates into a thick white curd, which settles to the bottom, and a thinner upper layer, which is the kumiss. This is ready to draw off and drink the next day and tastes much like buttermilk. A wealthy man with hundreds of horses can easily provide for all his household. Our host had to provision three yurts: his own, his parents', and the servants', providing for about twenty-five people in all.

During one of the rounds of kumiss in the main yurt, a servant dragged a sheep to the door; the animal must be blessed before being slain. We stretched out our arms, palms heavenward, muttering the prayer, "Allah ekber rakmet" (God is great, we thank Thee). The ritual was completed by stroking our beards or, if beardless, our chins. The eastern Turk is meticulous in observing blessings. No animal is butchered on a festive occasion, no one gets up to leave after a meal, no ceremony is complete until, after a moment of silence with palms outstretched, the Beneficent Provider is invoked.

In summer the meat is cooked outside the yurt at a fire hole. Every bit of the sheep is used: the meat is eaten, the hide cured with the sediment of the kumiss churning and the intestines saved for bologna. We assembled inside the yurt and took our places in a semicircle, Sayan Beg and I in the center as usual. A boy appeared with a hammered copper ewer and bowl. Setting the bowl in front of us, he ran a stream of water from the long-spouted pitcher into it; we washed our hands and dried them on the towel he carried slung over his shoulder. Ala Beg led the festal procession, carrying the enormous bowl of mutton. The largest platter was for the honored guest and contained the head, part of the tail, and a piece of the loin. Ala Beg set it down in front of Sayan Beg, who picked up the head and handed it to me. I stripped a portion from the cheek and handed it back. He cut off both ears, a large slice of the jowl, and passed what was left to a waiting servant. "Take it to the Baba." This was our host's father, who lived in a separate yurt.

Then, gathering in three groups around the kettles of meat, the Begs pulled their knives from their sashes and began cutting the meat into small bits. After all the bones had been scraped clean of meat, bowls of meat juice, unsalted but seasoned with pepper, were brought in and the traditional long Turkish towel was spread around, each one putting a section over his knee. The meat bits were dipped in the juice and eaten; more juice, more dipping, more chewing; silence save for the lusty smacking of lips, licking of fingers and other uncamouflaged gustatory noises. The Turk, like the Chinese, believes in a time for eating and a time for talking and is horrified when the two are indiscriminately mixed. Even Ala Beg, whose tongue was ever on the rampage, seemed to become a different person as he sat before the meat bowl; he dipped and chewed, his whole being absorbed in the process.

It was amazing how quickly a fat sheep could disappear. When the meat was eaten, the men attacked the bones, breaking them and sucking out the marrow; then there was a veritable sucking chorus. The waiting women and children began where we men had left off, and the powerful tongues and lips of the servants ferreted out any marrow that the children had left. The circle of dogs snarled and fought over what remained. Although everyone had more meat than he really wanted, the game of finding a shred of flesh continued until the bones were meatless and marrowless. Then the boy with the pitcher and towel made the rounds again. All eyes began to wander, the lolling feasters straightened up, we stretched out our palms heavenward, "Allah ekber rakmet," the motion of stroking our chins and the feast was over. So was all strenuous endeavor for the remainder of the day.

The Kyrghyz and Kazakhs marry their daughters off for a price, just as Marco Polo related that they did six hundred years ago, and as they probably had been doing for untold centuries before the Venetian visited Asia. Bridal prices run from as high as forty *kara* and a thousand *yanduk* (forty horses and a thousand sheep) for the daughter of a very rich man to as low as one kara (a cow or a horse) for a poor servant girl.

And then one evening, after we had listened for long hours to a twanging two-string lute, Sayan Beg announced: "We have found peace among the Kyrghyz tribesmen; we must keep our promise and visit the pastures of the Kalmuks."

Next morning horses were rounded up, saddles thrown on and we were off. The sun was well up before we reached the lowlands, splashed across several small streams and came at last to the primitive cantilever bridge thrown across the Tekes River. There were men at the bridge who would lead the horses across for a fee. A man walked across, swaying dizzily above the rushing, muddy torrent. One of the bridge horsemen took a horse across; the flimsy log ladder, laid between the two juts of bridging, danced and swung.

"Every four or five summers," Ala Beg had said, "some horseman is carried to his death when the bridge rots out; then the structure is rebuilt." Humbly I brought up the rear. Nor did any others of our party venture to lead their own horses across. Once over the bridge, we were in the land of the Kalmuks.

The Kalmuks are frequently spoken of as being related to the Mongols, when, as a matter of fact, they are Mongols. In centuries past there was a great confederacy of western Mongol tribes, the Olot; the present Kalmuks represent the remnants of this great horde. The name has been given them by the Turco-Tatar tribes among whom they live; it is probably derived from the Turkic verb *kalmak* ("to remain"). The history of the Kalmuks is obscure. However, it is certain that in the seventeenth century they occupied the whole region in and around the Tekes Valley. Late in that century they fled the tyranny of the Chinese warlords and crossed the Russian steppes to settle along the Volga. Eighty years later the Chinese emperor Chien Lung (1736–96), in a frantic search for some settlers to create a buffer state in the Tekes Valley region, made an attractive offer to the Volga Kalmuks, and the majority of them returned to set up their yurts again in the Tekes Valley grasslands. Some remained, however, and still form a settlement of Mongols, the Russian Kalmuks, along the Volga.

They are, in truth, a squalid race, reputed never to change their clothes or wash. When one coat wears out, a new one is put on over it, and not until it rots off do they discard a garment. In spite of Ala Beg's education of Arduch, the Kalmuk boy, the little fellow was not even up to Kyrghyz standards of cleanliness. But their filthiness does not prevent the Kalmuks from gaining riches. Their flocks of sheep are countless, and herds of horses blacken their pasturelands. Their wants are few, their standard of living at rock bottom and their only expenditures an occasional sheep or horse bartered in the bazaar for gold and silver bracelets and earrings for a daughter of the household.

Altan, a prince by birth, was the ruler of the Tekes Kalmuks, subject to the superior orders of the Great Lama. He wore a neat little velvet hat and a loose-fitting coat and long pants, which were heavily padded to keep out rain, sun and cold; from beneath his coat cuffs protruded a garment once white but long since changed to a grimy gray. In his twisted sash he carried a combination knife, chopstick and steel toothpick case. His head was cleanly shaven save for a knot well back in the center of his scalp, and from this hung a long braided pigtail with a silk tassel tied on the end. As their hair thins out with age, the Kalmuk men add strands of human or horse hair to the pigtail to keep it at a respectable length.

In the Kalmuk yurt we sat, as was the custom in Kyrghyz yurts, in a semicircle facing the door. In front of each two of us was a footstool on which were placed such various Mongol concoctions as ground wheat sweetened with sugar or goat's cheese dried and cured in the sun. The latter might have been palatable had it not been thoroughly mixed with hair. Since the women prepare the cheese, it is no wonder that it is adulterated, for the Kalmuk women wear long braids of false hair. They are most commonly fashioned from a horse's tail, but the wife of an especially important man may have braids of hair cut from their own Kalmuk dead or bought from the Chinese in the bazaar.

Altan's wife, all decked out in her regal yellow domed hat, was serving the party the famous Mongol arrack, or distilled milk, which is prepared by distilling the kumiss. It looked just like water, but I had heard that it was more potent. Therefore, I looked askance at the silver goblet that Altan's wife handed to Sayan Beg, and which he passed on to me, seated as I always was on his right. Sayan Beg noticed my hesitancy.

"Drink it," he snapped. "Don't insult them." This was the only time I had ever incurred his disfavor. I began sipping it. "In one gulp," he urged. "It is a rule among Kalmuks, the first three goblets at one draught." And then, of course, I was inveigled into drinking a fourth.

The next day I suggested that we visit the monastery. The chief himself had never been inside the walls and was eager for the trip; he dispatched a request to the Great Lama, who sent back a priest to assure us that he would be honored by our visit.

Each Kalmuk tribe has its own lama monastery, which is taboo to women save on the one or two festivals a year when women as well as men are welcomed within the temple grounds. On these occasions, so it is whispered among the Kyrghyz, there are bacchanalian orgies. My Tatar students had said that it was the custom for the Kalmuk bride to spend the first two nights after the wedding at the lama city. However, when I asked Ala Beg, he declared that the practice had been discontinued twenty years before when a report of it reached the ears of the Tibetan Grand Lama. Although the Divine Lama may have endeavored to raise the morals of his distant flock, the Kalmuks are still far from bordering on the puritanical.

The Great Lama of the Tekes is the richest man of his flock. His pastures are boundless, his flocks countless, and by the mere gesture of a hand or careless order he can add vast riches to his name, for the Kalmuks are fearful of divine power and worship him as a god.

When we arrived at the monastery, the old lama was waiting to receive us in his gold-brocaded robe. One of his priests brought in a skin of kumiss, and we drank the ceremonial three bowls. The lama's home was a two-room structure—one small room to eat and sleep in, the other a large room for his gods. A massive altar stood against the center wall. In front of the centrally seated Buddha were dozens of small, copper, offering cups. Some of the cups held milk, others grains and crumbs of bread, but all were quite fresh and recently set out.

"Don't fear," whispered Ala Beg at my elbow, "they don't waste the gifts. Every morning they offer a prayer of thanksgiving to the Buddha—happy that he has received their offerings; then they empty all the little cups into the great iron kettle, throw in anything else they happen to have on hand, and boil up the hotchpotch for their one daily meal."

When I questioned the lama as to whether he had been to Tibet, he brought out a long, narrow, red-and-white-striped envelope of the Chinese variety. Tenderly he drew out and unfolded a long sheet of paper, brown and frayed at the edges.

"It is a letter from the Dalai Lama of Tibet," he said, casting a sidelong glance at me to catch my look of admiration. "As a young priest I went on a pilgrimage to Tibet, and for seven years I remained there, studying the holy writings and learning the mysteries of the Great Buddha. Since my return, the Divine Lama has sent me several letters."

The lama called one of his priests and gave directions for showing us around. As we stood in the main assembly room of the temple, I commented to Ala Beg on the size of the great central Buddha.

"But that is only their second Buddha. There is a Buddha somewhere in the temple that is of solid gold; I have never seen it, but the Kalmuks all over the valley speak of it with awe and reverence and look to it as their true and greatest Tekes god."

I stepped over to Sayan Beg, who was looking at the strange collection of idols with unfeigned curiosity. "Ala Beg says there is an even greater Buddha of solid gold. Why not ask the priest if we can see it?"

The chief spoke to our guide, who sent word of our request to the lama. A priest came back bringing the lama's permission for the chief, Ala Beg and myself to visit the place of the Great Buddha. Led by the priest, the three of us clambered up a steep back stairway. We found a felt yurt pitched in the center of the large, second-story, paneled room. The priest reverently lifted the yurt flap, went through a series of obeisances, and motioned for us to enter; however, he did not approach the altar or allow us to do so. It was quite similar to the usual Kalmuk altar, but the foot-high Buddha was of yellow gold, and hung about its neck were dozens of strings of what appeared to be precious stones.

For several days we were entertained at the chief's yurt. Sayan Beg spent the day meeting with the important Kalmuk stock owners, while the rest of us lay about, talking, or rode off to visit some nearby yurts. Early one morning three Kalmuks rode up to the yurt, apparently on official business. Fastened to their saddles were elaborately tooled leather flasks; these they brought into the yurt, loosed the silver goblets strapped to their belts, and began to pour out arrack for the company. "It is a formal invitation to the yurt of Arduch, the little Kalmuk," whispered Ala Beg. We each drank our ritualistic three goblets, and the chief's Tatar mother taught me a valuable lesson. When she was offered a fourth goblet of arrack she merely touched her lips to the cup and handed it back; and lo! the emissary drank it himself. I tried the same procedure and found that it worked in my case too. Whenever I was offered a goblet after the first three, I had merely to touch my lips to it and return it; it was an insult to me should the one who offered not drink his own returned cup.

Soon after the official invitation had been completed and the Kalmuks had left, we mounted and rode off to make the visit. There was the inevitable cry for a show of horsemanship. Ala Beg challenged anyone to a real "horse and rider" battle. One of the younger Kyrghyz accepted the challenge, and they rode off, parrying, thrusting and finally ending in a clinch. Neither could unseat the other; their mounts seemingly had joined in the sport and galloped along, ever veering and turning flank to flank. Finally, Ala Beg grabbed the reins and drew his horse to a standstill. The other Kyrghyz, thrown off balance, fell from his saddle. "Hurrah, Ala Beg, hurrah!" shouted Foo Ben Yee, while the loser, rubbing one shoulder good-humoredly, clambered back onto his horse.

We rode abreast into the Kalmuk circle of yurts. Waiting to meet us were Arduch and his lama-priest brother, who had come from the monastery. To greet us, they stiffly clasped their hands in front of them and gave a short, choppy curtsy. They ushered us into a large, new yurt; one could see by the thick mat of grass that it had been only recently set up. We took seats on mats and blankets.

"Yesterday I superintended the setting up of this yurt on clean ground," whispered Ala Beg. "Whenever Kyrghyz are to be entertained in

Kalmuk yurts, the Kalmuks call on me to make the preparations, for the Kyrghyz cannot stomach the usual Kalmuk filth. It is I who must butcher the sheep for today's feast too. These 'heathen' Kalmuks simply knock a sheep on the head and boil it, blood and all. That is forbidden in our Koran; so I must see that the sheep is slain and bled in the Muslim manner, otherwise we Kyrghyz could not eat the meat."

After we had drunk the inevitable initial three cups of arrack, footstools were set up and stocked with the sugared flour and dried cheese. We were interrupted in the business of sorting the bits of cheese from the hair when a sheep was dragged to the yurt door. Lifting our palms heavenward we muttered the blessing and stroked our chins. The Kalmuks are past masters at aping the ways of others whenever so doing is either polite or politic. Yet asking a blessing is not aping but a genuine respect for an admirable custom. Arduch told me that even in their own Kalmuk gatherings they frequently carried out this Chinese Muslim ritual.

While Ala Beg cooked the mutton, Arduch showed me the encampment. The scene was similar to that in a Kyrghyz camp: males talking, females toiling. The women, dressed in filthy garments and decked out in even more grimy-looking horsehair headdresses, were milking sheep tethered in a double row facing each other. The milkers were mostly older women, that is, relatively old, for the dirt, toil and smoky yurts make the average Kalmuk woman wrinkled, leather-skinned and misshapen long before she reaches forty.

The younger women were all beads, buttons and braids. Their husbands ordered the older wives and women to do the hard, manual labor and let these younger "beauties" sit around and look pretty for as many years as they can. They do light work in the yurt, sewing garments of homespun and acting as mistresses of ceremony when their husbands have guests.

Momentous news awaited me at the chief's yurt: my permission to leave the country, now five long months overdue, had at last arrived. In the morning I must start my trek back across the Chinese border into Russian Turkestan, through Tashkent, Samarkand and Bukhara to Iran. As I lay in my blankets, feet toward the fire, looking out the round hole in the yurt top, it seemed as if life in the Tekes was the only reality—the rest of the world revolved in a realm apart.

CHAPTER 5

Seven Years in Tibet

Heinrich Harrer, 1954

Heinrich Harrer was born in 1912 in his mother's ancestral home at Knappenberg, a small village in the Noric Alps of southeast Austria. Throughout his childhood and adolescence, the surrounding mountains attracted him powerfully, and he soon became proficient at alpine sports. Since then his life has been a crescendo of adventure. In 1936, he was a member of the Austrian Olympic ski team. Two years later, his name became engraved forever in the annals of mountaineering as one of the four who made the first ascent of the Eiger north face (Harrer 1965; Rowell 1977; Rogers and Harlin 1991). The outbreak of World War II found him in the Himalayas of India (now Pakistan) after completing a reconnaissance of the murderous Nanga Pabat. He and his Austrian companions were promptly interned in British prisoner-of-war camps, where he avidly read the most authentic books about Tibet (Bell 1924, 1928) while making physical and mental preparations for his escape into that neutral but forbidden country. That was the beginning of his enduring Tibetan saga (Harrer 1954, 1984, 1992; DiRusso 1992).[1] The passages collected in this chapter describe the nearly fatal ordeal of his walk, together with his Austrian colleague Aufschnaiter, as a fugitive across the barren heights of the immense Tibetan Plateau, followed by his years as an honored guest and significant employee in the Dalai Lama's Lhasa.

[After three escapes from British internment camps in India:] As I was loping along in the gray of dawn I found myself facing my first leopard. My heart nearly stopped beating as I was completely defenseless. My only weapon was a long knife, which the camp blacksmith had made expressly for me. I carried it sheathed in a stick. The leopard sat on a thick branch fifteen feet or more above the ground, ready to spring. I thought like lightning what was the best thing to do, then, masking my fear, I walked steadily on my way. Nothing happened, but for a long time I had a peculiar feeling in my back.

It may have been a little after midnight when I ran into a bear standing on his hind legs in the middle of my path, growling at me. At this point the sound of the swiftly running waters of the Ganges was so loud that we had neither of us heard the other's approach. Pointing my primitive spear at his heart, I backed step by step so as to keep my eyes fixed on him. Around the first bend in the track I hurriedly lit a fire, and pulling out a burning stick, I brandished it in front of me and moved forward to meet my enemy. But coming around the corner I found the road clear and the bear gone. Tibetan peasants told me later that bears are only aggressive by day. At night they are afraid to attack.

At last, on May 17, 1944, we [Aufschnaiter and Harrer] stood at the top of the Tsangchokla Pass. We knew from our maps that our altitude was 17,200 feet. So here we were on the frontier between India and Tibet, so long the object of our wishful dreams. On top of the pass were heaps of stones and prayer flags dedicated to their gods by pious Buddhists. It was very cold. We had almost no knowledge of the language and very little money. Above all we were near starvation and must find human habitation as soon as possible. But as far as we could see there were only empty mountain heights and deserted valleys.

On this stretch we first met the *kiang,* a sort of wild ass, which lives in Central Asia and enchants travelers with the gracefulness of its movements. This animal is about the size of a mule. It often shows curiosity and comes up to look at passers-by—and then turns and trots off in the most elegant manner. The kiang feeds on grass and is left in peace by the inhabitants. Its only enemy is the wolf.

[Expelled from Tibet and reentering farther west, more than seven hundred miles from Lhasa:] We had reached Tibet at one of the few places where Tibetan territory extends into the Himalaya range. We had a grueling climb to the top of a pass called by the Tibetans Bud-Bud La. This pass must be over 18,000 feet high. The air was unpleasantly rarified and the ice tongues of a neighboring glacier projected over the route.

I have a vivid recollection of one person whom I encountered on this stretch of road. This was a young nomad, muffled in a long sheepskin coat and wearing a pigtail, as all Tibetan men do who are not monks. He led us to his black tent made of yak's hair where his wife was waiting for him. She was a merry creature, always laughing. Inside the tent we found a treasure that made our mouths water—a haunch of venison. Our host gladly sold us a portion of the meat for an absurdly low price. He begged us to say nothing about his hunting or he would get into trouble. Taking of life, whether human or animal, is contrary to the tenets of Buddhism, and consequently hunting is forbidden. Tibet is governed on a feudal system whereby men, beasts and land belong to the Dalai Lama, whose orders have the force of law.

Our friend's wife had prepared a meal from the game her husband had killed a few days before and now got down enthusiastically to cooking it. We watched the operation and were somewhat astonished when she slipped off the upper part of her great fur mantle, around the waist of which she wore a bright colored belt, without a trace of shyness. The heavy fur mantle had hindered her movements, so she stripped to the waist and carried on happily. Later we often encountered similar examples of natural simplicity. It was with real regret that we parted from this friendly couple, when fully rested and with our bellies full of good fresh meat, we set out on our way. As we traveled we often saw the black forms of wild yaks grazing far away on the mountainside.

We had to cross another high pass, the Bongru La. Camping these days was no pleasure. It was very cold by night at 17,000 feet. Small incidents provided variety. Once it was the spectacle of a fight between wild asses. The combatants were two stallions, probably fighting for the lordship over the mares in the herd. Chunks of turf flew, and the earth shook under their hoofs. The duelists were so absorbed that they did not notice us as onlookers. Meanwhile the mares, greedy for sensation, danced around, and the arena was often hidden in a thick cloud of dust.

During the whole of our march we were repeatedly stopped by prosperous-looking mounted Tibetans, who asked us what we had to sell. As we had no servants and were driving a pack donkey, they could not imagine that we were anything but traders. We became convinced that every Tibetan, whether poor or rich, is a born trader and exchange and barter his greatest passion.

One morning we heard the sound of bells in the distance as a huge mule-drawn caravan approached the village. Soldiers rode ahead followed by a swarm of male and female servants and after them members of the Tibetan nobility, also mounted, whom we now saw for the first time. The senior of the two viceroys, whom they call *garpons* in Tibet, was arriving.

He and his wife wore splendid silk robes and carried pistols in their girdles. The garpon, a high official, is invested for the duration of his mission with the fourth rank in the hierarchy of nobles. In Lhasa he is reduced to the fifth rank. All the nobles in Tibet are ranked in seven classes to the first of which only the Dalai Lama belongs. All secular officials wear their hair piled up on their heads: monks are shaven and ordinary people wear pigtails.

Now again for weeks we were on the way. During the whole of the next month we passed no inhabited place of any size—only nomad camps and isolated *tasam* houses. These are caravansaries in which one can change yaks and find a lodging. It was long since we had seen a glacier, but as we were approaching the tasam at Barka, a chain of glaciers gleaming in the sunshine came into view. The landscape is dominated by the 25,000-foot peak of Gurla Mandhata; less striking, but far more famous, was the sacred Mount Kailas, 3,000 feet lower, which stands in majestic isolation apart from the Himalaya range. The faithful often travel thousands of miles to reach it and spend years on the pilgrimage. During their journey they live on alms and hope that their reward will be a higher incarnation in a future life.

We lived like nomads; for the past three months we had been sleeping mainly in the open air. We camped and cooked and made our fires in the open, whatever the weather, while the nomads could find shelter and warmth in their heavy tents. From time to time, we had a view of the Himalayas, which surpass in natural beauty anything I have ever seen. We met fewer and fewer nomads, and the only living creatures we saw on the right bank of the Brahmaputra were gazelles and *onagers* [small wild asses]. As we marched forward we caught sight, after a while, of the gleaming golden towers of a monastery in the far distance. Above them, shining superbly in the morning sun, were tremendous walls of ice, and we gradually realized that we were looking at the giant trio [of peaks,] Dhaulagiri, Annapurna and Manaslu.

On January 19, the roads were sufficiently passable to allow us to start off in company with a huge yak caravan. Ahead of us went a herd of yaks, carrying no loads, which acted as snowplows and seemed to enjoy the exercise very much. We were deeply impressed by a rock monastery in the neighborhood of the village of Longda. Seven hundred feet above the valley red temples and countless cells were perched like birds' nests on the rocks. Despite the danger of avalanches, Aufshnaiter and I could not refrain from climbing the rock face, and so obtained another wonderful view of the Himalayas. We also met some monks and nuns and learned from them that this was the monastery founded by Milarepa, the famous Tibetan saint and poet, who lived in the eleventh century.

The name Kyirong means "village of happiness," and it really deserves that name. If I can choose where to pass the evening of my life, it will be in Kyirong. There I would build myself a house of red cedarwood and have one of the rushing mountain streams running through my garden, in which every kind of fruit would grow, for though the altitude is over 9,000 feet Kyirong lies on the twenty-eighth parallel. When we arrived in January the temperature was just below freezing; it seldom falls below −10 degrees Celsius. The seasons correspond to what we have in the Alps, but the vegetation is subtropical. One can go skiing the whole year round, and in the summer there is a row of 20,000-footers to climb.

The staple food in this region is *tsampa*. This is how they prepare it. You heat sand to a high temperature in an iron pan and then pour barley corns into it. They burst with a slight pop, whereupon you put the corns and the sand in a fine meshed sieve through which the sand runs. The resulting meal is stirred up into a paste with butter tea or milk and then eaten.

In the middle of February we had our first Tibetan New Year. Rich and poor, all come full of devotion and with no inner misgivings to lay their offerings before the gods and to pray for their blessing. Is there any people so uniformly attached to their religion and so obedient to it in their daily lives? I have always envied the Tibetans their simple faith, for all my life I have been a seeker. Though I learned, while in Asia, how to meditate, the final answer to the riddle of life had not been vouchsafed to me. But I have at least learned to contemplate the events of life with tranquility and not let myself be flung to and fro by circumstances in a sea of doubt. The people did not only pray at the turn of the year. For seven days they danced, sang and drank under the benevolent eyes of the monks. In every house there was a party, and we, too, were invited.

Our contact with the industrious, peaceable villagers had become more intimate. They did not reckon their work by the hour but used every moment of daylight. As there was a shortage of labor in the agricultural regions, hunger and poverty were unknown. The numerous monks, who do no manual work and occupy themselves with spiritual matters, are supported by the community. The women weave their own cloth, and all the clothes are made at home.

The supremacy of the monastic orders in Tibet is something unique.

It can well be compared to a stern dictatorship. The monks mistrust any influence from the outside world that might undermine their authority. For that reason, some of the monks of Kyirong disapproved of our close contact with the villagers. Our behavior, which remained uninfluenced by any of their superstitions, must have given the Tibetans something to think about. We used to go by night into the forests without being molested by demons; we climbed mountains without lighting sacrificial fires, and still nothing happened to us. In some quarters we noticed a certain reserve, which could only be attributed to the influence of the lamas. I think they must have credited us with supernatural powers, for they were convinced that our excursions had some hidden purpose.

During the summer the authorities sent for us again and summoned us to leave Kyirong. In the meantime we had learned from merchants and the newspapers that the war was over. It was known to us that after the First World War the English had kept the p.o.w. camps going in India until two years after hostilities were over. We had clearly no wish to lose our freedom now and were determined to make another attempt to penetrate into inner Tibet. Our knowledge of the language was now good, and we had acquired a lot of experience. We were both mountaineers, and here we had a unique opportunity to survey the Himalayas and the nomad districts.

We had learned that in 1904 a British punitive expedition had marched as far as the capital. Since that time the world has possessed only a superficial knowledge of Lhasa, and no goal is more attractive to the explorer than the Dalai Lama's home. Our experience had shown us that high officials are much easier to deal with than subordinates. We felt that we would be all right once we got to Lhasa. So there was no doubt about our goal: but we were not so sure how to reach it. We were, of course, attracted by the much-frequented high road with its roadhouses. Going by it, we should reach Lhasa within a few weeks. But we risked discovery and arrest.

So we decided to travel through the northern plains, which they call Chang Tang. This district is inhabited solely by nomads with whom we could safely associate. Then, we thought, we could approach Lhasa from the northwest. No one expects foreigners to come from that direction, and it would be easier for us to slip into the town. Our plan, as a matter of fact, involved considerable dangers, and the icy blizzards we encountered in Sangsang gave us an idea of what to expect. Nevertheless, we set out on December 2, 1945.

Just as the sun went down and the biting cold began to penetrate our clothing, we saw, as if we had ordered it, a black nomad tent. It was pitched in the shelter of surrounding stone called a *ihega*. One finds these enclosures scattered over the whole of Tibet, as the nomads are always moving to new pastures, and when they do they put stone fences around their tents. The ihegas also help to protect the beasts against the cold and the attacks of wolves. The nomad flatly refused to allow us into his tent. We had to camp in the open.

Next day we reached the top of the pass and were astonished to find that there was no descent and that we had simply come to a high plateau. The view over the unending plain was discouraging. One seemed to be facing infinity, and the huge spaces would certainly take months to cross. As far as we could see there was no sign of life and an ice-cold wind blew over the snow.

Then we had a lucky day. We ran into a tent and got a warm reception from an old married couple and their son, who had been camping there for several months. This was the first time we had been invited into a nomad's tent and asked to spend the night. Our hosts were horrified to hear of the route we proposed to take and strongly advised us to give it up.

Next day, soon after setting out, we ran into a deep snowdrift. Walking with our inadequate footgear soon became a torture. Some of my toes showed signs of frostbite. We were worried about our yak, which had not eaten properly for days. We passed through undulating country till we came to a pass. On crossing it, what was our astonishment but to find no more snow.

We soon ran into a nomad's tent where we were well received and allowed to graze our yak to his heart's content. This time our hostess was a young woman. In her long, black pigtail she wore mussel shells, silver coins and various cheap ornaments imported from abroad. She told us that her two husbands had gone out to drive in the animals. They had fifteen hundred sheep and a great many yaks.

We were astonished to find polyandry practiced among the nomads. It was only when we got to Lhasa that we came to know all the complicated reasons that led to the simultaneous existence in Tibet of polyandry and polygamy. The two men, when they came home, greeted us warmly, as their wife had done. An abundant supper was prepared. We laughed and jested much, and, as is usual when the company consists of several men and a single, pretty, young woman, the latter got her share of teasing.

In winter the men living a nomadic life have much to do. They busy themselves with various household chores and for recreation go hunting with their antiquated muzzle loaders. The women collect yak dung and often carry their babies around with them as they work. In the evening the herds are driven in and the [yak] cows milked—though it is little they give in winter. At night the nomads sleep on skins spread upon the ground and, slipping out of their sleeves, use their sheepskin cloaks as bedclothes. The fire is the heart of the household and is never allowed to go out. As in every peasant's house, one finds an altar in every tent, which usually consists of a simple chest on which is set an amulet or a small statue of the Buddha. There is invariably a picture of the Dalai Lama. A little butter lamp burns on the altar, and in winter the flame is almost invisible owing to the cold and the lack of oxygen. Often enough we had to bivouac in the open. We suffered much with our hands, which were always stiff with frost, for we had no gloves and used a pair of socks instead.

We had been some time on the way when a man came toward us wearing clothes that struck us as unusual. He spoke a dialect different from that of the local nomads. He left us unmolested and went on his way. It was clear that we had made the acquaintance of our first Khampa. A few hours later we saw in the distance two men on small ponies, wearing the same sort of clothes. We slowly began to feel uncomfortable. We had no money and not even the most primitive weapons. The tent pegs we carried did not impress even the sheepdogs.

Next morning we went on our way, not without misgivings, which increased when we saw a man with a gun, who seemed to be stalking us from the hillside. We were no little surprised to receive a friendly welcome at the next tent. Everyone came out. They fingered our things and helped us to unload—a thing no nomad had ever done—and suddenly it dawned on us that they were Khampas. We had walked like mice into the trap. The inhabitants of the tent were two men, a woman and a half-grown youngster.

We had hardly sat down by the fire when the tent began to fill with visitors from the neighboring tents, come to see the strangers. We had our hands full trying to keep our baggage together. The visitors gradually drifted away, and we prepared to go to bed. One of our two hosts insisted on using my rucksack as a pillow and I had the utmost difficulty keeping it by me. The woman muttered prayers without ceasing. It occurred to me that she was praying in advance for forgiveness for the crime her husband intended to commit against us the next day.

We were glad when the day broke. The Khampa family advised us to keep to the southern road, as the nomads from that region were making up a pilgrim caravan for Lhasa. Now we saw their plan. Our lives were at stake. If we went there we would be heavily outnumbered and they could dispose of us with ease. As though we suspected nothing we went on a short way. The two men were now on either side of us, while the boy walked behind. The two men wore double sheepskin cloaks, as robbers do, to protect themselves against knife thrusts, and long swords were stuck in their belts. Their faces had an expression of lamblike innocence.

Aufschnaiter thought we ought first to change our direction, so as not to walk blindly into a trap. No sooner said than done. The Khampas stopped for a moment in surprise. Our manner of speaking seemed to intimidate them. They saw that we were prepared to go to any length, so they let us go, and after staring after us for a while they hurriedly went on their way, probably to inform their accomplices. There was now no question of going forward—we had to retrace our steps. Unarmed as we were, to continue would have meant certain death. There was nothing for it but to take the hard road through uninhabited country.

We took a shortcut, entailing a laborious and steep ascent, but leading, as we hoped, to the route we meant to follow. Halfway up the steep slope we saw, to our horror, two men following us in the distance. Then we saw them turn around and go back. When we reached the crest of the ridge, we understood why our two pursuers had preferred to turn back. Before us lay the loneliest landscape I have ever seen. A sea of snowy mountain heights stretched onward endlessly. In the far distance were the Trans-Himalayas, and like a gap in a row of teeth was the pass that we calculated would lead us to the road at which we aimed. Our escape from the Khampas was due to the desolation of the region, the nature of which brought us new obstacles to surmount.

[Walking over the immense and inhospitable Chang Tang Plateau, still infested by Khampas who even stole their yak at night, Harrer and Aufschnaiter temporarily joined two caravans, first with pilgrims and then with a high official, who was deceived by their expired travel permit:] We had already been walking for some days toward a huge chain of mountains. We knew they were the Nyenchenthangla range. There was only one way through them, and that was the pass that led directly to Lhasa. The prospect of an ascent to nearly 20,000 feet was paralyzing. At last we reached the summit of our pass, Guring La. Here we again found the typical cairns and fluttering over them the brightest-colored prayer flags I had yet seen. Near them was a row of stone tables with prayers inscribed on them—an imperishable expression of the joy felt by thousands of pilgrims when, after their long and weary march, they saw the pass opening to them the road to the holiest of cities.

Now came the great question: even if we managed to smuggle ourselves into the town, would we be able to stay there? We had no money left. And our appearance! We looked more like brigands from the Chang Tang than Europeans. Aufschnaiter wore the remains of a pair of Indian army boots, and my shoes were in fragments. Our beards were perhaps our most striking feature. Like all Mongols, the Tibetans have almost no hair on their faces or bodies, whereas we had long, tangled, luxuriant beards. For this reason we were often taken for Kazakhs, a Central Asian tribe whose members migrated in swarms during the war from Soviet Russia to Tibet. They marched in with their families and flocks and plundered right and left, and the Tibetan army was eager to drive them on into India. The Kazakhs are often fair skinned and blue eyed, and their beards grow normally. It is not surprising that we were mistaken for them and met with a cold reception from so many nomads.

It was January 15, 1946, when we set out on our last march. From Tolung we came into the broad valley of Kyichu. We turned a corner and saw, gleaming in the distance, the golden roofs of the Potala, the winter residence of the Dalai Lama and the most famous landmark of Lhasa. We felt inclined to go down on our knees and touch the ground with our foreheads. Since leaving Kyirong we had covered over six hundred miles with the vision of this fabulous city ever in our mind's eye. We had marched for seventy days and only rested during five. Forty-five days of our journey had been spent in crossing the Chang Tang—days full of hardship and unceasing struggle against cold, hunger and danger. Now all that was forgotten as we gazed at the golden pinnacles—six miles more and we had reached our goal. We mingled with a group of people and walked unhindered through the gateway into the town.

Ten days after our arrival we received word from the foreign ministry that we could move about freely. At the same time we were supplied with the splendid full-length cloaks of lambskin for which we had lately been measured. For each cloak sixty skins were used. On the same day we went for a walk in the town and in our Tibetan cloaks attracted no attention. We wanted to see everything.

The inner town is composed of nothing but stores. Shops extend in unbroken lines, and the dealers overflow into the street. There are no shopwindows in our sense of the word. American overshoes, dating from the war, are displayed between joints of yak's meat and chunks of butter. Provision stores contain, as well as local produce, American corned beef and English whiskey. There is nothing one cannot buy or at least order. The gaily dressed crowds of shoppers laugh and haggle and shout. Here you can see a nomad exchanging yak hair for snuff and nearby a society lady with a swarm of servants wallowing for hours in a mountain of silks and brocades.

The nomad women are no less particular in selecting Indian cotton lengths for their prayer flags. The common people generally wear the *nambu*, a sash made of pure home-woven wool, which is practically untearable. The sash or belt is about eight inches in width. The white nambu is hardly worn except by donkey drivers, as absence of colors is reckoned a sign of poverty.

In [Master of the Mint] Tsarong's house we were given a large room with European furniture, a table, easy chairs, beds and fine carpets. Next door we had a little room in which to wash. We also found something that we had missed very much up to now, a closet for the relief of nature. In this respect the habits of the Tibetans are casual to the last degree, and any place seems to be regarded as a suitable latrine.

The Parkhor runs in a circle around the cathedral, and most of the life of the city is concentrated in it. Many of the big business houses are here, and here all religious and military processions begin and end. Toward evening, especially on public holidays, pious citizens swarm over the Parkhor mumbling their prayers, and many of the faithful cover the whole distance in successive prostrations. But not only piety is represented in the Parkhor. You find also pretty women showing off their newest frocks and flirting a little with the young bloods of the nobility. Ladies of easy virtue are also there professionally.

Pleasure in the misfortune of others is almost universal, but somehow it is not ill meant. As they have no newspapers they indulge their criticisms of untoward events or objectionable persons by songs and satire. Boys and girls walk through the Parkhor in the evening singing the latest verses. Even the highest personages must put up with being pulled to pieces. Sometimes the government proscribes a particular song, but no one is ever punished for singing it. It is no longer heard in public but is sung all the more in private.

The English doctor had plenty of work. Every morning there was a queue of clients waiting before his door, and in the afternoon he visited his patients in the town. The monks tolerated in silence this intrusion into their territory. They could hardly do otherwise because it was impossible to ignore the doctor's success. The doctors of the British legation were the only qualified medical men in a population of three and a half million. Doctors would find a rich field of activity in Tibet, but the government would never allow foreigners to practice. The whole power was in the hands of the monks, who criticized even government officials when they called in the English doctor.

In point of numbers the Muslims form an appreciable part of the population of Lhasa. They have a mosque of their own and enjoy full freedom to practice their religion. One of the best characteristics of the Tibetan people is their complete tolerance of other creeds. Their monastic theocracy has never sought the conversion of infidels. Most of the Muslims have immigrated from India and have intermingled with the Tibetans. Their religious zeal led them at first to demand that their Tibetan wives should be converted, but here the Tibetan government stepped in and made it a condition that native women could marry Muslims only if they kept to their own faith.

When a man has several wives, his relations with them are different from those that prevail in a Muslim harem. It is common practice for a man to marry several daughters of a house in which there is no son or heir. This arrangement prevents the family fortune from being dispersed. When several brothers share the same wife, the eldest is always the master in the household, and the others have rights only when he is away or amusing himself elsewhere. The children of irregular alliances have no right to inherit, and all the property goes to the children of the legitimate wife. That is why it is not so important which of the brothers is the father of the child.

The monks live in strict celibacy and are forbidden to have anything to do with women. Unfortunately, homosexuality is very common. It is even condoned as giving proof that women play no part in the life of those monks who indulge in it. It often happens that monks fall in love with women and ask for their release so as to be able to marry them. This is granted without difficulty. In every family at least one of the sons is dedicated to the cloister in token of reverence for the church and to give the child a good start in life.

We asked our friends if there really were lamas who could hold up hailstorms or call down showers of rain, for this belief is firmly held in

Tibet. Many villages have regular weather makers. These are monks with a reputation for special skill in managing the weather. For the purpose of their magic they blow on conches, which make a vibrating sound. Tibetans do not recognize any physical explanation—for them all is magic and spells and the sport of the gods.

Dust storms recur regularly every spring and continue for about two months. The Potala Palace disappears, and at once everyone rushes for home. Even in one's sitting room one gets sand between one's teeth, as there are no double windows in Lhasa. The countless street dogs huddle together in corners. They are not usually so peaceful. One day Aufschnaiter came home with a torn cloak—he had been attacked by dogs, which had killed and devoured a dying horse; the pack had tasted blood.

My favorite expedition was to a little mountain lake a short day's march from Lhasa. It was a peaceful, idyllic, little place. Herds of wild sheep, gazelles, marmots, and foxes sauntered casually by, and high in the blue the lammergeier wheeled in his flight. To all these creatures man was not an enemy. No one would dare to hunt in the neighborhood of the Holy City. The flora around the lake are of a kind to quicken the pulse of any botanist. Marvelous yellow and blue poppies grew on the shore.

In the following years I had several opportunities to stay in the Potala as the guest of friends who lived there. Life in this religious fortress resembles, one supposes, that of a medieval castle. Hardly an object belongs to the present day. Everyone goes to bed early. In contrast to the brisk social life in the city there are no parties or entertainments. From the shrines of the holy dead emanates an atmosphere of mortality, which makes the whole palace feel like an enormous tomb. I could well understand that the young ruler was happy when he could move to his Summer Garden.

We paid official visits to each of the four cabinet ministers. Responsible only to the regent, these men represent the supreme authority in Tibet. Three of them are civil dignitaries and the fourth a monastic official. They all belong to the highest families and live in great style. The minister-monk, Rampa, was one of the few official monks who belonged to the aristocracy. The way in which the political situation was developing must have been causing him secret anxiety. He was much interested in our views on Russia's policy and told us that in the old scriptures it was prophesied that a great power from the north would overrun Tibet, destroy religion and make itself master of the whole world.

The cathedral has the same defects as the Potala does. Externally it is grand and imposing, but internally it is dark, full of corners and un-friendly. It is full of treasures. Only the butter lamps on the altars shed their flickering gleam. The only creatures who benefit from the offerings are the mice, which climb in thousands up and down the heavy silk curtains and gorge on the butter and tsampa in the bowls.

There are in Lhasa celebrated carpet weavers who come to the houses of the nobles and weave carpets of the desired size and shape on the spot. They sit on the ground with a wooden frame in front of them and knot the brightly colored hand-spun wool into classic designs: dragons, peacocks, flowers and the most varied forms of ornamentation. The wool is incredibly durable, and the colors, made from bark from Bhutan, green nutshells and vegetable juices, remain fresh for ages.

Tibet contains considerable deposits of gold, but modern methods of mining are unknown. Since ancient times they have been scooping out the soil in the Chang Tang with gazelle horns. Many provinces must pay their taxes with gold dust. But there is no more digging than is absolutely necessary, for fear of disturbing the earth gods. Many of the great rivers of Asia have their sources in Tibet and carry down with them the gold from the mountains.

Every year dramatic performances are given on a great stone stage outside the inner garden at Norbulingka, the Dalai Lama's summer palace. Vast throngs come to see the plays, which go on for seven days from sunrise to sunset. They are performed by groups of male actors who are not professionals. Only the comic parts have spoken lines. One could not but be astonished at their frankness. They go so far as to give a performance of the oracle, with dance and trance and all, which brings down the house. When monks and nuns begin to flirt together on stage, no one can stop laughing, and tears roll down the cheeks of the sternest abbots in the audience.

The ten thousand monks of Drebung are divided into groups. In some houses you will find only Mongolians or Nepalese or students from a particular town such as Shigatse. The great cloisters of Drebung, Sera, and Ganden—the three pillars of the state—play a decisive role in the political life of Tibet. The cloisters are the high schools of the church. For that reason every lama—and there are more than a thousand of them in Tibet—must be educated in a monastery. Even during the Dalai Lama's visit to Drebung, these incarnations attended all the ceremonies and sat in the front seats—a regular concourse of the gods!

I was privileged to witness a drama that certainly no other person of another faith has ever witnessed. In front of a dark grove of trees a great multitude of red-cowled monks, perhaps two thousand of them, squatted on the gravel, while from a high place the Dalai Lama preached from the Holy Writ. The fourteen-year-old boy had been studying for many years, and now his knowledge was to be tested before a critical audience. His performance that day would show whether he was destined to be the instrument of the monks or their ruler.

The Dalai Lama sat down on the gravel so as not to emphasize the superiority of his birth, while the abbot stood before him and punctuated his questions with the conventional gestures. The Dalai Lama answered all the questions that were put to him, even the "teasers," with readiness and good humor and was never for a moment disconcerted.

After a while the antagonists changed places, and it was the Dalai Lama who put the questions to the seated abbot. One could see that this was not an act prepared to show off the intelligence of the young Buddha; it was a genuine contest of wits in which the abbot was hard put to hold his own. I was deeply impressed by what I had seen and heard, and felt genuine admiration for the presence of mind of this god-boy from a humble family. He almost persuaded me to believe in reincarnation.

I could hardly imagine that the young ruler, still a minor, would override all conventions and summon me directly to see him. He seemed to me like a person who had for years brooded in solitude over different problems, and now that he had at last someone to talk to, wanted to know all the answers at once. At last he noticed that I had hair growing on the back of my hands and said with a broad grin: "Henrig, you have hair like a monkey." I had an answer ready, as I was familiar with the legend that Tibetans derive their descent from the union of their god Chenrezi with a female demon. Before coupling with his demon lover Chenrezi had assumed the shape of a monkey, and since the Dalai Lama was one of the incarnations of this god, I found that in comparing me with an ape he was really flattering me.

With remarks such as this our conversation soon became unconstrained. I now felt the attraction of his personality, at which during our earlier fleeting contacts I had only guessed. His complexion was much lighter than that of the average Tibetan. His eyes, hardly narrower than those of most Europeans, were full of expression, charm and vivacity. His ears stood out a little from his head. This was a characteristic of the

Buddha and, as I learned later, was one of the signs by which as a child he had been recognized as an incarnation. He was tall for his age and looked as though he would reach the stature of his parents, both of whom had striking figures. He had beautiful aristocratic hands, which were generally folded in an attitude of peace. He always wore the red robe of a monk, once prescribed by the Buddha, and his costume differed in no way from that of the monastic officials.

To my surprise I saw that he had been transcribing the capital letters of the Latin alphabet. He insisted that I should immediately begin to teach him English, transcribing the pronunciation in elegant Tibetan characters. He had charged me to give him lessons in English, geography and arithmetic. In addition, I had to look after his motion pictures and keep him conversant with world events. When I gave him for homework ten sentences to translate, he usually showed up with twenty. He was very quick at learning languages, as are most Tibetans. It is quite common for people of the upper class and businessmen to speak Mongolian, Chinese, Nepalese and Hindi.

On August 15, 1950, a violent earthquake caused panic in the Holy City. The epicenter must have been in South Tibet. Hundreds of monks and nuns were buried in their rock monasteries. Towers were split down the middle, leaving ruined walls pointing to the sky. The evil omens multiplied. Monsters were born. In blazing summer weather, water began to flow from a gargoyle on the cathedral. The people had hardly got over their fright caused by the comet, which in the previous year had been visible by day and night like a gleaming horsetail in the heavens. Old people remembered that the last comet had been a precursor of a war with China.

News came from East Tibet that Chinese cavalry and infantry were concentrating on our frontier. On October 7, 1950, the enemy attacked the Tibetan frontier in six places simultaneously. The National Assembly now sent an urgent appeal to the United Nations for help against the aggressors, claiming that their country had been invaded in peacetime on the pretext that the Red People's Army could not tolerate the influence of imperialistic powers in Tibet. The whole world knew, they pointed out, that Tibet was utterly free from any foreign influence. If any nation deserved the help of the UN, it was Tibet. Their appeal was rejected. The whole of Tibet was occupied by Chinese troops. There is famine in the land, which cannot feed the armies of occupation as well as the inhabitants.

Wherever I live, I shall feel homesick for Tibet. I often think I can still hear the wild cries of geese and cranes as they fly over Lhasa in the clear, cold moonlight. My heartfelt wish is that this book may create some understanding for a people whose will to live in peace and freedom has won so little sympathy from an indifferent world.

CHAPTER 6

Hunza: Lost Kingdom
of the Himalayas

John Clark, 1956

John Clark (1909–94) was born in Chicago and graduated from the University of Illinois in 1931, majoring in geology, in which he earned his doctorate at Princeton University in 1935. As an officer in the U.S. Army Corps of Engineers on the staff of General "Vinegar Joe" Stillwell during World War II in China, Clark explored nine thousand miles of roads and trails in Kansu and Sinkiang, the longest ground reconnaissance in U.S. military history. This enabled him to witness the tyrannical activities of the Chinese in Sinkiang, who were uprooting the Uighur farmers and the Kyrghyz and Kazakh herdsmen to make room for their own population growth. Meanwhile, the clever Russian communists were infiltrating the area with free clinics, local-language schools and small-scale industries for the indigenous people. Clark decided he could do even better and undertook his personal two-year project in the Pakistan district of Hunza.[1] He discovered that the idyllic image of Hunza was based on highly exaggerated myths and that it was actually experiencing an environmental crisis. Nevertheless, his enlightened program, which is the subject of this chapter, was so effective that its continuation was opposed by local officials who felt that their personal authority was being threatened.

[June, 1950:] I was going back to the highest, driest cordillera on earth. The battered C–46 of the Orient Airways bounced on the updraft before it slid precariously between a pine tree and a rocky ledge, and we were across the Babusar Pass, flying quietly over the canyon of the Indus River, a silvery almond ribbon two miles below us. Nanga Parbat, the Naked Peak [26,660 ft.], reared its terrible crest two miles above us to the right, so massive that it took fifteen minutes to fly past.

In Karachi, I had hired Haibatullah Hojeh, an Uzbek refugee from Russian Turkestan, to act as my interpreter. With seven pack horses loaded with supplies from America, we were off on horseback for the final three-day trek to Hunza. This small country of twenty-five thousand people, high in the Central Asian peaks, had only one horse trail running from north to south [before the construction of the hazardous Karakoram Highway] and a trail from east to west, which not even a horse could follow. My object was to attempt to show the members of one Asian community how, within their own efforts, they could use the resources they already possessed to better their own lives. My plans included setting up a craft school, distributing vegetable seeds, starting a medical dispensary and the geological survey.

We entered the terrible gorge that the Hunza River has cut through the Kailas range. For fourteen miles, we crept along the foot of the cliff, beside the thundering stream. As we emerged from the canyon, the trail ran along the south flank of the Karakoram. Finally, it angled across the face of a dull, brown, rocky ridge and suddenly came to the edge. Here below us was the heart of Hunza: a great, open trough stretching far away into the distance with mountains closing in again above the narrow canyon at the far end. The terraced fields, yellow-green with ripening barley, climbed the low slope from river to mountain foot. High above towered Ultar Peak [24,700 ft.], white in the azure blue, alone and aloof as an ancient god overlooking his temple. The green and yellow of life below, the raw brown and black of the rocks above, and the stark blue and white high over all: this was Hunza.

Ayub, the seneschal, opened the door of the mir's palace at Baltit. I could feel its friendliness even while I was greeting the mir.

"You like my new room," he smiled. "But it is really very simple. The rug is red Bokhara, which my father bought from a caravan. The furniture—you would not believe, would you, that it was all made right here. The wood is apricot, and the cushions are full of wool. You see, my Hunzas know how to make things out of the materials at hand. Will you have tea with us?"

"Yes, thank you."

"Why don't you just settle in the guest house permanently? My cooks can feed you, and there would be no trouble."

This was the last thing I wanted to do. The people of Hunza would always regard me as an outsider if I remained the mir's guest.

"Thank you, Mir Sahib, but I believe that may be unwise. When my dispensary is opened, patients will be coming day and night. You wouldn't want them tramping under your windows, waking you. Besides, they would ruin your flowers. If it isn't inconvenient, I think the old castle would suit me perfectly."

"As you wish, John, of course. But it isn't really fixed up. If you don't mind that, you're welcome."

In the usual sahib system, three servants and four villagers care for one man's needs. My system was quite different. Haibatullah, Hayat, Beg and I drew clothes from a common storage locker, so we all dressed alike. They ate at my table with me. We were an outfit, not a master and caste servants. They were gentlemen at heart and responded proudly to being treated like humans. As a result I had perfect loyalty, no grafting, and a smooth-running outfit.

Except for dirty-white cotton clothes and bare feet, my patients looked about like the usual people to be found in an American doctor's waiting room. Their diseases, though, were quite different. Madut had chronic dysentery; Hobi had malaria; the old lady had sore eyes. With smoke in her eyes every mealtime of her life, it wasn't surprising. I asked Beg to announce that the hospital would be open every morning but never in the afternoon; there were many other things to do, and I was optimistic enough to believe that I could make Hunza conform to a schedule.

My own training consisted of a minor in anatomy, a year's college course in first aid and public health, and some very practical information from doctors of Billings Hospital in Chicago, Johns Hopkins in Baltimore and the United Mission Medical Council. Best of all, I had the wonderful modern medicines, sulfas, penicillin, atabrine, undecylinic acid and others. Of course, a real doctor could have done much more than I did. However, these people had been without any medical attention for three years. In my two trips, I was to treat 5,684 patients. Most of the people who came to me were helped or cured by the simple things I was able to do for them. Five or six would probably have died if treatment had not been available.

One of the finest things I have ever seen in an Islamic community occurred here. A man brought me his wife, who was suffering from ringworm all over her chest. It was naturally necessary for her to strip to the waist; she dropped her shawl and removed her blouse while he looked on.

I explained to him that this treatment must be repeated every day for a week, so they came again the next morning. The third day, she came alone. Knowing how Muslim men feel about having others view their wives, I sent her right back for her husband. He entered the dispensary and said in bored tones, "Oh, Sahib, don't be silly! We know we can trust you with our wives. I'm much too busy on my farm to come with her every day. You treat her, and it will be all right."

If this had happened one hundred miles to the south, the woman and I would both have been killed. These people were much more sensible and truly moral than were the rigidly fanatic Muslims. After all, the basic reason for the purdah and the heavy veils is the necessity for distrust. The Hunzas were more liberal because they were more decent and almost never unfaithful to their mates.

On the Fourth of July, a celebration was plainly indicated, so I decided to go camping with Hayat to the nearby Hyderabad canyon. A number of veins of pegmatite crossed the bare, rock walls, and in one of these veins huge crystals of muscovite mica flashed in the sun. The talus below the cliffs was littered with sheets of mica a foot across. Sheets of this size could be used in electric insulation and were worth several dollars a pound. If this deposit was large enough, it would be a real source of income to Hunza and Pakistan. Best of all, it would give employment to many local people because mica must be mined and trimmed by hand.

On my second geological trip, looking for mica in the next canyon west of the original prospect, Beg and I left Baltit in the evening and camped for the night in the *dak*-bungalow. Above the snout of the Shishpar glacier, the trail rounded the nose of ice and followed the lateral moraine, a high ridge of loose boulders, sand and clay, which the glacier had dropped between itself and the vertical rock wall. Finally we reached a great bowl, two miles long and a mile across, where eleven glaciers previously had met to form the source of the one we had been following. Surely this is the greatest view in the Asian cordillera: three 25,000-foot peaks around us, eleven glaciers in sight at once and the rock walls going up sheer and clean for three miles.

I had learned that the pegmatites did continue northwestward but that they contained no valuable mica in that direction. At breakfast the next morning the usual thundering sound shook the air, and one big glacier vanished temporarily behind a rolling white cloud of avalanche snow dust. Together we crept out on the rim of a great mountain buttress, like flies on the shoulder of God. We rounded a curve, and there suddenly was the whole sweep of the Hunza Valley, tiny below us, and the great rock peaks above. Sherin Beg sat down.

"What are you doing?" I asked.

"Looking at my mountains," he murmured. He showed me then the meaning of worship, which is a quietly deep emotion that our bustling analytical minds must relearn.

One afternoon, Amir Hayat and I left on a hike up the Ultar Nullah [canyon]. Here, in days not so long ago, six mighty glaciers had crashed down from the encircling peaks to form the main Ultar glacier. At the place of their joining they had gouged out a little basin, now a beautiful alpine pasture, the rocks covered with a loose mat of grass and flowers. The air was filled with trills and gurgles of meltwater dripping and trickling among a thousand boulders and the jarring crash of ice dropping over a great glacier falls. I chose a small terrace that lay next to the water and the protecting wall.

"This will be our wildflower garden," I told Amir Hayat. "Your first job will be to build a rock-and-thorn wall around it, so the goats cannot break through. Afterward, dig the ground with this pick"—I gave him a light prospector's pick—"and then plant your wildflowers" [for export of local alpine seeds to Europe and the United States].

In early August, Hayat, Amir Hayat, little Ali Johar and I took an overnight trip up the Ultar Nullah to inspect the wildflower garden. Brown *Satyrid* butterflies flitted through the bright sunshine in the canyon, and Ali Johar flitted after them [collecting for the Carnegie Museum in Pittsburgh]. We stopped for lunch at the sheep camp, then pushed higher in the hope of catching some *Parnassids*.

When we reached a perfectly vertical, granite cliff with two cracks across it, Hayat stuck his fingers in the upper crack and bare toes in the lower and started sliding across, with his whole body hanging out in space, two hundred feet above the rocks below. There was nothing to do but follow. We worked up to the bare, rounded granite beside a glacier at 15,000 feet, and there, between little snow flurries that melted as they fell, we caught some butterflies—blues and some small ones I didn't know.

Next morning, Amir Hayat took me to see his wildflower garden. He had cultivated a patch about twenty feet square. He had transplanted wildflowers until the whole place was a jungle but had not separated the different kinds. Once they went to seed, we wouldn't know one variety from another. I had not taken the time to teach him in detail what I wanted. The fault was mine.

"You have worked faithfully and done well, Amir Hayat," I said. "Continue to tend it and harvest seeds for me as they ripen." I would have to teach him, tactfully, to assemble his wildflowers by species in order to avoid offending him.

[On a trip to Gilgit:] Beg and I started up the Murkui Nullah, led on by occasional pebbles of pure magnetite iron ore in the stream bed. We found no more iron, but in a side nullah a great vein of copper ore made a green-and-blue streak across the dark mountain face. In a pine woods at about 11,000 feet, with patches of September snow lingering in all the shadows, I followed the lateral moraine of Dunyor glacier about two miles up toward Rakaposhi [25,551 ft.]. A fine, big eagle circled me but decided I wasn't edible and went on his way. There were also some crested chickadees, some magpies, several red-billed ravens, a rusty roustabout water ouzel, two or three kinds of eagles and one rare but very beautiful little black-and-white bird that I could not identify. The ridge of barren moraine gravel overlooked the black, hackled ice of the lower glacier and faced the green, pine-clad slope of the main ridge, while Rakaposhi towered overhead like the gleaming white wall of Paradise.

I spent the next day finishing my reports for Mr. Gurmani [minister for Kashmiri affairs, into whose jurisdiction the Gilgit Agency, including Hunza, had recently been transferred]. The first report described the copper and iron in Dunyor Nullah, with rock samples to demonstrate it. Last came a very carefully worded report—possibilities of placer gold in the area.

I also wished to hand in a report suggesting that they establish a sandpaper factory in Gilgit or Aliabad, using Hunza garnets as abrasives. Pakistan was at that time importing all of its sandpaper from England and was getting an ordinary, low grade, glass paper. I made three samples of sandpaper, sifting ground garnet through our flour sieve and an old shirt, using a paper bag and Duco cement for a base. Those were not ideal materials, but the sample worked.

The mir and his family had moved to the Ghulmit oasis, twenty-three miles up Hunza Canyon, for their annual winter stay. As there was not enough wood at Baltit to keep the palace heated throughout the winter, and Ghulmit had abundant firewood, the royal family spent two months there each year, ostensibly to hunt but actually to keep warm.

About two miles south of Ghulmit, the trail runs across bare granite streaked with pegmatite veins. I had crossed these veins before, but this time a wet, blue crystal glinted at me, and I stopped to look. Beryl! And the feldspar next to it was albite, not the usual orthoclase. Most pegmatites are nothing but coarse-grained granite, but every so often a pegmatite develops all sorts of weird, rare minerals—gemstones, lithium ore and other things. Beryl and albite feldspar are usually one's first intimation that a normal feldspar is becoming valuable.

The evening of December 18 was Tumushuling, the great celebration of the Hunza year. At dusk, the mir, Ayash, little Bapu [the crown prince], and the old wazir arrived in state at the castle. The floor was jammed with at least a hundred men and boys. The servants brought in great platters of chapatis, meat and rice, with plates of butter. This was the mir's traditional feast of harvest and thanksgiving, in which his people were to share. For the first time, the white expanse of faces turned toward me was actually friendly. As each man whose eye caught mine gave a companionable smile, I knew that I was being accepted. Maybe within a year or so I would actually be considered a Hunza.

Ayash Khan hunched close to me. "Now, Sahib," he purred softly, "you will hear the traditional song in honor of our dynasty. It is a very long song, because it tells the story of Hunza for more than six hundred years. Since our people have no writing, this is the way we preserve our history."

The epic song continued through the history of Hunza, king by king, for almost twenty minutes. When it still had at least two hundred years to go, a flurry stirred in one corner of the listening crowd, and a half a chapati sailed through the air at the chanting choir. In a flash, gobs of butter and torn pieces of chapatis were being hurled in all directions. The mir and Ayash chuckled with enjoyment of this excellent brawl, until old Momayr, a local character, received a large chunk of butter directly in his eye. The mir hastily stood up, which brought everyone to their feet and stopped the performance before it could get out of hand. That afternoon, we attended a big Tamasha with dances in the mir's palace yard. Three or four brief fights broke out, because everyone in Hunza was mildly exhilarated with wine. The whole celebration was rugged, lusty and eminently human.

Between Tumushuling and Christmas Day I settled down to running my school and treating medical patients. Since the nine boys had never seen a real woodcarving, I smoothed up a panel of mulberry wood and started to carve a floral design. Mulberry is a beautiful, golden wood. Inlaid with dark brown walnut, pale tan apricot and touches of red juniper, we would have a good range of colors without using any stains. The boys became much interested as the design developed, especially when I started to inlay. All of the boys now realized the goal toward which they were working. Hayat promptly started an inlay project of his own, a mulberry pipe.

The mir and his family had a big Christmas dinner for me—undoubtedly the first Christmas that had ever been celebrated by a Hunza royal family. We ate in the family dining room, a cozy place with a fireplace and a big, red rug on which bolsters and thick cushions were scattered. A servant spread a white cloth on the rug and we all sat around it. The rani (queen) and all the children ate with us because, as the mir explained, "You are our brother and a member of the family, so it is perfectly proper." This was the greatest honor that a Muslim king could bestow.

On January 6 my morning dispensary was interrupted by a magnificent earthquake. A deep subterranean rumble sent all of us running out on the castle roof. Then came three hard shocks a minute apart, with continuous waves between. The old castle swayed and creaked. It was so flexible that it was practically earthquake proof. As the earthquake stopped, the really spectacular scene began. Tremendous avalanches thundered down every nullah. The great snow cloud from the avalanche in our nullah was a wild, tumbling mass of cold air and powdered snow two thousand feet high. When it struck, the castle shivered again, and we had to lie flat to avoid being blown off the roof.

The mir was to arrive on March 19 from his winter vacation, and Hunza prepared a proper welcome. Bapu came first, on a black pony, led by Ayash, then the rani and younger children, riding yaks. The rani, properly veiled, was dressed in a shapeless black cloak, but the forty female servitors who followed her on horseback flashed red and green and white in their brightest clothes. After a proper gap in the parade, the mir appeared, riding on a white horse, followed by his train of servants. He dismounted and walked slowly forward, while his old men crowded in to bow and kiss his hand. No returning father ever received a more fervent greeting from his children. As the procession approached the palace lawn, Beg's family broke into the flag and sword dance, with cloaks and flags swirling to the wild music of rejoicing flutes and drums.

One of Beg's ancestors had carried the standard of Safdar Ali, the dynasty founder, who came from Iran six hundred years ago; the flag-bearing privilege had remained with his family ever since. It was typical of

Hunza's primitive tribal structure that this family, economically one of the poorest, should be able to retain a noble social position through its hereditary status and good character. The Aga Khan School boys staged a torchlight parade, and there was general rejoicing because the king was home again. Fire means much to the Hunzas; it was probably of major importance in their pre-Islamic religion.

One afternoon, as I was writing in my office, Burhan and Nasar Mohammed came tumbling in. A man from Altit was outside, they shouted, and wanted to buy the mulberry table and chair the two of them had just finished making together. Were they permitted to sell?

"Why, of course!" I said. "Let Mano set a fair price, then stick to it. Do not bargain!"

Mano [excellent teacher and carpenter] inspected the chair and table gravely, then said, "Ten rupees for the chair and eight for the table." And so it was. Nothing more fortunate could have happened. This sale was a turning point in the history of our school. The boys suddenly realized that they weren't just servants carrying out a sahib's whim, but young men learning a useful way to make a better living.

I had imported American vegetable seeds to improve Hunza's food supply. The mir kindly furnished a good-sized vegetable plot close by his palace. It had already been plowed and manured. My boys enthusiastically volunteered to help. Within an hour they had the soil nicely worked with hoes and rakes. Then we used the hoes to build raised rows for planting, with ditches between for irrigating and fertilizing, and round hills for our cucumbers and melons. All this was new to the boys, as it was to the mir's gardener.

Potatoes, melons, carrots, cucumbers and peppers were not new to the boys. A few Hunzas grew dry beans, but green and wax beans they had never seen. Our garden had a few rows each of beets, endive, lettuce, radishes, turnips, yellow pear tomatoes, brussels sprouts and parsley. The first time we irrigated, the boys appreciated the advantages of the row-and-ditch system over the old broadcast planting and flooding. None of the neighbors showed the slightest interest. It wasn't *dastur* [traditional].

The boys willingly tried the new vegetables. They loved radishes and beets and warmly approved of brussels sprouts, green beans and turnips. I gave small packets of seed to Beg, Hayat, Suleiman and Burhan, who turned them over to their fathers; by midsummer new American vegetables were flourishing in several Hunza gardens.

Actually, there is no true soil in Hunza, only powdered rock. All of the nourishment for crops has to be built in with manure. Irrigation washes out even the manure nitrates almost as fast as the farmers put them in. Hunzas have exceeded even the Chinese in their utilization of every square inch of land, with terraces on slopes at an angle of up to sixty degrees. Sometimes they actually create fields by repeatedly flooding a bare granite face behind a retaining wall. This is certainly the most desperate expedient of land-starved people anywhere on earth, yet visitors have written about Hunza as the land where everyone has "just enough" and there are no poor!

The climate is ideal for apricots, mulberries and grapes. Hunzas are good horticulturalists. They have practiced grafting apricot trees for over sixteen hundred years. Each vigorous, fully mature tree produces a tremendous yearly crop. The trunk and main branches grow to be as large as forest trees. My woodcarving school cut some planks of apricot three by eighteen inches, twelve feet long. If you go to visit, you are usually served tea with a side dish of apricot nuts and dried mulberries as a confection.

There is no coal or petroleum in the entire Gilgit Agency, so wood must remain the source of heat. The growing population has cut all the junipers around each large oasis below Ghulmit. The men of Baltit now climb the high cliffs in Ultar Nullah to gather wild rose canes and sagebrush for winter firewood.

There are not more than two dozen cows in the entire main oasis. There is no pasture within a day's herding distance of the settlements, so the cows must depend on leaves and straw for food. On this diet they give a few pints daily of very thin milk, for a very few months of the year. Given the same diet, sheep and goats produce more milk.

Late in May, the flocks move up to summer pasture at 12,000 to 15,000 feet, with a few men and boys from each community to herd. The herders milk into gourds (never washed) and shake this gourd for a short time, until the butter forms. They wrap the butter into ten- and twenty-pound pats, which they wrap loosely in birch bark and then bury in sheep dung to protect it from rats until someone packs it down to the village.

Each family owns so few animals that they can butcher but one or two a year, which they do at Tumushuling time in December. As one sheep lasts a family about one week, this means that the average family gets meat for one or two weeks per year. Since visitors always come in summertime, this also explains the ridiculous tale that Hunzas are vegetarians by preference. As their diet is deficient in oils and vitamin D, all Hunzas have soft teeth, and half of them have the barrel chests and rheumatic knees of subclinical rickets. "Happy, healthy Hunza, where everyone has just enough!"

But more important than wool, meat or milk is the manure the flocks produce. Without it, the grain would die in a single year and the orchards would not yield fruit. It accumulates nightly within the corrals in the summer pastures, and the shepherds dig out lumps of it, which they dry on the roofs of their little huts. They take loads of manure and butter on their backs whenever they go down-canyon to their villages. The winter accumulations in the village corrals are always mixed with leaves and straw, because the people haven't learned to build mangers and the sheep tread some of their fodder in with their manure. This is the basis for the tale that the Hunzas make compost.

The serious part of this whole matter is that there is no winter pasture, the high summer pastures are seriously overgrazed, and the amount of manure produced at present is not adequate. Also, the climate is rapidly growing drier and warmer, so the summer pastures will deteriorate with increasing rapidity. Within twenty years, the best climatic conditions for pasture will be at 13,000 and 14,000 feet, but here the rock walls are almost vertical and grass cannot grow. The Hini and other lower oases are drying up, and the upper country cannot support a large population. With pastureland deteriorating and the water supply decreasing, Hunza is headed for grim days.

From Hini, Suleiman and I climbed the steep canyon to the northwest. A short distance up, we came to a massive cliff. I chipped a piece off, stared, then clambered up the face, chipping flakes every few feet to make sure. There could be no doubt—here was fine-grained magnesian marble, as beautiful as the best Carrara! Rapidly I estimated the volume in sight— fifty million tons and certainly at least that much more buried under the slope. With the creek for water power and the garnets six miles away for abrasives, the marble could be worked into the pierced fretwork panels that the Muhammadan people so love in their mosques and tombs. Here was a real resource for Hunza! I resolved to encourage the mir to build a small factory to make panels for export.

There are not the frequent wife beatings in Hunza that one sees in China, nor is there much infidelity. The women are expected to do the housework, weed the fields and help with harvest, a fair division of labor, as their small, barren houses require little attention. The man ploughs, plants, irrigates, harvests, climbs the mountains in search of firewood and tends the flocks. The average woman can look forward to three to five children who live to grow up and one or two who do not. The legend of "birth control in Hunza" arises from the habit of nursing each baby for about eighteen months, during which time intercourse is forbidden. It does not prevent a normally fertile couple from producing six to nine children. Hunzas are emigrating to all the neighboring states, and still the overcrowding grows worse each year.

On the way back down the canyon, Burhan said to me, "Sahib, I've been thinking a lot about jeeps. Look—my father's fields are there below us, and our house is way over there, a long walk. Always we have to carry all our wheat and barley that long way home on our backs. We couldn't make a jeep motor, but couldn't we make a donkey jeep out of wood and let a donkey pull it?"

Burhan had independently invented the cart! He was a few thousand years late, of course, but no one else in Hunza had ever thought of such a thing. Hayat with the lathe, Burhan with the cart, Suleiman at woodcarving, and Mirza at art had now shown definite signs of creative thinking. This was more important than the achievement of any of my immediate projects. I must see that they had their chance to go ahead.

Definitely I had not won all of Hunza. New ideas were bound to be opposed, in Hunza as everywhere else. The boys were naturally inspired by the idea that they were competent to learn and to do anything others could. The adult community was grateful for the dispensary and enjoyed without gratitude the high wages I paid but bitterly resented the boys' adoption of Western attitudes.

In a close-knit family, the father or grandfather is absolute head. Since the old man is steeped in custom, any suggestion of change or experiment is a challenge to his authority. A progressive young man must either yield or risk being expelled from the family, from hope of owning land, and from hope of honorable marriage. Thus, the elders become a serious deterrent to progress.

I had developed a mild dysentery, which would not respond to treatment. This, like the enmity of certain officials in Gilgit, was to remain with me throughout my entire stay in Asia.

Col. Effendi, commander of the Pakistani armed forces for the Gilgit Agency, arrived in Hunza on his way to inspect the Misgar border post near Hunza's Chinese frontier. He was the grandson of a deposed amir of Afghanistan—Asia is littered with deposed Afghan royal families—and a patrician to his fingertips. It was obvious, he said, that from a military standpoint I was endangering the safety of the frontier—stirring up the local people. My presence so close to the border might incite the communists to raid Hunza, and he would so report to his government.

The moist, cloudy heat of a Karachi summer day seeped past the heavy blinds into the deep reaches of the spacious office. Mr. Mohammed Ali, the secretary-general of Pakistan, turned his drawn face and piercing eyes toward me again, as he had that day, more than a year ago, when I first arrived in Karachi. This time his eyes were kind and very sad.

"Doctor Clark," he said quietly, "we in Karachi understand exactly what you have been accomplishing up there in Hunza. We want you to know that we deeply appreciate it; we realize the difficulties you have faced. But many circumstances—both internal and otherwise—have arisen to complicate the situation. How long are you planning to stay in Hunza?"

"My funds will run out in November," I answered. "I had hoped to remain until then." (I had planned to go to America, recoup finances, buy equipment, recover my health and return to Hunza.)

I knew now that I could finish my stay but would not be allowed to return. The worst that [anti-American] gossip had accomplished was to influence Col. Effendi's military report. My project was dying because of the communist threat, Col. Effendi's report, and the disturbances in Punial [between Sunni Muslim rajas and their Ismaili subjects].

Mano and Rachmet Ali asked me if they could give the boys a farewell party in the castle. I agreed at once, so we had another party—an evening of cheer and good companionship. Sherin Beg and Mirza came to me quite shyly that same evening. Their family, they said, wanted to give me a farewell meal at their father's house. I replied that I would be honored.

After dinner, Mirza returned carrying a fine white Hunza cloak. His father hung it over my shoulders. A wide band of beautiful embroidery bordered the whole cloak, and a complicated floral design decorated each breast. This, I knew, meant several months of work by the women of their family. These people, the real gentlefolk of old Hunza, were thanking me for what I had tried to do.

On November 8, we left for Gilgit, Hayat, Beg, Mirza, Rachmet Ali and I. The old wazir met us as we passed the front gate; I dismounted to say goodbye. "Salaam alaikum, Sahib," he said. "We are sorry to see you leave." From here on, it was necessary to dismount and walk almost the whole six miles of the main oasis, shaking hands and taking salutes the whole way. The people were as grave and reserved as usual, but they were giving me a kind farewell.

CHAPTER 7

On the Roads of Central Asia

Vladimir Ratzek, 1972

Vladimir Ratzek (1918–80) was born in a hamlet south of Moscow, the son of an Austrian horticulturalist and a Russian mother who was a teacher. When he was still a child, his family moved to Central Asia, where his father was chief forester for the governor-general of Turkestan. When Ratzek accompanied his father to the upland forests, he became addicted to the mountains. After a series of brilliant first ascents and rescue operations, he was awarded the rank of master of sport of the USSR at the age of twenty-two, and two years later he was elected president of the Kyrghyz Alpine Club. He was then called into the army as a lieutenant in the topographic service and served at Tashkent as an officer in charge of developing alpine troops until his retirement in 1974. He became a Distinguished Master of Sport, the highest official rank in Soviet mountaineering[1] and earned a master's degree in glaciology from the University of Tashkent, where he also taught a course in regional studies, his profound knowledge of which is reflected in this chapter. During his final years, he was scientific secretary for the Uzbek Academy of Sciences.

Central Asia is a land of vast and powerful contrasts. It reaches from below sea level to above 7,000 meters, where snow-draped crags pierce the sky and slopes plunge into deep ravines. These changes give birth to a great variety of climates, landscapes, natural life and cultures. We experience these contrasts on a 2,000-kilometer tour in a light automobile, beginning and ending at Tashkent. It brings us into contact with the Turkic peoples of Uzbekistan and Kyrghyzstan, and with the Iranian peoples of Tajikistan, in remote mountain regions of the Pamir-Alai. Because

77

of high passes, the tour should not start before the beginning of July and should be completed by the end of September.

Going east from Tashkent, the capital of Uzbekistan, past the metal-lurgical quarries and cultivations of Angren, we cross the 2,446-meter Kamchik Pass. Sheep and cows graze near the pass, also a herd of a high-bred horse called a *tabun*, which provides milk, transportation and games. This is our entrance to Ferghana, "the jewel of Central Asia," an extensive valley between the Tien Shan and the Pamir-Alai. The upper part of a great Asiatic waterway, the Syr Darya, flows through it to the west, past melon fields, vineyards, orchards and even oil wells.

In the Uzbek part of the valley, between its Tajik and Kyrghyz portions, in a green oasis at 450 meters altitude, the ancient city of Kokand was first built in the tenth century, destroyed by the Mongols in the thirteenth, and rebuilt in 1732, including the palace of the Khudoyar Khan, which resembles a Samarkand *medressa* [a religious school of higher learning]. With a population of 133,000, it is now a manufacturing center for textiles, clothing, shoes and machinery. Its outlying villages are famous for traditional ceramic art. One of these, Kanibadam, has a name that means "the birthplace of the almond." It was, in fact, the original source from which almond trees spread throughout the south of the USSR and beyond, especially those for the large, sweet, softshell "*kandak-badam.*"

Our road follows an ancient silk route, past the larger Uzbek cities of Ferghana and Andijan, to Osh, a major city of Kyrghyzstan with a poly-glot population of 120,000. Near the eastern end of the valley, close to the Uzbek boundary, at an altitude of 900 meters, it has a pleasant climate with cool nights. Its most prominent feature is a limestone pinnacle 260 meters high in the center of town. Called the Mountain of Suleiman, it was a traditional Islamic holy place where pilgrims came to worship and be healed and women embraced hallowed stones in the belief that this would help them to conceive. The Soviets closed this shrine as a center of obscu-rantism and converted it into a city park. The adjacent mosque is now a regional museum whose Neolithic and Bronze Age artifacts show that Osh has been inhabited for thousands of years.

The road south from Osh to the Pamir, through spectacular mountain pastures, passes a village with hot springs where city folk come to bathe and relax in the local *tchaikhana* [teahouse]. The road follows an old caravan route until it turns east into China on a footpath over the Tereklavan Pass, the only one on the great Silk Route that could be used all year round. Camel caravans and armies crossed it for centuries, but many people and animals perished while crossing it in winter, as shown by their bones on the ground near the top. Farther south the road passes fifty *kurgans* [burial mounds] of unusual design. Some are twenty meters square with a ditch around the base, while smaller ones have the same shape, each in a ring of stones. They are thought to be the graves of Saka-Scyths, people of Iranian stock who lived in Central Asia in the first millennium B.C.

Climbing the crest of the Alai range, the road crosses the Taldyk Pass at an altitude of 3,650 meters, the highest point of our route. It commands a vast panorama across the wide Alai Valley to the soaring snow peaks of the Trans-Alai, which is the north front range of the Pamir. Its crest is the boundary between Tajikistan and the Alai Valley in Kyrghyzstan. A few kilometers west of the Pamir Road, the 7,134-meter Peak of Lenin, formerly Kaufmann, is the highest point of the Trans-Alai. Steep hairpin turns lead down from the pass to the village of Sarytash at an altitude of 3,200 meters in the upper part of the valley. It has an automobile repair and service station, dining room, shops, post office and hospital. A nearby bridge over the westward-flowing Kyzylsu [Red River] carries the road, which crosses the valley and the Trans-Alai into the eastern Pamir.

Without crossing the bridge, our route follows the valley west along the base of the Alai Mountains, whose steep south slope is free of snow except at the tips of the highest peaks. Their maximum height is 5,881 meters at a summit that has no name. The length of the Alai Valley is 135 kilometers, and it widens to an impressive 22 kilometers. Its pastures are famous for horses, sheep and yaks, tended by herdsmen and their families ensconced for the summer in felt yurts. Up to a million animals enter the valley each summer by footpaths over the Alai Mountains from the Uzbek, Tajik and Kyrghyz parts of Ferghana. A new breed of sheep is adapted to live there in concrete shelters all year round.

Some forty kilometers from Sarytash, a second bridge crosses the Kysylsu from the *kishlak* [hamlet] of Kashkasu, where a small shop sells nomad rugs. The bridge leads to the pastures, which are mostly south of the river, including those in the high side valleys between spurs of the Trans-Alai. At the foot of Lenin Peak, a high valley called Edelweiss Meadow is used each year by the International Mountaineering Camps, which have been attended by climbers from sixteen foreign countries and from Soviet Europe and Asia.

The Kyzylsu is fed by snows of the Trans-Alai, whose north slope

carries fifty-three glaciers more than 2 kilometers long, including the 19.5-
kilometer Korzhenevsky glacier. Its foothills are richly colored by red,
green and orange rocks. Fossils have been found even at the crest of the
Trans-Alai, which was once submerged by the shallow Tethys Sea. At the
base of a rock south of Kashkasu, a sinkhole leads into a large limestone
cave called Zinnan. At the end of the nineteenth century, Kurban-Dzhan-
Dakhta, the despotic female ruler of the Alai region, punished men by
leaving them to die in that cave bound with yak-fur rope.

In the village of Darautkurgan in the western part of the valley, where
a nineteenth-century fortress was built by the khan of Kokand, archaeologists have unearthed a settlement from the first millennium B.C. A bridge
at Darautkurgan crosses the Kyzylsu toward the Tersagar Pass, which
leads south to one of the world's largest temperate-zone glaciers, the 77-
kilometer Fedchenko in "the icy heart of the Pamir." In a ravine south of
the village, a large yak ranch is maintained by the collective farmers of
Tchonalai. The yak, which is more commonly called *kutas* in the mountains, is a large animal weighing up to half a ton. Its rich milk yields cream
and yogurt that are prized as great delicacies. It also provides wool, meat,
leather and fuel from dung. It is a widely used beast of burden, capable of
carrying heavy loads and fearless in crossing turbulent streams. Like
skilled alpinists, yaks have reached altitudes of 6,000 meters. They are
native to Tibet, where the fierce wild yaks have been used by Tibetans to
repel foreign visitors. The yaks of the Pamir, with their large horns and fur
hanging to the ground, have the same fierce look, but they are peaceful, at
least to their owners.

West of Darautkurgan, the climate is more arid and the rich pastures
gradually give way to thorny Acantholimon. As the valley becomes narrower, the floodplain is covered with wide meadows and thickets of sweetbrier, barberry, hawthorn, mountain ash, sea buckthorn, honeysuckle and
clematis. The sea buckthorn, called *dzherganak,* is especially prevalent. Its
nutritious berries are used to make jam and can be dried. Among the
wildlife of this mountain region are eagles, marmots, bears, ibex and the
huge *arkhars,* also known as Marco Polo sheep. Unlike the ibex, which
prefer the crags, the arkhars like to graze on open meadows but depend on
the alarm whistles of their constant companions, the large Central Asian
capercaillie grouse. The lord of the peaks is the snow leopard, which is
careful, patient and wise. One can travel in Central Asia for years without
seeing a single one of these large, spotted cats, but they are there.

People are coming into the mountains more and more. They penetrate places where silence reigned only a decade ago. Some come to explore the interior; others plough the virgin soil; a third group builds animal shelters; a fourth builds roads and bridges. The flow of tourists grows each year. People in large numbers, even if not there all the time, force animals and birds to leave their habitual homes and retreat higher into the mountains where it is cold and food is scarce. When people come with vehicles, helicopters and guns, one can imagine how the habitat of the animals shrinks.

The Alai Valley ends at the village of Ulugkaramyk. At its altitude of 2,240 meters, which is the low point of the valley, it is surrounded by agriculture, especially potatoes. Standing on a slight rise, the village is guarded on the east by crumbling walls from the early Middle Ages, testifying that invaders came mainly from the east. To go west from here, one has to ford a bridgeless tributary of the Kyzylsu. On our entire itinerary, this is the greatest obstacle to travel with a light automobile. One must obtain help from a tractor or a truck, both of which are common in the fields around the village.

The road then crosses the boundary from Kyrghyzstan into Tajikistan, from the Turkic- to the Iranian-speaking region. Here, in a canyon above the Kyzylsu, the road becomes extremely narrow, barely adequate for a single transport vehicle. The places where two vehicles can pass are few, and the traffic is sparse. This road did not exist before 1965, when it was built by the joint efforts of the collective farmers on both sides of the boundary to establish a link from Tajikistan to the Alai. Before that, this was a trail for mules and camels, in places over shaky walkways called *ovrings,* made from branches placed on logs beaten into the side of a cliff. After climbing to 2,800 meters, the road drops back to the river near the kishlak of Koshat, where the ruins of a caravansarai are a remnant of the great Silk Route from Termez and Dushanbe through the Alai Valley to Kashgar and eastern China.

Across the river from Koshat, the gray Muksu joins the red Kyzylsu at a hilly moraine that brings to an end the Trans-Alai range. The name Muksu refers to fire worshipers who once lived in this region. This moraine marked the end of the ancient Muksu glacier, which was 164 kilometers long, now reduced to the still gigantic Fedchenko glacier. Below the junction the combined river is called the Surkhob, which later joins the Obikhingou to become the Vakhsh, which, after junction with the

Pyandzh along the frontier with Afghanistan, becomes the great Amu Darya or Oxus River. This variety of names is just the way different peoples called the rivers in their own districts.

West of Koshat, the mountains across the river, which are even mightier than the Trans-Alai, form the Peter the Great range. Its eastern tip rises to the highest point in the USSR, the 7,495-meter Peak of Communism. From Dombratchi, the next hamlet below Koshat, one can look southeast and see this peak and the 7,105-meter Peak of Eugenia Korzhenevskaya. This is the only spot where one can see these giants from an automobile road. At Dombratchi, a light wooden footbridge crosses the main channel of the Surkhob and gives access to hamlets on its left bank when the river is low. In summer, when the glaciers melt and the river is full, the bridge goes only halfway across. The rest of the way one has to use a ferry made from inflated animal skins. Before the era of helicopters, such inflated skins were the only way that explorers and climbers could cross the wild rivers of the northwest Pamir. Even with helicopters now overhead, local people still do so. Crossing on an inflated skin is dangerous. Many have died that way.

Below Dombratchi, we detour 30 kilometers north to the sanatorium and vacation home of the collective farmers at Tandykul. In places the road is difficult for a light automobile. At Tandykul we rest in one of the guest houses, have our meals in the dining room, and bathe in the naturally hot mineral water. The most pleasant part of the bathing is not in the tubs but in the hot springs themselves. These are small pools in the earth, filled with hot water. When one enters these pools, black mud rises from the bottom and darkens the water, but the mud has healing properties and does not cling to the body.

Back at the Surkhob, at an altitude of 1,900 meters, the town of Dzhirghital is 30 kilometers down the river in a deep ravine, which allows few glimpses of the snows on the crest of the Peter the Great range. The town is filled with lush green trees and has a population of 10,000. This, too, is a good place for a rest in the hotel, with meals in the restaurant, and for thorough inspection of the car plus any repairs that may be needed. From here, the Surkhob Valley widens and goes on for another 120 kilometers. This is the famous Karategin, a legend-filled corner of Tajikistan.

In the past, Karategin was an isolated and backward region ruled by independent local princes. In the late nineteenth century, explorers found not a single town or place where there could be a bazaar and observed that money was virtually unknown and the people extremely poor. They wore clothing made from homespun textiles and made their own utensils, knives, swords and tools. Their Tajik dialect, like that of other Pamir mountain people, differs from the language of lower Tajikistan. Until 1932, when a road was put through, men carried loads from the outside on their backs or dragged them on primitive sledges, crossing the river on inflated skins. In winter, the herds were poorly fed so that even now the cows and sheep of Karategin are among the smallest in the world. The situation improved in Soviet times with the construction of towns, kishlaks, shops, clubs, hospitals, schools, libraries and child care centers.

Over the entire length of the Surkhob Valley, the Peter the Great range encloses it on the south. The highest point in this section of the range is the 4,973-meter Saganki Peak, about halfway down the valley. The eastern half of the valley is enclosed on the north by the Alai range, which ends almost directly across from Saganki Peak. There the Alai divides into two parallel branches: the Zerafshan range, which encloses the western half of the Surkhob Valley, and the Turkestan range farther north, which passes south of Tashkent to beyond Samarkand. West of the Surkhob Valley, south of the Zerafshan, the Hissar range forms a third branch north of Dushanbe.

In the wide part of the Surkhob Valley, the river flows gently in shallow branches. The valley is open to the west, with 700 millimeters of annual precipitation, more than twice as much as Tashkent receives. Being shielded on the north by the Alai and the Zerafshan, it has a mild climate in spite of its relatively high altitude, which ranges from 2,000 meters on the east to 1,000 on the west. It has more than two hundred days without frost each year, which enables the local people to grow rice, tobacco, corn and grapes.

In addition to their poverty, the people of Karategin have suffered from frequent earthquakes. In 1949, the district center of Khait and ten other villages were destroyed by a violent earthquake, which also caused a mountainside to slide into a lake, from which a muddy mixture of earth and water flowed over Khait and buried it more than ten meters deep. That village is no longer on the map. Such destructive mudflows, called *sels*, not always caused by earthquakes, are not uncommon in Tajikistan and elsewhere in Central Asia.

Situated near its western end, the largest town in the Surkhob Valley is now called Garm. In former times it was named Rapsha, the legendary capital of Karategin. In the early Soviet years, Garm was where several battles were fought between the Red Army and the Islamic Basmatchi rebels. The last such battle, a violent one, was in 1929. Garm is now a pleasant town with tall poplars and sycamores lining its streets.

West of Garm, a bridge takes the road across the Surkhob to its left bank, near the ruins of a kishlak that was also destroyed by a mudflow. This section of the road winds along the river in a deep ravine close to the foot of the Peter the Great range. In the upper part of the valley, one can pitch one's tent for the night almost anywhere without fear, but this is not recommended here. The rocky terrain with tall grass is teeming with poisonous snakes. In the morning one may find an unwanted guest in one's sleeping bag such as one of four different kinds of vipers or even a cobra. One should choose a place to sleep in an apricot orchard near a hamlet where the chance of meeting a snake is small.

At 34 kilometers west of Garm, the Peter the Great range ends where the Obikhingou, fed by the Garmo glacier in the northwestern Pamir, joins the Surkhob to form the Vakhsh. Here the road from Khorog, the chief town of the Pamir, 400 kilometers to the south, joins the Surkhob Road on the way to Dushanbe, which is 150 kilometers farther west. At this junction, the Karategin ends at the village of Komsomolabad, which has a dining room and an automobile repair shop. The way to Dushanbe then passes through cotton fields not far from the large Nurek hydroelectric dam.

Dushanbe is stretched out along the Varsob River at an altitude of about 800 meters. At the beginning of the twentieth century, it was a hamlet consisting of five hundred dwellings built of raw clay, surrounded by excellent fruit orchards but without a single building made of cured bricks. Before 1922, when Soviet power was established here after defeating the local Basmatchi, this part of Tajikistan was the eastern part of Bukhara. In 1929, Dushanbe became the capital of Tajikistan. In 1931, its population was 28,000. In 1970, it was 374,000.

Dushanbe is now one of the greenest cities in the Soviet south. The crowns of its trees have joined to shade its sidewalks and streets. The once treeless outskirts are now sumptuously clothed with decorative trees, productive orchards and forests from the foothills of the Hissar Mountains, whose pointed snow peaks are a spectacular backdrop that starts just north of the city. Our route into the mountains, past a lake in the city park, enters the Varsob Gorge, which the city people call Dushanbinki.

In the lower part of the gorge are mountain hamlets, rest houses, children's camps and scientific research stations. A botanical station of the Tajik Academy of Sciences, just beyond the village of Varsob, was active in the greening of the city and its surroundings. Farther on, a large complex of quarries extracts tungsten, galenite and fluorite from the depths of the gorge, which the river has cut through the bedrock of the mountains. The tungsten is used for high tensile steel and the fluorite is used in metallurgy, chemicals, optics and ceramics. Adjacent to the quarries are dozens of industrial buildings, dwellings, dining rooms, children's playgrounds, schools, a hotel, a hospital, a polyclinic and a palace of culture.

Forty-six kilometers from Dushanbe, a bridge crosses the Varsob to the hamlet of Gushara and the health spa of Hodzha-Obi-Garm at 1,850 meters altitude. Its hot springs have been well known since ancient times, and the development of the spa was started in the 1870s. As recently as a quarter century ago, an unusual form of healing was practiced here. A hole large enough to hold a person was dug into the earth and covered by a door adjacent to a rock. The patient entered this cellar and undressed. The door was closed and covered by a sheepskin. The inside then filled with steam percolating up through the earth. After a few minutes in this unique steam bath, the patient emerged and was wrapped in a cotton robe. The procedure was repeated two or three times a day. Now, with its forty hot springs, ranging from 38 to 95 degrees Celsius, the spa provides treatment under the supervision of qualified medical personnel. The radioactive waters combined with high temperature are useful for treating gout, gynecological illness and structural or peripheral nervous disorders. The hottest springs are used for the USSR's only institution giving radiological treatment with radon.

Above Gushara, the Varsob leaps like a mad deer over boulders brought down by earthquakes and mudflows. About 10 kilometers farther up, the Varsob begins at the junction of two nearly equal streams: the pure, blue, torrential Siama and the brown, turbid Zidda. The road follows the Zidda River into the interior of the range through a narrow cleft whose rocky walls are 1,200 to 1,500 meters high. In places along the bottom, cones of snow from avalanches, which fell the previous winter, remain throughout the summer. Local residents, workers, and youth scouts use these snow piles as iceboxes to preserve perishable foods. In some winters, avalanches cover the gorge completely to a depth of many meters.

At the hamlet of Zidda at an altitude of 2,820 meters, the annual precipitation is 1,500 millimeters. Here the jagged snow peaks of the Hissar crest come into view, as does the serpentine road that climbs its steep slope to the Ansob Pass through rich meadows of alpine flowers. The mountain Tajiks use many of these herbs and roots as medicines and in their cooking. Both slopes near the top have naturally carbonated mineral springs, which are refreshing stops for travelers but whose known output is as yet too small for commercial use.

The top of the pass, at an altitude of 3,379 meters, has an official meteorological station, a botanical station of the Tajik Academy of Sciences and an electrical research station for the study of high-altitude problems of high-voltage transmission lines. The mountains attract electrical storms. Trekkers and climbers are familiar with the tingling, buzzing and crackling of the charged atmosphere, with their hair and eyebrows standing on end and with the localized glow of Saint Elmo's fire. These are signals for hurrying to less-exposed places to avoid being hit by powerful lightning, which may follow soon.

The Ansob Pass is usually opened for vehicles early in July, and sometimes at the end of June, when the south side is free of snow, but deep snowfields on the north slope must be cut through by bulldozers. Before bulldozers were available and the road was opened by manual labor, it was customary to sprinkle coal dust or dark earth on the snow about two weeks in advance. The dark surface absorbed solar heat and accelerated the melting of the snow so that the amount of manual work required was significantly reduced. Skiing from the top continues till the middle of July, which is a popular time for training ski troops when they can be brought to the top by car.

This is the beginning of Kokhistan, "the country of mountains," which stretches 300 kilometers east to west and 80 kilometers south to north, all within the territory of Tajikistan. It starts at the crest of the Hissar, includes the entire Zerafshan and ends at the top of the Turkestan range. The highest points of these three ranges are, respectively, 4,491, 5,494 and 5,621 meters above sea level. From the Ansob Pass, the icy peaks of the Zerafshan dominate the panorama.

From the bridge across the Yagnob River below the north slope of the Ansob Pass, the Yagnob Valley, which extends 90 kilometers to the east, is one of the least accessible and most desolate areas in all of Turkestan. That part of the valley still has no automobile road. It is a region of excellent pastures surrounded by soaring peaks, which are crowned with permanent snows and glaciers. The population is poor, and to this day they speak among themselves in a unique language unrelated to those of the surrounding regions. Based on documents of the first century A.D., the Yagnobi language has been shown to be related to Sogdian, an ancient and extinct Iranian language. The paths in the Yagnob Valley are so difficult and dangerous, with steep climbs and unstable, narrow ledges over deep precipices, that warnings in the Arabic script were cut into the rocks and can still be seen. One of them says: "From you to the grave is only a single step. Tread as lightly as a teardrop on your eyelid."

Near the bridge, the kishlak of Ansob, at an altitude of 1,273 meters, had the misfortune, at the end of the nineteenth century, of a bubonic plague epidemic, brought in by pilgrims to the nearby grave of the Ishan Dzhandokush. Looking east from the kishlak, one can see a concrete enclosure at the top of a hill, which contains the graves of 237 residents who died from the plague in 1898. On the slope about 300 meters west of the kishlak is an unusual tower that strongly resembles a minaret. Actually it is a natural pinnacle formed by erosion of the conglomerate with a large, flat stone at the top. Such pinnacles are not uncommon, but this one is so perfect that it appears to have been built by a master builder.

High on the north slope of the Hissar, at an altitude of 2,180 meters, west of Ansob, the famous little lake of Iskanderkul is named for Alexander the Great, whose Graeco-Bactrian army is thought to have invaded this part of Turkestan. It is a lake of unusual beauty, enhanced by icebergs, which are always floating in it after falling from the glaciers above. The lake was formed by a rockfall. A legend is that Alexander was so irritated by the resistance of the local people that he ordered a stream to be dammed up with rocks, and when the water rose he ordered the dam to be opened so that the water rushed down and destroyed the hamlets of his opponents. Issuing from the lake, the Isakander Darya now flows steeply into the Yagnob at the bottom of the valley.

This valley is closed on its western end as well as on the east. The outlet from the valley is a river formed by the junction of the Yagnob and the Iskander Darya, called the Fan Darya. It has cut a narrow gorge 30 kilometers long all the way through the bottom of the Zerafshan range to join the large Zerafshan River on the north side, near the village of Ayni at the foot of the Turkestan range. In 1932, in the ruins of an ancient fortress in the upper part of the Zerafshan Valley, below its enormous glacier, a shepherd stumbled on a cache of Sogdian documents older than any that were known before. Ayni is a large village with a hotel, restaurant and telephone-telegraph service. It is named for a well-known Tajik writer, Sadriddina Ayni (1878–1954). In the center of the village is a tall minaret called Varzominor, which was the name of the village when the minaret was built in the eleventh century.

Conspicuously thriving north of the village, orchards of apricot and mulberry trees provide the favorite fruits of the mountain people. In pre-revolutionary times, the fruit of the mulberry tree was one of the staples in the diet of the local people. These trees, colloquially called breadfruit trees, are highly productive with little attention and are especially adapted to the mountain environment. They can be seen growing everywhere, on stony slopes and village streets as well as in private gardens. For hundreds and thousands of years, the mountain people were accustomed to depend on mulberries as a food that often saved them from hunger. Even today, when so many other types of food are available, mulberries have not lost their significance. They are used to make flour, halvah, and a sweet drink called *bekmes*. Their role in the diet of the mountain Tajiks is like that of potatoes in the European Soviet republics.

The berries begin to ripen at the end of July or early August. Each family prizes its mulberry orchard and keeps it absolutely clean. Chickens and lambs are not allowed to enter. The succulent berries fall on a plat-form where women and children gather them in wooden bowls several times a day. Nets covered with clean, dry straw are often installed under mulberry trees so that the berries are not damaged when they fall. The gathered berries are spread out on the flat roofs of the houses to dry. The dried berries are ground into flour, which in turn is pressed to form a highly nourishing and delicious solid mass called *tut-pist*. In Soviet times, the mulberry leaves have also been used to cultivate silkworms, from which the manufacture of silk has become an important auxiliary activity in the mountains of Tajikistan.

From Ayni, a road leads west down the Zerafshan Valley to the ancient treasures of Pendzhikent and the glories of Samarkand. Our route, however, takes us north to the 3,351-meter Shakhristan Pass across the Turkestan range. This pass, like the Ansob, is also rich in alpine flowers in a spectacular mountain landscape. Going down the north slope, the road passes through an extensive forest of juniper trees. In the western part of this forest, within the borders of Uzbekistan, a vacation complex is being built for trekking and winter sports in a region whose precious natural ecology is being protected by the establishment of the Uzbek National Park.

We continue our journey north through the city of Uratyube in the Tajik part of the western Ferghana Valley. Ruined fortifications show that it was already an important town in Arabic times before the tenth century. Its buildings, encrusted with colorful tiles, are typical of the Timurid style of the fifteenth century. Its people still work at their various traditional crafts, including camel's hair embroideries and textiles, square skull caps called *tyubiteykas,* colorful robes, wooden and metal utensils and tasteful jewelry of gold and silver with semiprecious and precious stones.

We return by way of what is still called the Hungry Steppe. In an ancient legend, a beautiful queen who can't decide between a strong and a handsome suitor promises to marry him who waters that steppe. The strong man starts to dam up the Syr Darya with boulders, while the handsome one, advised by a sorcerer, spreads reeds on the steppe to give the illusion in the sun that it has already been watered. This fools the queen, who orders the wedding. In despair, the strong man kills himself. When the sun goes down, the queen sees the deception and kills herself too. This legend expresses an early wish for irrigation of the steppes, which has now been done [and also foreshadows its tragedy, with depletion of the Syr Darya and the Aral Sea having become an ecological, economic and human disaster].

The return to Tashkent completes our journey through Ferghana, Alai, Karategin and Kokhistan, experiencing the contrasts of nature and culture in the mountainous heart of Central Asia.

CHAPTER 8

The Discovery of Victory Peak

Vladimir Ratzek, 1975

*Pik Pobedy was crucial in both the triumph and tragedy of Ratzek's life.[1]
On an expedition to the central Tien Shan in 1937, he climbed the 5,697-
meter (18,691 ft.) Nansen Peak from which he saw not only Khan Tengri,
then thought to be the highest Tien Shan summit, but also what appeared
to be an even higher but unknown one farther south. A few years later, his
group of five military topographers established its height at 7,439 meters
(24,406 ft.), second highest in the USSR. With the impending defeat of
Germany, he prevailed in having it named Pik Pobedy (Peak of Victory).
His group also identified several nearby peaks, passes and glaciers not yet
shown on any maps, including a major north-south range (the Meridian
range). These were extremely rare geographical discoveries at that time.
All five of the group were jointly awarded the Gold Medal of the Soviet
(now Russian) Geographical Society, of which Ratzek was elected an
honorary member in 1980. A few days later, he guided its members on a
Tien Shan field trip, at the completion of which he succumbed to a fatal
heart attack. Afterward, he was further honored by two snow peaks being
named for him, one each in the Tien Shan and the Pamir (Kalinin 1984).*

The highest point in the Tien Shan mountain system, the Peak of Victory
(Pik Pobedy), is situated on the Kokshaltau range, forming the left wall of
the large South Inylchek glacier. A climbing group led by A. Letavet in
1937 was the first to notice, in the panorama of the Tengri Tag group, that
this peak is higher than Khan Tengri, the Kyrghyz name for the famous
"Ruler of the Skies." Khan Tengri had been generally revered as the
highest peak of the entire Tien Shan, which is a Chinese name meaning
"heavenly mountains."

The following year, Letavet returned with three others to climb the unknown summit, which they tentatively called Little Star, the name of the tributary glacier just below it. On September 19, they climbed to the wide, snow-covered ridge east of the highest point, which they could see protruding through thick clouds 3 to 5 kilometers to the southwest, some 500 meters above them, and named it the Peak of the Twentieth Anniversary of the VLKSM.

However, in 1931, an expedition led by M. Pogrebetsky noticed this peak and named it the Peak of Sacco and Vanzetti, in honor of the two revolutionary workers who had been executed in America, without questioning the notion that Khan Tengri is the highest Tien Shan summit. Actually, this unnamed summit is clearly visible in the well-known panoramic photo of the Tengri Tag, which was given at the beginning of this century to the Russian Geographical Society by the mountaineer Count Gotfried Merzbacher and is kept to this day in the society's library in Leningrad.

In 1940, I led an expedition that was making a film of Kyrghyzstan (operator A. Samgin, assistant P. Opryshko) to the central Tien Shan. We observed this summit several times from panoramic points in the Terskey Alatau range (Berkut Pass) and the Sarydjas range (Achik-Tash Pass). From both points, with the aid of a telephoto lens attached to the motion picture camera mounted on a tripod, we made a horizontal transit from Khan Tengri to the unnamed summit. This procedure gave us the opportunity to be quite sure that a peak higher than Khan Tengri was hidden in the central Tien Shan. At that time, we were convinced that it was about 500 meters higher than the "Ruler of the Skies."

In 1943, as the leader of a group of mountaineers and the consulting guide, I was included in an expedition of topographers in the Khan Tengri region. This special high-altitude enterprise, led by the engineer P. N. Rapasov, was divided into teams of eight to ten men, including my group of mountaineering instructors. Before leaving for our work in the field, the topographers were directed to make particular observations of the summits on the Kokshaltau range south of Khan Tengri, where the peak had been hiding.

In August 1943, upon returning from one of their series of flights for aerial photography in the region of Khan Tengri, the pilot Bogomolov and the navigator Arutyunyantz told me, at the airport in Przhevalsk, that they had clearly seen an enormous peak that was significantly higher. They had been flying above the summit of Khan Tengri with their altimeter reading about 8,000 meters. Thus, as early as 1943, Soviet geographical science stood on the threshold of an outstanding discovery—establishing the height and geographical coordinates of the highest summit in the Tien Shan.

During the period when its height was being definitively calculated and independently verified, the head of the topographical section of the Central Asia Army Command, Col. Shapkin, set up an authoritative commission, which finally established that 16 kilometers south of Khan Tengri, above the Little Star (Zvezdotchka) glacier, a mountain massif rises above a great ice wall, in the center of which is a cone some 440 to 480 meters higher than the wall. This very spot is the highest summit of the Tien Shan, which earlier groups had variously called by several provisional names.

The name of this summit as the Peak of Victory (Pik Pobedy) was established upon my proposal, first expressed in *Komsomolskaya Pradva* on November 18, 1944. The name Pik Pobedy first appeared in 1946 on the large-scale map based on the 1943 fieldwork. Until then, no one had dared to challenge the preeminence of Khan Tengri as the highest point of the Tien Shan, as recognized by a whole series of domestic and foreign explorers.

During one of the first reports about the discovery of Pik Pobedy at the jubilee meeting of the Central Asia Geographical Society (December 1945), Professor N. Malitsky expressed an interesting thought: "Isn't Pik Pobedy the real Khan Tengri, which was known from deep antiquity?" For the next thirty years, Professor Malitsky's question gave me no peace. Wasn't that the answer to the riddle of Khan Tengri? And now we can answer it. Yes. The Tashkent professor was right. Today's Khan Tengri is really Kan Too, while Pik Pobedy is the real Khan Tengri. How could this have happened?

Prior to the time of P. P. Semenov's journey through the central Tien Shan in 1857, two outstanding summits were known: Khan Tengri and Kan Too. Moreover, the first of these was known to Semenov from historical documents, while the second was so named by the Russian explorer's Kyrghyz guides. It was then that Semenov, having no information about the location of Khan Tengri, gave that name to the most outstanding summit that he saw, the present Khan Tengri, even though his guides called it, in their own way, Kan Too, which means "Mountain of Blood" in the Kyrghyz language. One cannot thus assume, as Semenov did, that Khan Tengri and Kan Too are identical. These are two different summits.

In the Kyrghyz national epic *Manas* (pt. 2, "Semetey," in the line-by-line translation of the poem by V. N. Schneideman, from the manuscript version of the oral text of Sayakbay Karaliev in the archive of the section of national history of the Academy of Sciences of Kyrghyzstan at Frunze), it is stated that the highest mountain in the Kyrghyz domain is situated at the source of the Temirsu, the "Iron River," which flows from the north slope of the Kokshaltau.

On one of the earliest maps of this region, made by Col. Venyukov, it is clearly seen that the mountain called Khan Tengri lies on the watershed ridge, on the north of which are the sources of the river Sarydjas, the lower part of which is called Aksu or Kumaryk. Among these sources is the "Iron River" Temirsu. Southeast of the Khan Tengri knot are shown the sources of another river, the Muzart. The positions of these rivers on the map precisely determine the place that is now the location of Pik Pobedy.

Work on the topographical map based on data from the 1943 expedition was completed in Tashkent by the Red Army topographer Rashid Zabirov, who is now the well-known Soviet glaciologist and director of the Physical Geography Research Station of the Academy of Sciences of Kyrghyzstan at Pokrovka on the shore of Lake Issyk Kul. As finished by him, the map showed contour lines and altitudes but hardly any geographical names. This was indeed the last part of our country where summits, glaciers, passes and even entire ranges did not have proper names. The authors of the map were faced with the question of giving corresponding names to the objects on the map.

The first name entered on the map was that of the newly discovered range, stretching from south to north, which expedition leader Rapasov proposed to call the Meridian range. A more difficult problem was that of the summit whose height was a new record for the Tien Shan. The topographers wanted to call it the Peak of the Army Topographers, but we insisted on the previously proposed name—the Peak of Victory. In addition, there was another, very high summit with an altitude of 6,873 meters. Its existence became evident only after preparation of the map. It lay on the southern part of the Meridian range, at its junction with the Kokshaltau range.

In 1946, in connection with the discovery of the highest point of the Tien Shan, we had to make many appearances before the learned men of Moscow in the big auditorium of the old building of Moscow University, before the editors of the newspaper *Pravda* and the magazine *Around the World*, and finally in the severe headquarters of the Soviet Geographical

Society in Leningrad. The listeners were most varied—learned men, journalists, mountaineers, many of whom had taken part in the recent Great War for the Fatherland. They warmly supported the idea of calling the highest point in the Tien Shan the Peak of Victory. In 1946, after making these appearances in Moscow and Leningrad, I had a private visit with General Mark Karpovitch Kudryavtzev, the ultimate authority on topographical matters. The conversation went something like this.

"The people," reported the lieutenant from Tashkent [Ratzek], "request your agreement to name the '7,439' peak in the Tien Shan the Peak of Victory."

"Good," replied the general, "I do not object."

Upon my return to Tashkent, it turned out that the map already had had its first printing, and in the southeast corner of the sheet, near its edge, next to the mark "7,439.3," was the name Peak of the Army Topographers. However, the head of the department, Colonel Serge Alexandrovitch Shapkin, took the matter very seriously and said: "Since we have an order from the highest command, we will carry it out."

As a result, on the topographical map, and later on the map of the Soviet Union and on maps throughout the world, the name Peak of Victory, or Pik Pobedy, made its appearance. Even now, on the first edition of the topographical map, one can see that, next to the mark "7,439.3," the name Pik Pobedy is printed in red, while the name Peak of the Army Topographers is transferred to the highest point of the Meridian range.

Thus, the summit, seen by various explorers since 1931 and variously named the Peak of Sacco and Vanzetti, of the Little Star, of the Twentieth Anniversary of the VLKSM and of the Army Topographers, came to be officially called the Peak of Victory, symbolizing the victory of the Soviet people and their armed forces over Hitler's Germany.

The full significance of the discoveries and investigations after 1943 in the Tien Shan consists not only in the determination of the height and coordinates of the highest summit but also in the finding that the Tien Shan knot is not just the Peak of Khan Tengri but a whole range, called the Meridian range, standing just east of the dethroned Khan Tengri.

The discovery of the Peak of Victory, the highest summit of the Heavenly Mountains, is now thirty years in the past, but it still arouses heated discussions and misunderstandings. Who discovered it first? The mountaineers claim that the credit is theirs and the topographers that it is theirs. Who is right?

Actually, the Peak of Victory was discovered through the efforts of many explorers and expeditions, working in the eastern part of the central Tien Shan, in the Khan Tengri knot, during the first half of the twentieth century. But the priority, evidently, has to be given to those who measured its height, determined its geographical coordinates and, finally, gave it its name. This was the team of five men [P. N. Rapasov, V. I. Ratzek, A. F. Kokhsharov, P. Y. Gamaleyev and A. M. Arutyunyantz] that was awarded the Gold Medal of the Geographical Society of the USSR in the name of P. P. Semenov, the first explorer of the great mountain system of the Tien Shan.

CHAPTER 9

The Icy Heart of the Pamir

Vladimir Ratzek, 1980

Being surrounded by Afghanistan, Turkestan and China, the true core of Central Asia is a roughly rectangular area called the Pamir, where the world's highest mountain ranges mingle with each other in a complex knot. Its northern half is approximately bisected by the northward-flowing Fedchenko glacier, which is one of the longest, if not the longest, in the temperate zone (77 km or 48 mi.). That glacier and the magnificent world of ice around it are the major topics of the passages collected in this chapter, which includes important observations of high-altitude natural history. They are parts of Ratzek's guidebook for "tourists" (high-altitude trekkers), which includes crossing glacier passes up to 6,000 meters (20,000 ft.) high. He begins and ends with a hymn to the Pamir's icy heart and a plea for the preservation of that unique part of the world. After World War II, Ratzek was assigned to a cartographic survey of the Pamir, many parts of which were still blank spots on the map, and as the leader of military expeditions he successfully climbed a number of its highest peaks, including all three that exceed 7,000 meters (23,000 ft.).[1] His studies of glaciology were brilliant but included some memorable moments.[2]

In our time, when science and technology are modifying our native landscapes, people strive to find fragments of nature preserved in their virgin state. In high mountains, nature sternly guards those of its sectors that have not yet yielded to the influence of man. There, as in earlier times, one can still hear the howling of blizzards, the roar of avalanches and the crunch of hard snow, and one can look into a glacier's depths through crevasses that plunge into the green-blue gloom.

In the shape of a quadrilateral that stretches 250 kilometers from north to south and 275 kilometers from west to east, the Pamir is a high mountain region, one-eighth of which is covered with glaciers and permanent snow. In its northwest quadrant, a glaciated area of 3,000 square kilometers, is the largest single concentration of ice and snow outside of the polar latitudes. This is the icy heart of the Pamir, a sanctum of high mountain nature and truly one of the wonders of the world. This labyrinth of glaciers and steep, intertwining, snow-covered ranges cannot be compared with any other place. It is truly unique.

Bounded on the east by China and on the west and south by Afghanistan, with India and Pakistan not much farther south, the Pamir is at the latitude of the Mediterranean Sea, but its harsh environment is like that of polar regions, with the added hazards of intense radiation and rarified air that are characteristic of high altitudes. Its climate is unusual too. Hot days alternate with frosty nights, and in the midst of a heat wave snow can suddenly fall. All this is the fault of extreme altitude, combined with great distance from the oceans, in the center of Asia's continent.

Nature produces two main types of ice, one of which is formed by the freezing of water and the other by compaction of fallen snow in the mountains and polar regions. Glaciers thus depend on precipitation in the form of snow and on a climate that produces it. For precipitation to occur within arid Central Asia, moisture carried in the atmosphere must be lifted upward by air currents so that it condenses at lower temperatures above. The mountains of the Pamir are instrumental in this process. Figuratively speaking, they squeeze the moisture out of the air, saving part of it in the concentrated form of glaciers.

Glaciers are reservoirs of water in solid form from which nature can obtain needed water during dry years or seasons. Twenty years ago, when the need to protect nature was not so keenly felt as now, experiments were made to accelerate the melting of glaciers for irrigation by sprinkling them with carbon dust to retain solar heat. More recent knowledge shows the need to do just the opposite, to protect glaciers from excessive melting, which is partly the result of man-made forces in the form of atmospheric pollution, with a negative effect on water resources and nature itself.

All moisture coming to the Pamir from the north, west and south is retained by peripheral ranges, where the precipitation can be substantial, feeding its numerous glaciers and the great rivers of Soviet Asia. This leaves little precipitation for the Pamir's eastern part, an arid tableland mostly over 4,000 meters high, which is drier than most deserts. The dryness there has lasted millions of years, so that the landscape is remarkably free from erosion, though dotted by the moraines of ancient glaciers.

Throughout the Pamir, however, the air is extremely arid, causing rapid evaporation on any surface. On one occasion, we saw an avalanche fill the air with dense snow dust, but all of it vaporized before settling on the ground. Another time, when the sun came out after a heavy snowfall on the southern slope of a mountain, we thought the snow would melt, but instead the thick cover of snow just disappeared into the air as vapor, leaving bare, dry earth within two hours.

The dryness also causes the remarkable temperature differences. If one walks in the sun near a shaded cliff, one side feels the heat of the sun while the other shivers because the cliff is several degrees below freezing. In the eastern Pamir, on July 9, 1934, the temperature was 33 degrees Celsius at 1 P.M., but −6.4 degrees only three hours later. That is the kind of temperature change that shatters rocks, forming piles of rock debris over much of the Pamir.

Forming a natural boundary between the eastern and western Pamir, the Academy of Sciences range and its southern extensions bisect the Pamir from north to south. At its northern tip, this range rises to 6,297 meters at the Peak of Muzdjilga, the highest point in a group informally called the Mazarsky Alps, being across the Muksu River from the pasture of Altyn Mazar. On a spur 20 kilometers westward, the Peak of Eugenia Korzhenevskaya, at 7,105 meters, is the fourth highest in the USSR. From there the Academy of Sciences range winds its way southward for 108 kilometers. Its southern tip is marked by the 6,439-meter Peak of the Communist Academy, at its intersection with the east-west Yazgulem range. About 10 kilometers east of there, the latter rises to 6,974 meters at the Peak of the Revolution.

Between these two great peaks, the Yazgulem range forms the southern boundary of the great Fedchenko glacier, which is the main core of the glaciated area in the northwestern Pamir. Flowing north on the east side of the Academy of Sciences range, the Fedchenko glacier has a length of 77 kilometers and a total area, with its tributaries, of 652 square kilometers, thus one of the largest temperate glaciers on earth. From where it begins, at an altitude of 6,280 meters, it flows down to its tongue at an altitude of 2,910 meters. This massive glacier and its tributaries "drown" the spurs of its neighboring ranges to such a depth that they form a landscape of a truly Antarctic appearance.

The common terms "eternal snow" and "eternal ice" are misleading.

Even in the huge Fedchenko glacier, the mean age of its solid substance is only 230 years. This is simply a matter of dividing its length of 77 kilometers by its average speed of 350 meters per year. The reality is not quite so simple, because in this glacier, with its depth of up to 900 meters and its width of about 3,000 meters, not all parts of it move at the same speed in straight lines. According to calculations taking this into account, a complete change of its substance, within its volume of 96 cubic kilometers, requires about 1,000 years.

The 3,000 square kilometers of snow and ice in the Pamir's icy heart include some fifteen hundred glaciers, thirty of which are of major size. In addition to the large tributaries of the Fedchenko glacier, these include the glaciers of Grum-Grzhimaylo (37 km, 142 sq km), Garmo (30 km, 115 sq km), Russian Geographical Society (24 km, 64 sq km), Sugran (22 km, 47 sq km) and Fortambek (27 km, 36 sq km).

The western Pamir is filled with steep, high mountains through which torrential rivers flow west and cut deep gorges, which are difficult to follow or cross. Between these gorges, the east-west mountain ranges mostly rise to over 6,000 meters. The northernmost of these is the range of Peter the Great, whose intersection with the range of the Academy of Sciences is crowned by the Peak of Communism, which, at 7,495 meters, is the highest in the USSR. About 15 kilometers west of this peak, the Peter the Great range rises to 6,785 meters at the summit of the Peak of Moscow, whose north face is a grandiose jumble of overlapping glaciers feeding the Fortambek glacier below.

At the crest of this section of the Peter the Great range is an unusual formation called the Pamir Firn Plateau. *Firn* is the term for ice in the form of large, interlocking crystals, which is the intermediate stage in the transformation of snow into solid glacier ice under pressure from its weight and movement down a mountain slope. Being almost level, at an average height of about 6,000 meters, this plateau is a remnant of the coastal shelf of the ancient Tethys Sea, which covered much of Central Asia in the Tertiary geological period. Later, when the Pamir Mountains rose under the pressure of plate tectonics, this piece of the Tethys Sea bottom was bodily lifted up together with the adjacent peaks. Thus, the Pamir Firn Plateau lies on a surface that is some 300 million years old. There are several similar but smaller formations in and around the Academy of Sciences range.

Rising about 2,000 meters above the Fortambek glacier, with an almost vertical north wall, the Pamir Firn Plateau has likewise a nearly vertical south wall of about the same height. Based on indirect seismic measurements, the accumulation of ice and snow on the plateau is estimated to reach a thickness of up to 150 meters. Covering an area of 30 square kilometers, it is actually a large glacier, but, being nearly level on the crest of a ridge, it doesn't flow in a single direction. Instead, it periodically spills over its north and south walls. Viewed from the Fortambek glacier, one can regularly see such avalanches of snow and ice. The largest of these outlets occurs from a break at the top of the north wall, through which large blocks of packed snow and ice emerge at least daily. These blocks shatter when they hit a ledge about halfway down, from which the debris of ice and snow bounces off and falls to the Fortambek glacier another 1,000 meters below, where it forms a large, white cone. This periodic bouncing of snow and ice is informally called the Trampoline glacier. It is an opportunity to observe the dynamics of glaciers at an accelerated pace.

Another unusual action of Pamir glaciers is periodic acceleration. This was observed in the 16-kilometer Medvezhy ("Bear") glacier in the early summer of 1963 and again ten years after that. The Bivatchny ("Bivouac") glacier, a tributary of the Fedchenko, was likewise observed to accelerate in 1978. The periodic acceleration occurs, not because of an increase in the volume of glacier ice but, on the contrary, as an interaction with excessive melting. Thus, when melting causes the tongue to recede, it no longer gives the same support to the weight of ice above, which then slides down more rapidly into the warmer zone below. In the process, the surface of the glacier is broken up into a fantastic jumble of uplifted slabs. This phenomenon occurs, however, in a few glaciers only and is not yet fully understood.

In addition, because of atmospheric dryness, Pamir glaciers evaporate greatly in addition to their melting. This is why they often have such a spectacular surface of enormous, jagged, ice towers in an irregular sawtooth pattern. On the Fortambek and Walter glaciers below the Pamir Firn Plateau, these towers form a ribbon of white ice down the middle of the glacier, being squeezed from both sides by a heavier load of rock debris on the surface. The rushing Bivatchny glacier developed a similar central ribbon of huge ice blocks.

One should not get the impression, from the preceding, that the icy heart of the Pamir is devoid of plant and animal life. In many places, at the side of glaciers, bushes, grasses and alpine flowers grow well above 4,000 meters, even up to 5,100 meters at the upper part of the Fedchenko glacier, while mosses and lichens grow higher still, up to 5,300 meters. On one of its large tributaries, the 50-square-kilometer Vitkovsky glacier, wild pigeons and larks were seen spending the winter at 5,000 meters but flew higher when the weather improved. Butterflies were seen flying upward at 5,700 meters on this glacier, and rabbit tracks were also seen.

On one occasion in the high Pamir, we saw a large flock of sand martins, which are not considered to be native in such areas, flying rapidly over the surface of a glacier, often dipping down, apparently to pick up something off the ice. Then we saw that on top of the ice were numerous black spiders, which normally move only in the heat of the day. The birds were apparently feeding on them. And what did the spiders eat? Probably microscopic organisms, the so-called green algae, which form "red snow." Other birds, such as jackdaws, ravens and snow finches, are residents of the Pamir up to 6,000 meters altitude. Even in the eastern Pamir, which is mostly an elevated desert, patches of alpine meadows thrive near the lakes and streams where *Parnassius* butterflies and hawk moths feed on the flowers.

Among the larger animals of the high Pamir are the mountain sheep and goats. The largest of these is the Marco Polo, or Pamir, sheep (*Ovis ammon poli*), first described by Marco Polo in the thirteenth century and not seen again by Europeans until the early nineteenth century. This huge animal weighs up to 200 kilograms, with massive spiral horns almost 2 meters long. It frequents high ridges not covered with snow such as those of the eastern Pamir. The Asiatic mountain goats of the species *Capra ibex* usually weigh about half as much, but their scimitar-shaped horns can be almost 1.5 meters long. They are residents of steep rock, ice and snow throughout the Pamir. They often rely on the large capercaillie grouse (*Tetraogallus himalayensis*) to warn them of danger from predators or hunters.

Once, when we were walking under a steep cliff formed by the moraine of an ancient glacier, we saw stones falling from above. Looking up, we saw a herd of about thirty ibex, including young ones, running off, perhaps to escape a snow leopard. At one point, they came to a deep ditch, washed out by a stream, which the adults could easily jump, but for the young ones it was a challenge. The leader of the herd, a old male, straddled the ditch with his front and rear feet until all the young ones made it across, after which he resumed his place at the head of the herd.

Snow leopards are now so rare that they are listed in the "Red Book" of endangered plant and animal species (as are the Marco Polo sheep), and they live only in the most inaccessible mountain strongholds. However, in the snow and on the clay near streams, one can still quite often see their large, round tracks. We have followed their tracks and observed that they, like expert mountaineers, avoid dangerous places, even walking around potential avalanche slopes. In 1950, we saw snow leopard tracks on the summit of the Peak of Lenin, which at 7,134 meters is the second highest in the Pamir and the third highest in the USSR. That is not the only time we saw animal tracks at such heights in the Pamir.

Before the 1950s, when helicopters began to provide easy access to the icy heart of the Pamir, it was reached only by occasional native hunters and by scientific explorers of the late nineteenth and early twentieth centuries, who crossed the dangerous rivers on inflated animal skins or air mattresses. It was really first penetrated by the 1928 Soviet-German expedition and several Soviet expeditions in the 1930s. Now this region is popular with scientists, climbers and trekkers, who cross the high passes around peaks and between glaciers. Trekking in the USSR is a major activity, which offers more opportunity to study the surroundings, and see more of them, than does climbing, which requires concentration on ascending rock, ice and summits. As of 1978, trekking associations officially recognized 311 mountain passes that had been crossed in the Pamir on foot. The highest of these, called the Zimovstchikov Pass (5,970 meters), first crossed in 1959, is the outlet from the Fedchenko glacier basin by way of the Vitkovsky glacier.

Why would one wish to travel on foot in this uninhabited mountain region with its hazards of sudden blizzards, avalanches, rockfalls, crevasses, accidents, sunburn, frostbite and all forms of high-altitude illness? This is the perennial question for mountain climbers and trekkers, but I answer it briefly: because it is difficult, interesting, beautiful, expansive and evocative of all one's physical and mental powers and because nature there, though sparse in plant and animal life, is of a special kind in this kingdom of crags, ice and snow.

CHAPTER 10

The Pamir Is Rising

Okmir Agakhanyantz, 1975

Okmir Agakhanyantz, who was born in St. Petersburg in 1927, is pro-
fessor of biogeography at Minsk, doctor of geographical sciences from the
Institute of Geography in Moscow, honorary member of the Russian and
Belorussian Geographical Societies, and academician of the Academy of
Sciences and Arts of Peter the Great. A geobotanist and a prolific scientific
and popular writer, he was a resident of Tajikistan for eighteen years and
has explored the Pamir almost every year since 1949. First as scientific
secretary and later as senior scientific fellow of the Tajik Academy of
Sciences, he was in charge of the main botanical laboratory at Khorog and
of the botanical expeditions at the high-altitude research station at
Chechekty at an altitude of 4,035 meters (12,300 ft.), making surveys of
the vegetation of the Pamir.[1] Even more than individual species, he stud-
ied plant communities because these are more readily correlated with
accurately dated geophysical changes over long geological periods, espe-
cially those involved in the formation of mountains.[2] Thus, the rate of
uplift of the Pamir concerned him greatly. In this chapter, he reports an
actual but almost ludicrous debate on this subject involving himself and
his scientific colleagues, including botanists and archaeologists, which
was resolved by definitive physical data. It began, however, on a quiet
evening with a herdsman in the mountains.

If mountains didn't grow, our planet would be something like a billiard
ball. But mountains do grow. When they stop growing, they fall into ruin.
True, they disintegrate even when they grow, but then their growth may
be faster than their destruction, and a mountain country arises. That is
how it is in the Pamir: it grows faster than it crumbles. Its heights are

enormous. Earthquakes testify to its continuing growth. Calculations are that over the past million years it has risen by 2.5 to 3 kilometers. This means that during this time the mountains rose one centimeter in three years. On the average. That's a good tempo for a geological process measurable over millions of years. All this is known.

That the Pamir is rising at a catastrophic rate is something I first heard about from a herdsman in the Tosion Gorge. The sheep were hurrying to reach their shelter for the night, but it was still broad daylight. We drank tea and talked about abstract things. The slope across the ravine was striped in many colors. Winding paths crossed it back and forth. This so-called pathness results from grazing. The flocks walk across the slope on various levels without losing altitude and gradually produce a multitude of light-colored paths. I was familiar with this but was interested to hear what my companion would say about it. I asked him. The herdsman looked at the slope and laughed.

"The mountain is growing. A cow stamps out a path at the bottom, but the mountain grows. The cow then stamps out another path lower down. That's why there are so many paths. The new ones are below and the old ones above."

I laughed and winked at the herdsman, letting him know I appreciated the joke. He burst out laughing, too, and slapped me on the shoulder, meaning the game was even, tit for tat, and let's call it quits.

But a few years later a scientific journal published an article by Cyril Vladimirovich Stanyukovich. He showed that the distribution of certain plants in the eastern Pamir that reproduce without seeds cannot be explained by present conditions. For example, near the warm springs of Djarty-Gumbez a fern grows at an altitude of 4,100 meters [13,450 ft.]. It has no spores and reproduces by its roots. But the nearest growths of this fern are 150 to 200 kilometers away. How did it get there? Cyril Vladimirovich postulates that the whole Pamir was warm in relatively recent times and this fern grew all along the rivers, but then it got sharply colder and this tiny island of ferns survived near the warm spring. Since temperature drops sharply with altitude, he concludes that the Pamir is now rising fast from a formerly warm, lower level. How fast, he doesn't say.

As a basis for such a conclusion, he relies not only on the fern but also on other plants whose range is getting smaller. This is not a herdsman saying tit for tat but a scientific article. Without numbers, admittedly, but a brilliant, enticing hypothesis creating a sensation. Fully in the style of

Stanyukovich, a talented and lively man. I read the article and set it aside without special emotion. After all, the rapid rise of the Pamir is only a supposition, and without quantitative indications one could ignore it for the present. Botanists are strange people. To explain the distribution of some blade of grass, they don't hesitate to move continents and build mountains. [This could be a play on words, since *bylinka* means both a blade of grass and a little legend.]

It didn't turn out that way. The hypothesis was seized upon, and articles on the same theme poured out one after another. Some just repeated what Stanyukovich had said, while others introduced new material proving the Pamir's rapid rise. All indications were indirect, but their combined effect was impressive. In the valley of Markansu, at an altitude of 4,000 meters, the archaeologist Vadim Alexandrovich Ranov unearthed an early human abode. In it were ashes from a bonfire, some weapons and animal bones. Their age was identified by the carbon radioactive method. It turned out to be a bonfire from 9,500 years ago. Two circumstances were surprising. The first was wood ashes. Today in Markansu there are not only no trees but almost no high-altitude desert plants of any kind. It is the most lifeless place in the entire Pamir. Cold and drought, bare rubble and tornadoes. The name Markansu [in Turkic] means "the valley of tornadoes." What timber could be here? But the bonfire was. That is a fact. True, a small bonfire, but one has to take it into account, like any fact. Second, the conditions under which people then lived were surprising. Even now, when we have tents, sleeping bags and warm clothing, life in Markansu is not cozy: we freeze, and our lips are chapped by the wind and dryness. How was it there for those early hunters? (That they were hunters Ranov established precisely.) But these difficulties could easily be set aside if one supposed that ten thousand years ago the Pamir was lower, and therefore warmer, with trees growing all around. Since the upper forest limit at these latitudes is 2,500 meters, sometimes up to 3,000, some scholars concluded that since the time the ancient hunters burned wood at Markansu the Pamir has risen by 1,500 meters. This implies that the Pamir is growing at the rate of 10 to 15 centimeters per year, maybe even 20. This is fifty to sixty times faster than the average of the past million years. The numbers are now stated!

Afterward another finding turned up. In the same eastern Pamir, south of Murgab, Ranov found a grotto with colored paintings on the walls. The drawings are ancient. Neolithic. This turned out to be the world's highest location for neolithic drawings: 4,000 meters above sea level. But most interesting was the content of the drawings. On the walls of the cave were drawings of a bear, a boar and something like an ostrich on human legs. There are now no bears or boars in the cold of the Pamir's highlands. Not to mention ostriches. First question: did the ancient artist see these animals where he drew them? If he did, one would have to admit that in those times bears and boars lived here, and these are essentially forest animals, meaning that there were forests, and therefore . . . In other words, we come once again to the insane tempo of the Pamir's recent rise. A second question: if the ancient artist saw these animals somewhere else (the nearest such place today is 200 kilometers from the grotto) and he made the drawings with the idea of so-called hunter's magic (the drawings show arrows pointed at the animals), could our ancestor have wandered so far, like a nomad, over the cold highlands, barely covered with furs? If he could, this also means that the Pamir was then lower, warmer and wooded.

There is still more. Already other archaeologists have discovered in the highlands ancient graves covered with logs. The age of the graves— from two to four thousand years. From where did they get the logs? This means there were forests near here not long ago. If so, the Pamir rose 1,500 meters not in ten thousand but in four thousand years, that is, at a rate of 25 to 37 centimeters [10 to 15 in.] per year? Exactly that conclusion was made.

This is getting somehow uncomfortable. Such a rapid rise in no way agrees with many other, fully established facts. For example, if the mountains are growing in such a rush, the rivers must be cutting into their beds at a comparable rate, that is, also very fast. This means that the groundwater level in the western Pamir (which rises together with the eastern Pamir) must be sharply dropping, and its meadows must perish in some one hundred years. But these meadows have existed for hundreds of years, which is established by documentary evidence. For example, Marco Polo saw them in the thirteenth century. This is the first contradiction. If the Pamir became a high mountain area in only ten thousand years, or even four thousand years, how can one explain that hundreds of species of its plants are so precisely adapted to the local high-mountain conditions? For evolution, such a short period is very small; it would take hundreds or at least tens of thousands of years, not just thousands. This is the second contradiction. There was a third, and a tenth, but these two would be enough.

Meanwhile, the hypothesis was becoming popular. Sensational! Journalists grabbed it. In the pages of newspapers and popular science magazines, colorful articles appeared under intriguing headings. In many articles the hypothesis was presented as absolutely proven.

Acquaintances asked me how it felt to be on the Pamir when it was rising like an elevator. My confident replies about how it felt and cautious ones about the Pamir's rise did not satisfy their thirst for the sensational. All this time I sat at my books, wandered over the mountains, searched the archives, verified published facts, compared them with each other, in other words, worked.

I must admit that the question of the rate at which the mountains were rising aroused in me a far from idle interest. Much depended on how it was resolved: the tempo of high-altitude plant evolution, the age of many plant communities, the fate of the meadows and forest plantations, the future of agriculture. It affected all discussions about nature in the mountain world. The hypothesis of the rapidly rising Pamir did not bother me personally, but it simply did not agree with generally known facts.

I published my disagreement with the hypothesis, calling attention to the various contradictions. A discussion began. I was supported by geologists, geomorphologists and paleobotanists. On the opposite side were my friend Ranov and several botanists and zoologists. Articles appeared one after another. Both sides gathered more new facts into their evidence. After a full measure of polemical articles with proofs, they started to seek refutations. And then there was another round of publications.

In debate, as is known, is the birth of truth. It is a complicated thing—this scientific argument. It becomes scientific only under strict rules: both sides seek the truth, do not indulge in angrily distorting the facts, maintain logic and respect the opinions of their "opponents." Otherwise, it would not be a scientific discussion but just an abusive quarrel, which would not lead to the truth. And, although the rules of debate are strict, one cannot get away from emotions and passions. Truth is not given to those who are indifferent. To the cold-blooded, yes—but not to the indifferent. Often, having received in turn one's share of arguments from the other side, one feels astonished: "Well how can he not see the obvious?" Afterward, realizing with a cold head that the "opponent" is not bound to see things with your eyes, you start to analyze the implications. And in that argument there are no kinsmen or near ones. Here, for example, is Vadim Alexandrovich Ranov. He is my old and close friend and at the same time my adversary in a scientific argument.

Ranov is an archaeologist. A specialist on the Stone Age. A brilliant expert on quaternary geology. Because of that, he is a skillful archaeologist. He knows where to dig. He is a very serious, deep and many-sided researcher and an excellent man. It is fully understandable, therefore, that in confronting Ranov in the role of an "opponent" it was necessary to proceed seriously, though he was not at all the leader of those who advocated the rapid rise of the Pamir.

This argument did not spoil our friendship. We continued the debate not only in print but also at home. We discussed our positions and sought the truth. If the debate of many years is compressed into a single dialogue of "for" and "against" the Pamir's rapid rise, it would be about as follows.

For: The remains of the bonfire in the ancient abode in Markansu, the logs on the graves.

Against: Pollen analysis of specimens from the abode show that the vegetation of ten thousand years ago was not a forest but the same as now—of the desert type. Even now, when we leave the Pamir, we burn the tent poles, and why should not the early hunters have done the same? Logs for the graves could have come from across the Sarykol range [i.e., across the present Sino-Soviet boundary] for the sake of a ritual burial. Even now Pamir people carry logs from far away.

For: And the drawings of forest animals in the grotto?

Against: The ancient artist saw them in a different place.

For: But then one must admit long-distance, nomadic travel by the early people, which is likely only in a milder climate.

Against: Why so? They did not spend the winter on the Pamir but were able to reach Markansu for the summer, and therefore they could wander long distances. They were simply hardy fellows. But these are all indirect data. Now geophysical measurements at often-repeated elevations show that the Pamir rises only 3 centimeters in a most active year of earthquakes. This is a direct fact.

For: The rise of the Pamir could have been uneven: 3 centimeters per year now and 20 centimeters per year a thousand years ago.

Against: But how about the meadows in the western Pamir?

For: This means that the eastern Pamir rose faster. And consider the ancient cirques, filled with glaciers, now found at high altitudes, proving the rapid rise of the Pamir.

Against: This is based on an incorrect estimate of the ancient snow line, which we have verified. But how to account for the facts established by the paleoglaciologists? They have calculated the material balance of the Markansu glacier and compared it with temperature conditions, and the calculation showed that from the time of the encampment the mountains rose only 200 meters.

For: And how did the ferns reach Djarty-Gumbez?

Against: By means of winds from the valley. Spores also fell in other places, but they germinated only near the warm spring and after that reproduced through the roots. But how about the rate of evolution?

And so forth, for more than fifteen years. Every "for" and "against" was an article. Or a paper presented at a scientific conference. Or just a discussion over a cup of tea.

If scientific truth were decided by majority vote, the question would have been resolved long ago. But in science, debates are not decided this way. Galileo was clearly in the minority, but the truth was on his side. It is another matter that the indirect indications of the Pamir's rapid rise were more easily refuted by the direct geophysical, paleoglaciological and pollen-spore data. But many implications of the opposing side required explanation. Sometimes this meant getting the facts more precisely or searching for defects in methods or theory. But sometimes the question remained without an answer. And for our questions the "opponents" did not always find a convincing answer.

Today we have many facts indicating that the tectonic rise of the Pamir in the last ten thousand years did not exceed 2 or 3 centimeters per year. These facts result from fundamental research, carefully verified. If only there were not those "damned" questions, always being thrown at us by the advocates of the rapid rise, we could sleep peacefully. But we don't have this peace, nor do we have the answers to some of the "damned" questions. And we continue to work.

CHAPTER 11

Osh, Ancient Trade Route City

Okmir Agakhanyantz, 1987

Between the Pamir and the Great Steppes and between Samarkand and China, Osh is the second-largest city of Kyrghyzstan. For Okmir Aga-khanyantz, Osh was a familiar place where he often stayed when going to or from his work at the eastern Pamir high-altitude research station at Chechekty. In this chapter, in addition to describing the city, its history and its surroundings,[1] he gives intimate details of local family life and current gossip. He explains how the caravan trade, for which the city was once important, has been replaced by its bustling traffic as a hub of expeditionary travel and supply, serving Russian, Central Asian and for-eign groups of earthquake specialists, archaeologists, surveyors, moun-taineers and prospectors for oil or gold. As a result, every boy who grows up in Osh dreams of someday becoming a chauffeur or the driver of a truck.

Different kinds of cities are found in the world: rich ones and poor ones; large ones and small ones; some that preserve traces of dying empires and some that are merely collections of boxlike houses; some that are marked on maps with bright stars and others that are marked only with the tiniest dots. There are all kinds of cities, but nowhere else is there one like Osh. It cannot be compared with any others.

This city's location is at an intersection among different currents of humanity. The town itself is in Kyrghyzstan, but 3 kilometers to the west lies the boundary of Uzbekistan. Caravans from Central Asia passed through it in ancient times. That is why it is inhabited by so many different peoples: Kyrghyz, Uzbeks, Russians, Ukrainians and Uigurs who once settled this region, emigrants from Kashgaria [Chinese Turkestan] and

Kazakhstan. Demographers surely know how to categorize its 250,000 residents by the nationalities to which they belong, but on its streets one can meet anyone at all. Osh is a city that is truly international.

It perched itself at the eastern tip of the Ferghana Basin in its very highest part. A little lower one enters the scorching deserts and the large cotton plantations, a little higher the glaciers of the Alai. The city sprawls beyond its periphery, imperceptibly merging with the farms. This also is an intersection. Some cotton fields lie close to industrial buildings, but a bit farther on are more town houses. It is hard to tell where the city ends and where the outlying communities begin. Osh is urban and rural at the same time.

It is green like all the cities of the Ferghana oasis. Along its irrigation ditches grow acacias, maples, catalpas, Lombardy poplars and plane trees. The same as everywhere in Middle Asia. Here they are not arranged in rows, and are not pruned or cared for, but grow as it were all by themselves, untended but luxurious. The impression is that whatever happened to be at hand was planted at random, and everything grew, unexpectedly forming an elemental landscape that is typically Oshian. Osh is just an overgrown park.

The cities of the Ferghana Basin are all flat, but Osh is distinguished by a unique silhouette. In the very center of the town rises a spire-shaped holy mountain that is seen from everywhere around, the Takhta-i-Sulaimon, "the Throne of Suleiman," or, in the vernacular, the Suleimanka. In the sixteenth century, Shah Babur, founder of the Great Mogul Empire, built a mosque on its summit and afterward conquered India, where he often longed for the cool nights of Osh, as he wrote in his well-known memoirs. Osh is a city of colorful history.

The bazaar of Osh spreads out at the foot of the Suleimanka. Not even the famous bazaar of Ferghana can compare with it in size and opulence. The position of the city at the junction between the mountains and the basin attracts mountain people as well as inhabitants of the plains. In the bazaar of Osh one can study geography, ethnography, handicrafts and the incredibly rich agricultural products of the Ferghana oasis. Here one can eat a fat *lagman* [a pasta dish] from Kashgar or a juicy *shashlik* made from a Pissarsky lamb, wash it down with kumiss [fermented mare's milk] from the Alai, get one's head shaved without soap by an Uzbek barber, buy a knife from Marghelan or a pair of *djuraby* [patterned wool stockings] from the Pamir, listen to *zurnatchi* [long oboe-type instruments] from Namangan, haggle over half a ruble for a pail of local tomatoes, and learn one's fate from an Uigur fortune-teller who skillfully throws down the bones. The bazaar of Osh is really a museum.

But that is not all. Osh is a huge center for transportation, portage and expeditions. Here are several large automotive establishments with thousands of vehicles and automobile repair shops, all because Osh is situated at the intersection between the Pamir, the Tien Shan, and the Ferghana Valley. The most widely practiced profession here is that of chauffeur. Next to that is being a mechanic, a maintenance man or anything that has to do with cars. The talk one hears in the restaurants, tchaikanas [teahouses] and parks is mainly about the condition of the roads, about spare parts, fuels and loads. Osh is mainly a city of chauffeurs and truck drivers.

The second most prevalent occupation in Osh is providing services for expeditions. Most of these are from distant places, but many are local—from the republic of Kyrghyzstan, from the district of Osh or from the city itself. The establishments include administrative offices, travel agencies, outfitters and just plain bases. On the streets of the city one can run into a colleague whom one once met at Leningrad, Moscow, Tashkent, Frunze, Vilnius or on a mountain trail. An unshaven man with a huge rucksack may turn out to be an academician [the highest academic rank in the USSR, as it is in France and the United States], while a pleasant girl in blue jeans may be an experienced geologist. Different makes of vehicles circulate through the city with signs identifying them as belonging to various expeditions. In the local sporting goods shops, one can find not only ordinary sneakers but also good mountain boots, which one cannot always find even in Moscow. A saddlebag among the baggage on a bus, a faded anorak on a restaurant guest or a customer bargaining at the bazaar with an ice ax in his hand—all these are common embellishments of the local color. They show how Osh is a city of those who work in expeditions.

Our base is a house on an outlying street of the city, with a courtyard, a garden, a storage building, a garage, an irrigation ditch, a shower and the warm hospitality of the Alexander Pavlovitch Derunov family. He is both chauffeur and manager of the base. We see each other typically about once a year and then only if I happen to find him at home. More often it turns out that Derunov is "up there" in the Pamir, and I might see him there, but if we miss each other en route then it will be only the following year.

Derunov's small sons are running around the yard. Future chauffeurs.

Around here one can ask almost any boy what he wants to be when he grows up, and he will surely answer that he wants to be a chauffeur. In Leningrad, the boys want to become sailors, in Siberia geologists, but here they even play at being chauffeurs. The boys make noises like an automobile horn, or shout to each other to shift gears or something of the sort. It is the game of the Pamir road.

I ask them, "Is your father home?"

"He's asleep. Got home late last night."

I throw my rucksack into the room reserved for visitors and take a long shower to wash off the grime from the sweltering, dusty road. A knock on the wall. The voice of Alexander Pavlovitch: "Welcome! When would you like to go 'up there'?"

"Hello! Even today."

"Today is not convenient, but Sushkov is leaving tomorrow morning and I'll give him a call."

The three of us spend a long evening together—Alyosha Sushkov, Sasha Derunov and I. There is plenty to talk about. The Pamir is big, the road is long, and there is enough news to go around. We three have much in common, too, from many years in the past. And what years they were!

We discuss recent events in the Ferghana Basin. A *sel* [mudflow] came down from the Alai and destroyed part of a settlement. Alyosha just came from there. A long column of trucks was held up in the disaster area. I know that place well. The sel comes down there regularly. When it gets really hot, the snow from the previous winter melts in the mountains and the water level in the narrow gorge rises 10 or 15 meters fast. It undercuts the banks, which consist of sedimentary rocks. Parts of the banks fall into the stream. This increases the water's destructive power. It is not even water anymore but liquid mud filled with stones. Its abrasive force scrapes off more rocks, which make it even more destructive. Finally, the stream of mud and stones bursts out of the gorge and rushes down into the valley with a roar, at the speed of an express train, and carries off literally everything in its path.

I once had the occasion to see that hamlet after a powerful sel. The spectacle of such damage in peacetime shook me up. But afterward, on a bare patch of earth, new buildings of some kind began to appear. I was always amazed at the stubbornness of people who persist in rebuilding their homes at the foot of an active volcano or in places with a perennial avalanche or mudflow hazard. Is it fatalism? Or just habit? I don't know.

We discuss other weighty questions. Someone turned over on the road in his truck. Someone married for the third time ("a wanderer, and a strong one!"). Someone bought a Zhiguli [a compact car designed by Fiat and made in Russia]. It is late when we say good night. Only three or four hours are left for sleep. We have to make an early start so that we can climb to the Taldyk Pass before it gets too hot. Beyond that pass there is no more fear of overheating the engine. There it does not get hot. There it is high.

CHAPTER 12

Geobotany in Folk Art and a Dream

Okmir Agakhanyantz, 1987

The scientific results from the work of Agakhanyantz occasionally came to light in unexpected ways. Once he had a casual visit to his camp from a local herdsman selling folk art stockings made by his wife. These stockings, or socks, called djuraby, *which are products of domestic craftsmanship in the Pamir and adjacent northeastern Afghanistan, are made of wool, which is dyed into intricate patterns handed down, like those of rugs, within each family for generations. Each dye is obtained from a specific plant. This led Agakhanyantz to find a remote stand of junipers, which his botanists had overlooked and which are extremely rare in the Pamir. Another time, in semidelirium from a fever while in his Pamir tent, Agakhanyantz had a detailed dream in which different groups of plants traveled toward these mountains and settled themselves at the proper altitudes on slopes facing the directions from which they came. Two years later, with a cooler head and further study of his botanical maps, Agakhanyantz found that his delirious vision was essentially correct. Such apparently accidental findings, reported in this chapter, could happen only to those who have reached a high level of perception after deep and prolonged study of their subject.[1]*

While Derunov and I were driving, the fellows completed the survey of the massif missing on the map, and it was left for me only to verify it by inspection. We also successfully corrected the old geobotanical map. It had been made in 1936 with a now outdated classification system. This was tedious, but the work progressed. After five days we considered the territory sufficiently studied. This meant that, sticking one's finger anyplace on the map, we could tell in detail the vegetative cover of that place, the soils, the productivity of the grasslands, the condition of the pastures and so on.

Expecting an early departure, the fellows under the direction of Markelych furtively started to pack some of the smaller equipment. I again looked over the outline of the completed itineraries and was more or less pleased. Complete satisfaction was prevented only at the north-western part, at the junction of the Shugnan and South Alichur ranges, within the natural boundary of Ayransu. There only two trips were made, and those incidentally on the descent from adjacent passes. But I know that on the way down people move much faster than on the way up, and because of that they are less careful and may miss something. In both cases the route was completed by Oleg and Tolik. I questioned them. Everything appeared to be correct, and I decided to break camp in the morning. But that evening we had a visitor.

He was an extremely tall native of the Shugnan, well along in years. He came to sell us djuraby. He pulled a whole load of them out of the *hurdjum* [saddlebag] slung over his shoulder and dumped them out on the tarpaulin, and our eyes were benumbed by the colorful patterns.

Djuraby are socks—or stockings, if they are long, sometimes coming all the way up to the groin. On the Pamir, djuraby are knitted from yarns made from dyed sheep's wool. The color is homemade by cooking herbs and is so stable that the djuraby wear out but their color is still just as bright.

Women of all ages knit the djuraby with homemade knitting needles, three and not four as in Russian villages. The pattern on the djuraby is not only a product of the master lady's fantasy but is also a geographical identifier. Each valley, even each natural boundary, has its own traditional, basic design with any desired variations possible within its limits. Because of that, by the pattern of the djuraby, like by the embroidery on the *tyubiteikas* [caps], one could tell in olden times from where someone came. Each knitter had her own taste and skill, so that each pair of djuraby was entirely individual in color and design. Occasionally they are true works of art. They are even sent to exhibitions of native crafts, including international ones.

The djuraby brought here were of the rug type. This means that they have colored pattern from bottom to top. Such djuraby are more beautiful and more expensive than those that have sections of white yarn. I picked out a pair of the rug type [we have such a pair, a gift from Okmir, maybe the same ones], and the others also bought some. We invited the salesman for dinner. His name was Naimsho. He said that his old woman knitted them all day on the upper pastures, but there was no one to whom to sell them. He heard that we were camping here and came. He was glad we liked them. His old woman was a master knitter but with a very bad temper. He laughed.

I started asking him which herbs were used to make which colors. Plants are known here by sight, not by their Latin names, so I asked that the herbarium be unpacked and began to show the plants to Naimsho. One that he recognized was the *macrotomia,* and he showed it to me on the pattern, saying that its red color was obtained by cooking the roots. Then he pointed to a house leek, which produces a violet color when cooked with added salt. And so we went through the herbarium page by page.

"And how are these dyed, my youthful friend?" asked Markelych, throwing his djuraby on the tarpaulin (he called everyone "my youthful friend").

These were the very cheapest djuraby, with a monotonous brown design.

"Why, this color comes from juniper. We cook the berries, dye the wool and boil it again afterward."

"How so from juniper?" I asked in surprise. "Does it grow here?"

"There is none here, but we take it from Ayransu."

I almost jumped. Juniper was shown nowhere on our map. According to Naimsho, on the left side of the Ayransu Valley is a ravine where juniper grows.

When our guest left, pleased with his sales and his reception, I announced that tomorrow we would not be taking the high road but going to Ayransu to verify the survey. Oleg and Tolik looked away embarrassed. They had missed the juniper. This can happen, and I was far from blaming them. I should have looked there myself.

Before going to bed I told the fellows about how we once failed to find the source of the lapis lazuli. We were working then in Garundar, in the basin of Shakhdar. We were doing a botanical survey. Our route was taking us upward. We could have gone up either the left or the right side of the river; for a botanical profile it would have been the same. We took the left bank because it had a path, though a poor one, while the right side had steep slopes all the way down and no path. We decided to come back by way of the right bank. But we got held up at the top of the ridge and being short of time came back by the same path. A few years later, a new source of lapis lazuli was discovered on the right bank. It was right on the surface, with pieces of lapis lazuli lying on the loose gravel, and they couldn't be missed. And we would have noticed them if we had gone down where we intended. Oh, this subjunctive mood: if . . . if only. And, though the discovery of the lapis lazuli source was not our problem, what a great side result that would have been . . . if only.

In the morning, we drove to Ayransu and then went on foot. We found the juniper stand. It was so small in area that it was impossible to show it on the scale of our map. Most of the trees were growing on the cliffs and the rest on the scree. Altogether about five hectares. Evidently, some time ago there were more. Junipers grow slowly, living up to five hundred years or even a thousand, having a dense wood, full of pitch, making glorious firewood and lumber for the ages. At first the junipers were cut below, where they were nearer, then the axes were taken higher. The only ones left here were a few in the most difficult places.

"And why, my youthful friend, do pines not grow here?" asked Markelych, jumping from boulder to boulder. "When I was in the Caucasus, I saw masses of pines, but I have not seen them in Tajikistan."

This was a new entry in his biography. I had thought that Markelych had knocked around only in the Pamir all his life.

"It is dry here, so they don't grow," protested I, reluctant to go deeper into that subject. Not knowing it himself, Markelych had stepped on a toe with a painful corn. [Agakhanyantz (1987) includes a later chapter discussing what happened to the pines.]

The outcome of our trip was a note on the contour map: "On the scree in the range of 3,400 to 3,600 meters, are fragmentary stands of juniper." That's all. Incidentally—as a factual note—this was not at all a bad result.

Of course, a high fever is enervating. But it also, on occasion, sharpens the imagination. While I was lying in the tent with a respiratory infection, the subjects on my mind acquired astonishing imagery. Rational procedures became graphic, resembling wide-screen color films. In one such "film," the brain, tortured by high temperature, formed a well-defined picture in space, similar to an enormous map. Within this blowup, different species and types of plants moved about with ease from place to place.

I saw the dry Pamir. Different forms of vegetation moved toward it from all directions, as though seeking to occupy as quickly as possible the new territory formed by rapidly rising mountains. Some types surged ahead of the others and distributed themselves on the dry slopes, each at its proper height. They congregated in those altitude belts with which they were familiar. Streams of other types of vegetation, unable to cope with the arid climate, faltered and broke into rivulets, which dried up and failed to reach the Pamir. A third group, taking advantage of the environmental climate becoming temporarily more favorable for them, somehow managed to arrive in those mountains. But the temporary improvement of the climate ended, and the rivulets of such vegetation, finding themselves in an area of drought to which they were unaccustomed, shrank into small lakes. The mountains grew and became colder and drier. The small lakes became even smaller and fewer. The only ones that survived were those that happened to have been placed on favorable slopes.

For immigrants from the west—from the Mediterranean, the Caucasus and mountains of Middle Asia west of the Pamir—the favorable slopes were precisely those that faced west. On them the precipitation was slightly greater, and its regime resembled that of the lands from which these new arrivals had come. The western slopes thus became the habitat of almond trees, *tomilliaras* and bladder campions. In their native lands, they grow on any slopes, but here their distribution is limited to the slopes facing the direction from which they came.

For immigrants from the north—plants of the steppes, certain meadows and juniper groves—just those slopes that face north were most favorable on the Pamir, offering a bit more moisture but being not quite so hot.

For immigrants from the south and southwest, such as those of the Hammadan deserts, only a few small islands have survived on southern or western slopes, from which they look out, as it were, toward their places of origin in the Hindu Kush and the mountains of Iran.

And how about the immigrants from the east? Those that live on plateaus at home have likewise settled on plateaus here. If their preference at home is for steeper slopes, on the Pamir they also established themselves on the more inclined slopes that face east. On those slopes, the regime of precipitation is most suitable for them.

This moving-picture film seemed to be conforming to a fairly logical rule: on the Pamir, the distribution of surviving migratory plants is limited to the slopes facing the directions from which they had migrated. After formulating this rule, I rapidly recovered from my illness and continued walking on the remainder of my trip, thinking about my new scheme with a cool head. I was already looking, not for confirmation but for contradictory facts.

I do not believe in the widely held view that an exception proves the rule. In my opinion, that thesis has no relevance to science. Every exception must be tested from a position that does not exclude the rule that has been formulated. And, if a hundred facts support the rule but a single valid fact contradicts it, and can be explained only by deviation from the rule, this means that the formulation is incorrect. At best, the rule might indicate a tendency but more likely just an incorrect opinion. Such are the laws of strict scientific logic.

With such an approach to the matter at hand, exceptions were found. Some could be satisfactorily explained—for example, those southerners that have already been mentioned. In the western Pamir, they grow on all slopes, not just on those facing west, as one might expect in accordance with the rule [since between these east-west ranges they must enter from the west]. But here, in the eastern part of their habitat, they usually establish themselves on gravel slopes, where the reserves of moisture are greater than on slopes of finely grained earth. Gravel occurs on slopes facing in all directions. These are not the preferable plant locations. But those southerners that have settled on good, fine earth rather than gravel are invariably on slopes facing west. So far everything fits.

Other exceptions did not yield to such explanations and could in no way be made to fit the scheme. Most of the high-altitude xerophytes [desert plants] are immigrants from the west, but the belt of xerophytic plants is expressed on slopes facing in all directions. This is a real contradiction. True, most mountain xerophytes are found on crumbling terrain, which one might say is not typical. If so, one would also have to say that the entire xerophytic belt is not a typical belt but something different. One could seek another explanation, one that does not disrupt the entire scheme. For example, this type of vegetation may have reached the Pamir long ago and had time to change from its original form in the course of adapting to its new environment, to such a degree that it can survive on all slopes. Why is this not an explanation? Other types of vegetation have changed under the influence of local conditions, so why should this correction not apply to them all? Moreover, it is not clear which types of vegetation arrived earlier and which came later and in what original forms. No, if a rule is to be put forward, everything must first be analyzed thoroughly, and afterward one may formulate the rule. In other words, again, "we'll sort it out later."

Sorting it out was achieved after two years. The formulated rule was more accurately called a firm tendency. It applied not only to individual species but to entire altitudinal belts: often a band of vegetation occurs on slopes facing the direction to which this type of vegetation properly belongs. Often, but not always. It is in this, actually, that a tendency differs from a rule. Incidentally, identifying a tendency is also not bad.

CHAPTER 13

A Night in the Year of the Pig

Okmir Agakhanyantz, 1989

*Almost exactly in the center of the Pamir, the large Sarez Lake, sur-
rounded by snow peaks whose ramparts plunge steeply into the water,
was formed in 1911 when an earthquake released a landslide that
dammed up the Murgab River. Agakhanyantz was eager to study its
effects on the local ecology, and, after unsuccessful approaches from the
east and west, he reached the lake on his third attempt over a high pass
from the south (1975). Before the lake was formed, its location was more
accessible, and it was even inhabited. The landslide buried one hamlet,
and the water slowly submerged another.[1] In this chapter, Agakhanyantz
(1989) tells the story he heard from the sole surviving witness to the
catastrophe. In addition to graphic physical descriptions, it records poi-
gnantly amusing details from the lives of the impoverished Pamir
dwellers. This was an interval of relative peace in their lives, when they
were subjects of the Russian and Soviet empires. Before that, they suffered
under the despotism of the khans of Kokand and Bukhara, from whom
they fled into the mountains to keep their children from being exported as
slaves. Now, in newly independent Tajikistan, they are persecuted as here-
tic Ismailis by the Sunni fundamentalists of the lowlands.*

During the night before the fifth of Nahun (the month of the male finger-
nail, or February) in the Year of the Pig (1911), in the *kishlak* [hamlet] of
Usoy, the young head of family Mirshaib Gurgaliev came out of his warm
hut into the frosty air and knocked on the door of his neighbor, Sulmamat
Karamkhudoev, with whom he had agreed to go to the kishlak of Sarez.
He began to wait. They had agreed to go together. Mirshaib, who had
married two years earlier, had to go to Sarez to buy an endpiece for his

plow from the smith. The old one was cracked and worn. This was just the time to go because his wife had gone to Rukhtch to visit her sick brother. He knocked again, but Sulmamat's old woman screamed though the door that the boss had already left.

Mirshaib became frightened that he would have to make the long trip alone, which was dangerous because it was said that the *voit* (the abominable snowman) had been seen there again. But then Mirshaib saw Nashmit Karamkhudoev, with whom he also had agreed to make the trip, coming out of his hut. The crafty old Sulmamat didn't wake them, afraid that he would be unable to keep up with the younger men and that they would laugh at him, saying, "Na boft musafet" (the old fellow can't make it).

The young men strode off rapidly upstream to the east. The kishlak of Sarez was a long way off, and they had to get there before sunrise. After that, the sun would warm the slopes and the melting snow could break off in "the white death"—an avalanche. After that one might not find a man at all, or, if found, he would be mangled to death with a mouthful of snow. The young men were well clothed and equipped, with padded robes under sheepskin coats, with *djuraby* (wool stockings) up to the groin, with homemade boots of tanned leather whose soles were sewn with yak fur specially cut against slipping [like sealskins used for skiing up hills]. In their hands each carried a *tchugurtchuk*—a 4-meter-long stake with a sharp metal point. This served both as a weapon and as an aid for vaulting over a crevasse or a stream.

A tchugurtchuk is an expensive thing. To find a straight and not too thick sapling of boxthorn or mountain ash, with sound and resilient wood, was no easy task in the deforested Murgab or Oroshor Districts. In Usoy or Sarez, tchugurtchuks are brought from Yazgulem or Darvaz and are sold for a high price. Sulmamat himself goes somewhere down the Bartang and brings back mountain ash stakes for tchugurtchuks. But where he gets them, he doesn't say.

The young men's pockets were stuffed with *bursaks*—round wafers baked from thick dough and butter, which do not dry out on the way. Nashmit, a bachelor, was going to Sarez for a celebration: the *pir* (a holy elder of the Ismailite sect in the Pamir) would be circumcising his son, which meant that there would be large crowds among whom Nashmit might find a bride. The population of Usoy was only fifty-eight, less than half of them women, all either old, married or too young. Besides, one should not take a bride from one's own kishlak because every one was closely related and the children would be unhealthy. But Sarez was a large kishlak, and a rich one, where many girls had grown up. Veils are not worn in the Pamir, and one can get a proper look at a prospective bride. For such an event, Nashmit was carrying a present in his breast pocket, a Chinese silk kerchief that his father had bought in a bazaar just for this purpose.

From Usoy to Sarez is 20 kilometers, but Mirshaib and Nashmit were reckoning the distance by the moon: when it would set behind the Lyangar horn, that would mean that Sarez was near. It was a very frosty night, but their rapid pace warmed them. About halfway, some three hundred paces ahead of them, a small avalanche came down with a crackling sound. The young men were surprised: an avalanche at night! They supposed that there must have been a light earthquake, which threw snow from the Muskol Ridge; otherwise, it could not be explained. For a long time they waded through the loose snow that had just fallen from above. Not far from Sarez, they caught up with Sulmamat, who muttered a greeting and said that there had been an earthquake; he had heard it.

The sun had risen when the three travelers entered Sarez and scattered among the huts of their friends to drink tea and get some sleep before doing their errands and attending the celebration. The celebration was a glorious success. The offering of food was sumptuous: the pir had five rams and ten chickens roasted, with an abundance of pickles made with salt brought from Rangkul, with freshly baked wafers and starched candies bought in Oroshor to decorate the tables. There was slapping of *rubobs* (tambourines) and dancing until dark. Earlier, before the celebration, Mirshaib had bought the endpiece for his plow and paid the smith five pairs of djuraby and five Russian pennies. He had expected to pay more and still had two pairs of djuraby left.

Nashmit, too, was happy, with his affairs of the heart going well. The travelers left the party late, by our time at nine o'clock. And they went fast asleep.

At twenty-three hours and fifteen minutes [11:15 P.M.], a strong shock was felt in Khorog [now the chief town of the Pamir but then a mere hamlet]. It was recorded even in St. Petersburg. In Sarez, everyone rushed out of their huts screaming and weeping. Two huts had caved in and four were cracked. From the west one could hear a wild roar. It merged with the crashing of avalanches. From the opposite bank of the Murgab River, one could hear the noise of rockfalls. The moon above Mardjanay began to dim. In the morning, everything was covered with dust, which thickly hung in the air, while the earth continued to shake.

Mirshaib ran off to Usoy. The grim Nashmit could barely keep up with him. Sulmamat stayed in Sarez, saying he would leave the next night. The young men, gasping for breath, alternately climbed terraces or descended to the Murgab River. But the dust in the air was so thick that they returned to Sarez, afraid that with such low visibility they would fall and smash themselves. Only on the third day did they leave. But they did not recognize the landscape. Rocks were falling from somewhere to the right, and the men had to walk below the steep bank of the river. But the going there was not easy either: the ice in the river had broken up and was floating in large blocks or climbing the bank. No such a thing had ever happened, not just in February but at any time before.

When the young men came to where Usoy had been, they could not see the kishlak. In its place rose a mountain of boulders. The height of this mountain was so great that one could not see the top from the bottom through the dusty air. The earthquake continued, and stones flew about, but Mirshaib and Nashmit climbed on the rockfall. The kishlak was not there—it was buried under the rocks. Mirshaib wept, remembering how a few days ago his father and mother had blessed him on his journey and how he had put a pinch of ashes from the hearth into his bootleg as a sign that he would not forget his home and would come back.

Beside him, with a gray face, Nashmit sat rocking and muttering the words of a prayer. Afterward he turned to Mirshaib and said that God was angered by something, since this was the good Year of the Pig, in which Mahomet himself was born, and now there had been such a disaster.

After some time, people from Sarez began to come. They looked, they sighed, they wept and they departed. From down the Bartang River, no one came, and Nashmit said that, probably, along the lower Bartang, everything was also buried under landslides and everyone had perished. Mirsaib shuddered: his wife was there in Rukhtch. Was it possible that she, too, had perished? Afterward the crafty Sulmamat appeared. He looked around, grieved aloud for his old woman and said that he had had a dream about an old man who told him to leave the kishlak or there would be a disaster, and so he left before the others. He had called to his woman to come with him, but she had scolded him and turned away under the blankets. The young men paid no attention to his lies: if there was any truth in what he said, it was that the woman had scolded him—

she was known for her bad temper, may Allah preserve her soul. All three were hungry and in shock. Where to go? Nashmit and Sulmamat, after taking leave of Mirshaib, returned to Sarez—their Muslim brothers would not, after all, allow them to be lost. But Mirshaib decided to go down to Rukhtch.

The young man climbed the rockfall and looked down the Bartang, but he could see nothing through the dust. Bearing left, he reached the pass over the rockfall and took a long time going down to into the channel of the Murgab. But the riverbed had no water. This frightened him, and, armed with his tchugurtchuk, he leaped rapidly from rock to rock. By evening he reached Rukhtch. In the kishlak everyone was weeping and wailing. Some huts had caved in and killed four people. The charming Gulmirzo, his wife's brother, had died, and Nukra, his wife, was weeping, shaking her heavy belly, expecting to give birth in one month. Mirshaib talked with his wife, stroked her cheek, told her about Usoy, took the djuraby and the endpiece for his plow from his breast pocket and said that he would have to stay in Rukhtch. The women wept for joy and thanked him, since he would be the only man left in their hut.

One had to go on living. Mirshaib attached his new endpiece to his late brother-in-law's old plow, ate a tureen of boiled beans and fell asleep. He didn't know then that by the time his grandchildren were finishing school he would be the only remaining witness to the catastrophe, and he would have to remember all this and tell it to a "good Russian peasant." Mirshaib lived well, and his old woman was alive, serving tea and offering wafers. And he always remembered that terrible night of the sixth (the eighteenth by today's calendar) of February 1911. "Nashmit now lives in Shadzud on the Gunt River, if he is still alive—he was quite sick. But Sulmamat died on the way from Sarez to the Gunt."

Two months after the destruction of Usoy, in April, Staff Captain Zaimkin came from Khorog to Sarez. He rode a horse and made his way across the rivers, coming from above, from the Pamirsky Post, down the Murgab River. When he reached Sarez, he was surprised that much of the land around it was not being cultivated. Zaimkin was unable to reach Usoy because the way was buried by boulders and the horse refused to go, while the staff captain couldn't go on foot because his boots were falling apart. He then sent express messengers to the headman of the Oroshor District, Kokan-bek. When these returned, he wrote down from their words that the mountainside had fallen and that the number of people killed had been fifty-eight in Usoy, ten in Savnob, four in Rukhtch, thirty in Pasor and forty in Nusur, as well as more than three hundred grazing animals. Zaimkin saw for himself that a lake had been formed in place of the Murgab River. According to the local inhabitants, the height of the dam formed by the landslide was 300 *sazhens* (640 m), which turned out to be close to reality.

Later, Zaimkin was told that the number who perished in Usoy was not 58, but 54, because 1 lad, 1 young peasant and an older man were in Sarez for the celebration, while the wife of the young peasant, who was visiting in Rukhtch, was alive and gave birth to a little boy. Zaimkin thus counted 138 people who had perished, but two months later it was verified that 45 men, 58 women, and 77 children had been killed, a total of 180 people.

Visitors began to come to the remote Sarez vicinity of the Oroshor District. During the winter after the landslide, a German arrived at Mardjanay. This was Arved Schultz. As early as 1912, he published an article about the catastrophe. In September of 1911, Zaimkin had made a second visit to the Sarez kishlak and seen that the water was rising half an *arshin* (about 36 cm) per day, with only 16 meters to go before it reached the kishlak. The peasants were bringing in their harvest rapidly and selling it cheap to the nomads because they all planned to move to a different, less dangerous area.

For this purpose, the Russian authorities provided a tract of uninhabited land on the upper part of the Gunt River. There, at the junction of the Gunt and the Toguzbulak, a new kishlak called Shadzud was built and settled by the people from Sarez. There was much land on the banks of the Gunt, which carried plenty of water, and Shadzud at 3,120 meters altitude (10,240 ft.) was a bit warmer than Sarez at 3,260 meters (10,700 ft.). In 1972, an old man living in Shadzud told me that the people in Sarez had lived affluently and did not respect those who were poorer, and therefore they did not respect God, so God punished them.

"But Usoy was a poor kishlak," I objected, "so why did God destroy it?"

"Well here you are, a learned man, and also a fool, forgive me, an old man. How could I know what God intended?"

"Then how did you know why Sarez was drowned?"

"That is the way people talk."

He obviously did not want to prolong the argument.

A small portion of the Sarez people settled lower along the Bartang. As was predicted, Sarez went underwater in October 1911. Now it is at a depth of about 240 meters. The only thing left above the surface is the spring coming out of the rocks some 300 meters above the kishlak. This high spring provided the kishlak with water for drinking and irrigation. Now the clear water flows down to the lake in a brook, along whose banks grow willows as before. They are like a bouquet on the grave of the Sarez kishlak.

After part of the Muskol Ridge fell, seismic shocks continued for several days, and rocks continued to fall for ten years. In some places, especially below the landslide, rocks fall in summer even today. To approach that part of the slope is simply impossible. The stones are not only falling down, but they ricochet sideways, giving one the impression of being under an artillery barrage, but without the same roar.

From the first year after the catastrophe, the stability of the dam formed by the earthquake was a cause for concern, with its potential danger for inhabitants of the lands downstream. Some tried to frighten the people living there, while others tried to calm them, pointing to other stable earthquake lakes. Meanwhile, the stories of former Sarez residents were embroidered with new and more horrifying details, which were the grist for sensational newspaper articles. Whom should one believe, and, most important, what should be done for the future?

To answer these questions, a thorough scientific study would have to be organized, staffed and provided with needed equipment, including transport on the lake. The funds for such an expedition were not forthcoming from the Imperial Academy of Sciences. Even financial help for the former Sarez residents had been gathered by means of private donations. St. Petersburg had other things in mind than a distant and not easily accessible mountainous corner of the empire.[2]

CHAPTER 14

A 600-Kilometer Solo Walk across Tajikistan

Okmir Agakhanyantz, 1975

Because of a bureaucratic circumstance,[1] Agakhanyantz found himself high in the Pamir and suddenly deprived of his botanical crew but with all of September still ahead and available for fieldwork. He decided to walk across Tajikistan to Dushanbe, which was his residence at that time. It was a unique opportunity to compile a continuous botanical profile over most of the republic, both vertically and horizontally. In addition, he made close contacts with local people along the way and experienced adventures: being the guest of honor at several weddings; taking a brief, unheroic part in a dangerous game to capture the skinned carcass of a goat while riding a horse in a wild cavalcade; encountering a swarm of huge, deadly poisonous vipers that blocked his trail in the mountains; and being arrested just short of his goal because the police considered that any person in such worn clothing, even carrying an ice ax, must be a suspicious character.

At the end of August 1959, a telegram was delivered to me in the mountains from the University of Tajikistan, demanding the immediate return of the students in my field crew to prepare for the coming academic year. There could be no argument. I was working for the Academy of Sciences of the republic, and the university was a different jurisdiction. The saddened students left that evening. The workmen in my crew could not replace the students, so I paid them off too. The entire crew fell apart.

The next day I was back at the Pamir Botanical Garden near Khorog, still full of fieldwork energy. Before me was the entire month of September, but without a crew there could be no thought of botanical mapping in the mountains. Disappointment occasionally proves productive, and that happened this time. It gave me an idea: what if I should use the rest of the field season to walk from Khorog to Dushanbe?

The more I thought about it, the more attractive it became. True, the distance is long—about 600 kilometers [375 mi.]. I had traveled on this route in a vehicle many times, also parts of it on horseback. But it is one thing to ride and quite another to walk. On foot, I would be able to look at everything thoroughly and think about it. And there was plenty to see and think about. After following the river Pyandzh from the Pamir and Darvaz, I would be able to leave the motor road and eventually reach Dushanbe in the Hissar Valley by way of the Tajik depression and Kulyab.

No sooner said than done. Gürsky [head of the botanical garden] approved. Since part of the route would follow the Afghan frontier, I would need permission from the border guards. They reacted favorably and forewarned their colleagues at the stations ahead.

Since I had to carry everything on my back, the contents of my rucksack were restricted severely: a light sleeping bag, a plastic groundsheet, an alpine-type Primus stove, an enameled mug that would also serve as a kettle, a spoon, a little bag of sugar, a package of crackers, tea, matches, tobacco, extra socks and a sweater. Into the pockets of my anorak I put the necessary documents and a notebook. I decided that heavy mountain boots, which would endure the whole trip, would be too cumbersome and uncomfortably hot. All along the way, I would be losing altitude, from 2,200 meters [7,200 ft.] at Khorog to only 600 meters [2,000 ft.] at Dushanbe. I decided to wear sneakers, with the idea of buying new ones in village stores when the old ones wore out. I packed a spare pair of "Keds" just in case. The pack became bulky but not very heavy. The plan was to depend on teahouses and dining rooms along the way, so food, which is always heavy, was excluded from the pack.

By 7 A.M. I was already at Khorog and walking toward the Pyandzh, down a street with poplars planted on both sides. I like that little town. In those days its population was only eight thousand but now it is twice that. The entire town is strung out like a necklace on a single street 4 kilometers long. It is squeezed into a narrow ribbon between the Gunt River and the rampart of the Rushan Ridge. Workmen on duty dipped water out of the *ariks* [ditches] and threw it on the asphalt to hold down the dust. The wet dust had a fresh and pleasant smell. In Khorog everyone knows one another, and I have many friends there; but now it was early, and I left town without seeing a single person I knew.

Walking along the Pyandzh in the cool shade of the Rushan Ridge is easy, but delays occur that are not according to plan. Seeing a traveler with a rucksack, every vehicle driver jams on his brakes, stirs up a cloud of dust and offers me a lift. That is the Pamir way. So as not to explain to each one that I am an eccentric who prefers to go on foot, I tell them that I am about to turn up into the mountains, literally just a few feet ahead. By noon I was covered with dust from the stopping cars and trucks, and the situation was no longer a joke. Later, when hearing a vehicle behind me, I pretended to be working and bent down to examine a plant through a magnifying glass. It worked. The most I got now was a greeting as the car drove by. I followed this strategy throughout the trip, and by the end of it my simulation of work had reached a virtuoso stage.

I had almost reached the *kishlak* of Porshnev when my feet began to sink into sand and the walking became harder. The riverbanks, terraces and lower slopes were covered with loose sand. It is brought there by the Pyandzh, whose level rises each summer from the meltwater of the glaciers, carrying silt. This regime is typical of Pamir rivers. For thousands of years, the Pyandzh, like a conveyor belt, has delivered the sand here. And mud too. When the water recedes, the sand is blown around by the wind, forming dunes, heaps and layers, while the fine dried mud is blown higher up the slopes. On the sand, almost nothing grew, except for a few specimens of cotton thistle and brambles. Plants have little chance to take root before they are buried by next year's portion of silt.

In one place, a quarry had been dug to obtain sand for construction at Khorog. A layer about 15 meters [50 ft.] deep had been cut through, forming an almost overhanging wall. The sand was still wet from yesterday's work and clearly showed the strata of differing thickness and composition. The thicker and coarser ones had been formed during hotter years when the glaciers melted more, while in cold years the layers were thin and fine. Perhaps in some cold years the water did not rise this high at all. The stratified wall was like a thermograph, recording the temperatures year by year for millennia, with the thickest layers at approximately twenty-year intervals. I decided to study this record more carefully and photographed the wall.

Toward evening I reached the kishlak of Porshnev, where the geologists had established their base, with laboratories, storage buildings, garages, workshops and living quarters. These are friendly cohorts for me. Among them I feel at home, close in spirit and interests. With them I spent the night, having walked 25 kilometers the first day.

In all, I walked for twenty-six days. If it had not been for the loss of time spent avoiding getting lifts, and a few other circumstances, I would have traveled faster. Actually, I was not in a hurry. I slept at the end of each day wherever I happened to be. Provisions were acquired at the local stores. My booklet was filling up with notes. I was losing altitude, but the nights were getting colder. Autumn was coming on faster than my descent into the warmer regions. In the first 100 kilometers I lost 300 meters of altitude.

Walking along the river, I had to be careful to identify the characteristic botanical profile formed by atmospheric precipitation. Going up the slope along the path of atmospheric moisture, it becomes colder, and the moisture is increased because the evaporation is reduced, which makes up for the lower precipitation and keeps the soil moisture about the same. Meanwhile, close to the river, the total moisture can be higher because of groundwater or widespread irrigation. Thus, following the river down, there were two different profiles, a xerophytic one in the drier places of atmospheric precipitation only and a mesophytic one in the more heavily watered places near the riverbanks. In places, I could see the impoverished, yellowish, thinner vegetation of mountain deserts: wormwood, brambles, *eurotia,* prickly grasses and cushion plants, with the stony soil showing through. But nearby, on the floodplains, I saw sedge meadows, small bogs, clumps of willow and sea buckthorn, while on the watered alluvial fans near the villages there were walnut, mulberry, apricot, apple and pear trees and sown grain that had just been harvested. In short, I was able to follow, from top to bottom, the belt of mesophytic vegetation along which the effect of increasing temperature was evident. Only the temperature varied, while the moisture remained stable and high. One could see the changes in vegetation from the cold of the Pamir to the subtropical domain below.

At first, the items entered in my notes were the rather cold-resistant plants of the flood banks: turanian willow, Wilhelm's willow, sea buckthorn and bog myrtle, while the saline meadows included growths of milk vetch, lyme grass and licorice. The first sign of warming became apparent on the fifth day of the journey. On a sandy terrace next to a cliff, from which springwater was flowing, there was a shrub of Bukhara almond. The altimeter here read 1,850 meters (6,070 ft.). The first harbinger, or "swallow," of the subtropical belt! Some 10 kilometers farther on, some tamarisk bushes appeared on the moist ground, a second harbinger, this one from the stifling thickets along the lower floodplains of Central Asia's rivers.

In one such place, I noticed a weathered inscription, partly concealed by bushes, hammered into a cliff at such a height that it could not be reached when standing on the road. The inscription must have been made when the flood terrace was higher than it is now. It said "Staff Captain D. Topornin passed here 18 VIII 1911." This distinguished topographer, as I knew, had investigated the tragic Sarez landfall of that year. I also knew of him as the brother of Eugenia Korzhenevskaya, for whom one of the four 7,000-meter peaks in the USSR is named. He had also been active in mapping the frontier with Afghanistan for the agreement between Russia and Great Britain in 1895.

Still following the Pyandzh, I headed for the kishlak of Shipad, where I planned to spend the night with an agronomist I knew. To reach the kishlak, one has to pass through a gorge in which the view always made me gasp. On the Afghan side, the river flows under an overhanging cliff, along which an *ovring* was built. [An ovring is a walkway made from matted branches resting on projecting logs that have been driven into cracks in the rock.] I have never seen a higher or more vertiginous ovring than this one. Clinging to the overhang, it climbs in a zigzag to about 200 meters above the river and disappears behind a projection of the rock. Only once have I seen a man actually walking on it. He looked like an ant crawling over bits of straw. There is a tale that a young girl threw herself off that ovring when she was being taken to the kishlak of a man she had been forced to marry but did not love. A sad story but quite appropriate to that dark gorge from which one can see only a thin strip of the sky. Once more, I was thankful that I didn't have to walk on that ovring and that we had an automobile road on our side of the river.

The kishlak of Shipad is situated at the mouth of the river of that name, which flows through a ravine cutting into the western tip of the Yazgulem Ridge. Once I had the occasion to walk through that defile. A narrow but turbulent stream flows along its bottom, coming from the Odudi glacier. Climbing the gorge, I had to cross it fourteen times. In one place I even had to climb up on the slippery rocks of a waterfall. At the upper end, close to the ridge itself, the ravine opens out into something like an amphitheater whose floor is covered with juicy grasses. Herds were grazing there. I was amazed. How on earth did they drive the herds up through the insane Shipad Gorge?

I wanted to ask the *chaban* [shepherd], but at that moment I began to shake with an attack of malarial fever, and with the sudden rise in temperature I forgot about the question. Now I remembered it and asked the agronomist who had received me so kindly. He thought for a moment, went outside and came back with a wizened old man. After drinking tea with lengthy ritual politeness, after questions about the old man's health, his children, his grandchildren and his great-grandchildren, after discussions about the perspectives for the weather and the harvest, the agronomist finally conveyed my question to the old man.

In reply I heard an interesting tale. The point was that, without its upper pasture, the kishlak would not exist. Today's collective farms include several kishlaks, and it is possible to use each other's pastures. Before that, it was impossible. To climb the gorge was difficult even without the herds. The flocks had to be carried across the torrent, and more than once. Not cows, of course, but only small animals like sheep. Later it was decided to prepare a trail, using combined local forces. They chopped at the cliff, turned over stones and made the way slightly better. But not good. Then the *pir* [the wise old man of the kishlak] announced that, from then on, every man who wanted to get married would first have to make one hundred paces of good trail. How the prospective bridegroom would do this was his problem. But without acceptance of the work, the pir refused to bless the marriage. And without the pir's blessing, how could there be happiness in marriage? After that, things began to go better. Each year, a few young men who were intending to get married would cooperate and work on the trail. It became possible to drive the flocks up the gorge on their own feet. In our time, this custom has been forgotten, and the trail has become bad again. But they still drive the herds up almost all the way and carry them only over a few torrent crossings.

Early in the morning, after a hearty breakfast with tea, I went on. At the mouth of the Yazgulem, I paused near a few sorry specimens of vari-leaf poplar. On the hot parts of the plains, they are seen sporadically. Here, at 1,700 meters (5,580 ft.), the poplars looked sick and desiccated. Relatives of these trees thrive in the Near East, where they are called Euphrates poplars, while another, related line grows east of the Pamir, on the sands of the Takla Makan, where they are called *tograk*. Meanwhile, their poor relations had scrambled up to this unnatural height, where they were confined to a sad existence.

Toward evening, at the mouth of the Khikhek River, I encountered the first fig tree, in full health, about 6 meters (20 ft.) high. It grew near the water, protected from the wind by a steep bank. The next such tree I saw only after three more days of walking. The Khikhek fig tree had clearly strayed by chance to this height of 1,650 meters (5,400 ft.). It is a typically subtropical tree.

Below the kishlak of Khikhek, the road narrowed to the absolute minimum. On the right was an overhanging cliff like the visor of a cap; below on the left roared the Pyandzh. If two cars met, one would have to back up several kilometers before they could pass. I had to squeeze against the cliff with my rucksack to let the cars go by, but even here the drivers offered to pick me up. My usual story didn't work. I could hardly claim to be climbing to the right just ahead. So I had to formulate a different version of my refusal, namely, that it was precisely this section of the cliff that I was studying. Meanwhile, some of those who had passed me before stopped again on their way back and exclaimed with surprise, "So you are still walking, Bearded One?"

At the mouth of the Vantch, I rolled out my sleeping bag on an ancient moraine among succulent annuals that had already dried up and a few bushes of saksaul-hammada. From a kishlak on the Afghan side, I could hear the call of the mullah above the muffled grumbling of the Pyandzh below. I lay and thought of the impending conclusion of the Pamir phase of my trip. Tomorrow I would not be going north, as I had up to now, but would follow the great bend in the river to the southwest through Darvaz.

The western part of the south slope of the Darvaz Ridge is exceptional in its natural environment. Here, from the north, the valley of the Pyandzh is enclosed by the arc of the Darvaz Ridge, which shuts off the cold air from that direction. The slope is open to the southwest. The absolute height of the valley here is 1,600 meters [5,250 ft.] and lower. The result is something like a warm cul-de-sac. This is the realm of the dry subtropics, with only 400 millimeters of rainfall per year, about one-half to one-third of that in the humid subtropics. But it is warm. Because it was autumn, I felt this not so much on my own skin as by the character of the vegetation.

By the end of the first day along the Darvaz bend of the Pyandzh, I came across some grapevines. Actually, I had seen some earlier, but in the role of horticultural decorations, while here the vines were maturing and fruitful. Near the springs along the sloping sides of the road grew giant erianthus grass. On flat riverbanks, they grew to 6 to 8 meters high. Later, instead of individual subtropical "swallows," I met whole flocks of them almost every day. Fig trees became common. The slopes had lost the barren look of the Pamir. Now they were scattered with shrubs of pomegranate, almond, jujube, Christ's-thorn, hackberry, pistachio, hawthorn, sweetbrier, woodbine, Regel's maples with three-lobed leaves, sumac and Judas tree. Incidentally, in Russia, the aspen is sometimes called the Judas tree because, ever since Judas hung himself according to biblical tradition, the leaves have continued shaking. Without questioning the tradition itself, I can say that the aspen has nothing to do with it because that tree does not grow in Palestine where the biblical events took place. But that is the habitat of the Mediterranean Judas tree of the genus *Cercis*. If Judas really did hang himself, it was probably on the *Cercis* tree, which, like the aspen, has round leaves that tremble at the slightest breath of wind. I felt that I was walking, not in the mountains of Central Asia but somewhere in the Balkans, perhaps in Greece.

After passing the district center of Kalay-Khumb, at about the halfway point of my trip, I turned off from the main road to Dushanbe, which crosses a pass to the north, and continued southwest on a new road used only by collective farm trucks and not by many of these. Traffic was sparse and with much less dust. I would have been able to make better time, with fewer offers of a lift, if it were not for another unexpected circumstance. I was now in a low, warm belt between 1,200 and 1,400 meters [3,900 and 4,600 ft.] elevation. Back in Khorog, where I had begun the trip 1,000 meters higher up, the harvest was just beginning. Here, the harvest was finished, and it was the season for weddings. From every kishlak I could hear the beating of the *doira* [a percussion instrument] and the wedding song "Yor-yory." The kishlaks were enveloped in the aroma of stewing pilaf [rice with lamb and spices]. According to local belief, a traveler who happens to attend a wedding brings happiness to the marriage, and I, as they say, was caught. I was desperately in demand. The first time, the bridegroom and his old father came to invite me. To refuse was impossible. This held up my trip for almost twenty-four hours.

At the next kishlak, I had to attend a grandiose wedding. The *dostarkhan* [food table] was set for three hundred people. After the meal, they arranged a *buskashi*, which in Russian we call "tearing the goat apart." It is, so to speak, a sporting game on horseback. Very old and traditional. A goat is killed, its head cut off, its skin removed, and the carcass is thrown into a ring. The horsemen dash into the ring from all directions. One has to seize the carcass while riding one's horse, gallop with it to the end of the field and throw it over the finish line. The winner receives a prize, which is usually symbolic. During the game, one can grab the carcass from another player, force him out of his saddle and the like. There are few restrictive rules and sometimes none at all. The game threatens the players with injury or worse.

In Afghanistan I saw an enormous buskashi with a good hundred horsemen. Here it was more modest, almost domestic, with only about twenty riders. Dust rose from the race ground, along with sweat from the horses, in a demonstration of early medieval and insanely wild daring. The spectacle is arousing. And it aroused me. After two rounds, I asked if I could take part. I was given a horse. The stirrups were dangling below my feet, but I managed to pull out into the leading group. Then two young men arranged themselves on either side of me, the horse came out from under me and I, in a flowing trajectory, crashed to the ground on my back. While I was trying to catch my breath with just a small swallow of air, the entire cavalcade dashed over me but didn't even touch me. The crowd was delighted. I barely managed to stagger back to my place. When the buskashi was over, I asked one of the young men who had unseated me to explain how they had done it so skillfully. He squinted slyly and said, "Come, get back into the saddle, and we'll show you." Laughter! I categorically refused.

After two more boisterous weddings, I understood that, if I continued with this chain of events, I would not reach Dushanbe before late autumn. It was necessary to try something different. At first I passed the kishlaks without stopping and slept at a significant distance from inhabited places. But the bridegrooms thirsting for happiness found me everywhere. Then I decided to change the itinerary with a detour through the mountains. The thought was based on the principle of altitudinal belts. On my way up, the weddings would not have started because the harvest would still be going on, while by the time I got down the other side the hymeneal revelries would have ended. So I hoped! At the kishlak named Dzhak, I turned up the river of that name and began slowly climbing away from the wedding noise and into the peace of a green ravine.

I was sorry to leave the lower zone, where the annual flooding of the Pyandzh enriched the vegetation of the meadows, which was becoming more and more interesting. On the banks of the river below Kalay-Khumb there were many poplars, and the silvery trees of eastern Babylonian willow stood out sharply, while thickets of tamarisk were being washed by the gentle green foam of the river's edge. All of this was interwoven with clematis vines and filled with tall grasses, among which one could see wild dogbane, malva and *incarvillea*. There were many reeds. But the willows and sea buckthorns were becoming fewer. True, such dense thickets occurred only where the flat riverbanks were wider. They were extremely interesting and were reminiscent of subtropical riverbank jungles.

However, after half an hour of climbing, I stopped regretting the change of itinerary. The vegetation of the Dzhak ravine is so magnificent that I could no longer think of anything else. After the sparsely wooded landscapes to which I had become accustomed during the previous week, the thickly forested slopes of the ravine produced an astounding impression. Near the stream one could see dense stands of walnut and plane trees, the latter of which in Central Asia are called *chinars*. Higher, the slopes were covered with maples, not the sparse growths of Regel's maples but dense forests of Turkestan maples with five-lobed leaves. The maples were accompanied by sweetbrier, *exochorda*, woodbine and hawthorn. Where the slopes became steeper, the bushy growth thinned out in the realm of the bean-caper (caltrop), pomegranate and Christ's-thorn. Having filled my pockets with the fruit of the pomegranate, I sucked the pleasant acid juice and admired the rich grasses and shrubs near the upper part of the forest. The feathery leaves of the *prangos*, which sting in the springtime, were harmless now. The dryness had extracted their poison. Having provided protection from damage by grazing animals while the plants were in their flowering and fruit-bearing stages, their stinging secretion had fulfilled its function and had now lost its strength.[2] Nearby, one could see the little umbrellas of the hawk-nuts, the white disks of *malva-altea*, the fruit of the *eremurus* gathered into pigtails of little balls, the brown withered plants of the yellow groundsels, the pale mauve bellflowers and the touch-me-not (yellow balsam).

These were the real mountain forests. In this part of the Darvaz, on the Khozretisho Ridge, the annual rainfall is plentiful, and the forests grow, while in all of the Pamir-Alai only 3 percent of the area is wooded. What I was seeing is now a rarity in Central Asia.

My enthusiasm was noticeably dampened by the fantastic abundance of snakes. I have never seen them in such numbers. Large, fat *gyurzas* [the deadly poisonous *Vipera lebetina* Linnaeus] were lying everywhere on the path, basking in the autumn sun. Luckily, the cold of the season made them lethargic and less aggressive than usual. In my sneakers, I was constantly vulnerable to a fatal bite and had to watch my step every moment. When they saw me, the snakes hissed with a whistling sound, and most of them crawled away. But a few stubborn ones refused to yield the right of way. These I had to kill with the blade of my ice ax. The next morning a gyurza was cuddled up to the outside of my sleeping bag. I couldn't wait to get above the tree line and out of the realm of the snakes.

When the sun finally lit up the ravine, the growths of sweetbrier that had crowned the forest belt were left behind, and I strode through fragrant meadows of Saint-John's-wort, mountain flax, thyme and herbs. Finally climbing through the alpine zone, I crossed the Valvolak Pass at an altitude of more than 3,400 meters [11,150 ft.] where it was very cold. I wanted to get back to the warm air but had to spend one more night jumping around to keep warm rather than sleeping, unable to keep a fire going with dried alpine plants and rapidly using up the fuel of my Primus. Starting down at dawn, I reached a tiny kishlak, where an ailing old woman fed me some hot pea soup and tea. At the next kishlak, I bought new Keds and threw away the old ones, the reserve pair, which were torn to shreds. Now I was ready to continue on the last 200 kilometers of the trip.

After duly attending yet another wedding, I came down through the forest zone, which was thinning out, and at last got back to the Pyandzh. The valley here is botanically rich but unfortunately disfigured by deforestation. The river continues southwest, but I turned right, over the steep east slope of the Khirmandzhay Pass, which for some reason is also named for Alexander the Great, and reached the village of Kulyab. Here nothing suggested the thriving vegetation of Darvaz, either on the mountain slopes or on the floodplains of the river. All around were steep hillocks, yellowish brown with dried grass. One had to look closely to see the wheat, rye and darnel. Gone was the freshness of the mountain air. It was hot and dusty, a completely different environment. Southern Tajikistan is a huge depression with a subtropical climate and short-lived, annual plants. The monotony of the landscape is really oppressive. In Kulyab I barely overcame the desire to give up the whole enterprise and take a flight to Dushanbe. In life there are many such temptations, if one only yields to them!

After that I still had seven days on foot. I passed through the oasis of Yaksu in the low hills of Kangurt, which was once a residence of the emir of Bukhara. This brought me to the river Vakhsh at a place where its rocky banks come very close together, only 5 or 6 meters apart. One could cross it here on a wooden bridge by car as well as on foot. Confined within this tortuous slit, the mighty river roared far below but could hardly be seen from the bridge. There are many legends about this place: about a young girl who threw herself in because of a tragic love affair; about a *bogatyr* [a superman hero-knight] who chopped out the gap in the rock with his sword; and about a Red Army soldier who escaped from the Basmatchi [a movement of Islamic rebels who fought the Soviets from 1917 to 1923] by leaping on horseback over the gap, which then had no bridge. The last one, about the Red Army soldier, is said to have really happened. Now this is the site of the giant Nurek hydroelectric dam, and the kishlak of Nurek has become an important city.[3]

The monotonously burned-out, hilly terrain was now replaced with steeper slopes where pistachio, almond and bean-caper woods were growing. After crossing the pass of Zardolyu, I finally saw the Hissar Valley spread out below. I was walking like an automaton. My goal was now not far away, but the process of getting there had become an ordeal.

On the twenty-sixth day, I reached the village of Ordzhonikidzeabad, with only 18 kilometers to go. But these I did not manage to cover on foot. The fault was not mine. It was due to the vigilance of the local militia [police]. In all honesty, I cannot blame the good faith of the militiamen. Judge for yourself: brown from the sun, sweaty, dusty, with a scraggly beard, a worn-out shirt, torn sneakers, a grimy rucksack, a knife in the belt and an ice ax in the hand—such a figure could attract attention. I had also fallen into a muddy ditch at the outskirts of the village, which didn't improve my appearance. While I walked through the village, the militia stopped me twice to check my documents. The third time, I was escorted to the local militia station, with a convoy of gleeful children bringing up the rear. It took three hours for the militia to verify my identity. Fortunately it was a working day, and after getting a telephone call from Dushanbe, the chief of the militia sighed wearily and allowed me to proceed. I realized that civilization and my appearance of the moment were incompatible. Leaving the militia station, I boarded the first bus to Dushanbe.

By now it didn't matter to me. I had walked 580 kilometers, and was riding the last 18 like a city dweller. So I did not walk quite all the way from Khorog to Dushanbe. But I did get a complete profile, including the cotton fields of the last stretch, which do not belong to geobotany.

It was a useful trek. I observed the vegetation of the Pyandzh Valley between the altitudes of 2,200 and 900 meters [with a detour to 3,400 m]. I noted the transitions between the mountain and valley sections and could define the geobotanical boundaries between the different altitudes more precisely. But, most important, I obtained a more intimate picture of Tajikistan, its people, its hot valleys and its awesome mountains. And the more I walked, the more convinced I was, and not for the first time, that these mountains hold all, for the sake of which I was born.

CHAPTER 15

Mountain Song

Okmir Agakhanyantz, 1987

The native music of Central Asia is less extensive and less familiar than that of most other parts of the world. It has inspired a few favorite pieces in the standard classical repertoire: Balakireff's Islamey, *Borodin's tone poem* On the Steppes of Central Asia *and the* Polovetsian Dances *from his opera* Prince Igor, *which formed the basis for a Diaghilev ballet with Roerich sets and the Broadway musical* Kismet *(fate). Previous chapters include examples of indigenous music performed at bazaars, monasteries, feasts to celebrate weddings and circumcisions and intimate evening meals in nomad yurts, featuring lutes, horns, percussion instruments and voices. Belaiev (1975) has published original words and English transla-tions for many Turkestani songs.[1] The great sage and Nobel laureate of India, Rabindranath Tagore, wrote (1916): "The true poets, those who are the seers, seek to express the universe in terms of music. . . . This world-song is never for a moment separated from the singer. . . . It is his joy itself taking never-ending form. It is the great heart sending the tremor of its thrill over the sky" (142 ff.). Once, when Agakhanyantz was alone in the high Pamir, as he recalls in this brief, poetic chapter, he heard an impromptu love song drifting up from far below. This song and his reac-tion to it have much of the quality described by Tagore.*

One day we climbed out into the zone of the steppes. The soil scientists marked off their observation points and went back down. So as not to climb back here again on the way back from Dushanbe, I stayed to describe the vegetation of this area. Then I climbed another 300 meters or so and reached a steeper slope. The smog of the "Afghanetz" [the local name for a dusty wind from the south, like the sirocco of the Sahara] was left below. Here, on the height, the air was clean and transparent. Tired from the climb, I gave in and lay down. I wanted to sleep at least an hour.

The sky was so blue that it was almost purple. In it two vultures were flying. They moved in circles, as though they were guardians of space. The steppe on the steep slope was soft and aromatic, dominated by the spicy odor of origanum. The noise of the river far below could scarcely be heard. Its faraway sound accentuated the abnormal silence. I lay on the grass of the steppe in delight. Not a single thought was in my head. I was too lazy even to think about how good it was here. And it really was good: the grass, the sky, the gentle sunlight and a vague expectation of happiness. Like in one's youth.

And then I heard a song. Somewhere far away from me a young, male voice was singing. In the silence I could hear every word. The voice sang about a young girl. The words in the Tajik language seemed to enfold themselves into a beautiful garland: "Little berry, my little berry! My sweet little berry! My flower of spring! Come to my home and breathe into it your soul!" The tune was improvised and drawn out, but in the mountains that is the only way to sing. Any rhythmical melody would have torn apart the silence. This one wove itself into it, not destroying the charm of the mountains or the calmness. The song seemed to carry the sorrow of the ages. That, undoubtedly, is how the children of the endless steppes sang in ancient times. Only he could sing like that who has enormous space in front of him, who is not in a hurry to go anywhere, who is far from care and rejoices in the given fate of the day, the sun, the mountains, the space and his love. "Little berry, my little berry . . ."

I lay without moving and listened. The voice moved off and then the song faded away. But the breeze rustled and brought it back to life again. I lay and listened to the wind-song and thought about things vague but approaching generality. About how we live wrongly, losing something big in our cares, forgetting how to distinguish the good from the inferior, fretting about trifles and grieving about nonsense. But the years fly, and so life leaps away in a hurry. But here are the mountains, a reproach to our anxiety. It is frightening to think that one can live one's entire allotted time in the city and never see the mountains, never feel the scale of our life, never hear that song . . .

CHAPTER 16

A British Pamir Tragedy

Anatoly Ovtchinnikov, 1966

Dr. Anatoly Ovtchinnikov was born in 1927 in the Soviet part of Karelia, in a small fishing village on the eastern shore of Lake Oneinda. He is a professor of mechanical engineering at Moscow Technical University and one of Russia's leading mountaineers.[1] In 1962, he and John Hunt, of Everest fame, were coleaders of a British-Soviet expedition to the Pamir, during which two of its outstanding climbers, Wilfrid Noyce and Robin Smith, fell to their deaths from the Peak of Garmo. Hunt and several companions left for England to bear the sad news, leaving Malcolm Slesser as leader of the remaining British group, which included the famous Joe Brown and Ian McNaught-Davis.[2] This chapter by Ovtchinnikov is the only eyewitness account of the accident. It includes an amusing passage on how the British spent their leisure hours in camp, and it concludes with the memorial ceremony for Noyce and Smith. It gives a clear picture of the tragedy and its main causes, that is, snow-filled crampons and a collision with a knob of snow, which diverted the fall from a gentle to a precipitous slope. These points are both absent from the published accounts by Slesser (1964a, 1964b) and Hunt (1978), neither of whom witnessed the accident.

"Friends, we have lost Wilfrid and Robin," came the sound of a muffled voice.

Together with Ovtchinnikov and Sevastianov, they had reached the summit of the Peak of Garmo (6,595 m). On the descent, worn out by many hours of hard climbing, Noyce and Smith had slipped on the slope: the packed ice was covered with snow, but the snow was soft, and filled up the teeth of the crampons.

Here is what the eyewitnesses tell.

After climbing intermittently, pitch after pitch, the group assembled on the crest of the Academy of Sciences range, at an altitude of 5,500 meters, and set up a camp. The following day they had to sit in their tents, waiting for the strong wind to calm and allow visibility.

The British climbers even here did not forget their comfort. Ours usually squeeze in five to a tent, they only three. Ted Wrangham even put on pajamas for the night. Each one killed time in his own way. Noyce read, made entries in his diary and puffed on his inseparable pipe. Robin Smith, preparing for his doctoral dissertation, studied a course in philosophy. To the question, what is primary, mind or matter, he pointedly replied that this was equivalent to the eternal argument about what came first, the egg or the chicken? The two Anatolys [Ovtchinnikov and Sevastianov] took turns dueling with Ted Wrangham in a game of checkers. Derek Bull, who had the duty, prepared supper. By evening it began to get colder, a sign of improving weather. Before going to sleep, we climbed 300 meters up the ridge and cut steps.

Our scheduled deadline was approaching, and our food supply was running low. Noyce proposed to attack the summit on June 24. This meant climbing about 1,100 meters and coming down the same day. Because of intense cold, the start was set for 6 A.M. The boots of the Soviet mountaineers were soaked and gave us fear of frostbite. The boots of the English fellows were also wet, but the fleece slippers that they wore inside protected them from the cold.

In the lead rope, the two Anatolys and Wilfrid, in the second, Derek, Ted and Robin. The lead rope moved fast to warm up. The second one moved slowly and immediately lagged behind. The first complication was a section of piled-up ice. The English screw-type ice pitons proved useless here. Even Wilfrid was unable to put in a single piton. We had not brought other pitons because of their great weight. We had to find a way around.

At that moment, Robin came up and informed us that Derek and Ted had turned back but that he wanted to keep on climbing. Wilfrid then cut the rope and tossed the end to Robin. The rest of the way up the snow-rock ridge, we continued in mixed ropes [Noyce-Ovtchinnikov, Sevastianov-Smith]. On the rocks approaching the summit, the Soviet climbers invited their guests to take the lead. In spite of his weariness, Robin led this part of the route skillfully and in a qualified manner.

The group was on the summit at about 3 P.M. They photographed the signed notes left by the Georgian climbers on the traverse of the Darvaz wall, then took pictures of themselves and had a bite to eat.

On the descent, after the rocky section of the ridge, we had to put our crampons back on. Meanwhile the British, with Vibram boots, had come down over the rocks wearing crampons. So as not to lose time, Smith unroped and suggested to Sevastianov that "Wilf and I will go down together, and you will catch up with us anyway." While the Soviet climbers were putting on their crampons, the British disappeared down a dip in the slope. When they reappeared, Sevastianov, still tying his crampons, noticed how the British pair slipped down the slope. The slope below the dip is gentle, with an easy exit to a plateau. The Soviet climbers didn't worry.

Alas! Having reached a considerable speed while slipping over the slope, even where it was not steep, Robin and Wilf crashed into a knob of snow, which threw them off to the left, where, after 15 to 20 meters, there was an iced-up rock cliff down which they fell for 800 meters. This happened at 6:30 P.M. in the thirteenth hour of the day's movement.

Within an hour, the pair of Soviet climbers was back at the assault camp, where Ted and Derek met them and agreed to the proposition of descending straightaway. They had seen the fall of their companions and had no doubt that they both had perished immediately. (Afterward, the doctor examined them and confirmed this opinion.) By now it was dark, and the climbers spent a sad night, drying out their thoroughly soaked boots.

Early in the morning, the foursome began the descent. Ted and Derek were powerfully shaken by what they had seen. We had to take special care in providing security with the 90-meter rope. In the second half of the day, on the upper plateau, they met Hunt, who was on his way down from the first ascent of a 5,640-meter then-unnamed peak [now called the Peak of Sodruzhestvo, which means "mutual friendship"]. The Soviet climbers asked Derek for a detailed account of what had happened and suggested immediately going back to those who had perished. Hunt was of a different opinion: if there was the slightest hope that Wilfrid and Robin were alive, it would be necessary to go to them, but now it was better to go down to the rest of the expedition members.

While crossing the middle plateau, the Soviets offered to bring down the bodies of those who had perished so that they could be buried. But the British, in the tradition of sailors, bury those who perish on the spot where they died. On the morning of June 26, climbers got up to the perished ones: they were lying side by side at the edge of a *bergschrund* [large crevasse]. The force of the fall had torn off one of Noyce's boots.

The giants of the Pamir were glumly quiet. The silence was shattered only by the sound of falling rocks. Heads are uncovered. Hunt reads a prayer. The deep ice crevasse will keep the bodies of our companions in its dark bosom forever. A signal rocket curves up into the sky.

A few days later, not far from the base camp, the Soviet climbers built a pyramid of rough stones and wound it with a black ribbon. They fitted an ice ax into a niche at the summit of this model of the peak and at its base engraved the names of the two who had perished and the date of the accident. From this spot, on a clear day, one can see the shining ice and the eternal snows of Garmo.

CHAPTER 17

International Pamir Climbers

Anatoly Ovtchinnikov, 1972b

In the northeastern Pamir, three Germans of the 1928 Soviet-German expedition (Krylenko 1929; Rickmers et al. 1929) made the first ascent of the 7,134-meter (23,406 ft.) Lenin (formerly Kaufmann) Peak, which till then was thought to be the highest in the USSR. They reached it from the glacier world to the south, but an approach from the north was later found to be easier, through the high pasture of Achik-Tash, which is used by yurt-*dwelling herdsmen and is informally called Edelweiss Valley. Since 1967, it has also been used as a base camp for international mountaineering, with two higher base camps for climbing in the northwestern Pamir. For years, Ovtchinnikov was the chief trainer, that is, in command of mountaineering for all three camps.[1] Lenin Peak has been climbed more often than any other mountain of 7,000 meters or higher, but it has also been a killer, notably in 1974 when eight Soviet women died in a blizzard at the top (Craig 1977) and in 1991 when forty-three eastern and western Europeans were buried by an avalanche at Camp 2, only one of whom survived. This chapter is Ovtchinnikov's dramatic story of one of the first international summers in the Pamir.*

The year is 1969. This time, the meadow of Achik-Tash is settled earlier than in 1967. As soon as July 14, above the camp spread out here, flags have been raised by the countries taking part in the international assembly of mountaineers. Those that accepted the invitations this year were Austria, Bulgaria, Hungary, East Germany, Italy, Poland, Rumania, France, West Germany, Yugoslavia, Mongolia, Nepal and Japan.

Outwardly, under the Peak of Lenin, everything appeared about the same as in 1967. Actually, however, there were sharp distinctions from the

148

alpiniad held here two years ago. It was hard to say whether it was simpler then, with 300 representatives from eight countries and a ratio of 5 to 1 from the USSR, or now, with about 100 persons from fourteen countries and a ratio of 1.5 to 1 from the USSR. Moreover, the average level of qualification for the participants in 1967 was noticeably higher than for those who came in 1969. All this could not help but complicate this year's endeavor and influence its results.

The Trainers' Council of the assembly, consisting mainly of Leningrad mountaineers and headed up by A. Ovtchinnikov, was faced with a difficult problem: how to organize climbs for such a large number who were so differently prepared, so that each participant could have the joy of reaching the summit of the Peak of Lenin without the feeling of being a burden to the others but under his own initiative, determination and even inspiration on such a significant ascent.

Work began under pressure to familiarize the participants with the tactics of high-altitude climbing worked out in the Soviet Union over many long years, with emphasis upon the routes on the Peak of Lenin, on intermediate bivouacs in snow caves, and especially on the assurance of safety during the ascent. The representatives from foreign countries were offered individual consultation with the trainers for choosing their route and working out plans for its achievement.

The teams from Austria, Bulgaria, East Germany, Italy, Poland and France immediately announced their intentions to climb independently of each other but with essential participation of Soviet climbers. The groups from Mongolia, Yugoslavia and Japan preferred to make the ascent primarily as members of a Soviet team. The climbers from Hungary, Nepal and Rumania formed an international group and invited the Soviet trainer K. Konoplyev to be their leader.

To provide cooperation and offer help in case of need, a team of Soviet climbers was established with the special assignment of following up all the climbs and descending last from the summit.

Weather conditions in the region of Lenin Peak in the summer of 1969 were not the best: almost every team appearing on the slopes en route to the summit encountered low clouds, snowfalls and strong winds. This was especially unfavorable for the climbers from Kyrghyzstan, for the "Burevestniks" [a Soviet climbing club], the French and the Italians, who were the first to start out on the ascent. In a blizzard with strong wind and almost no visibility, at each step the climbers sank deep into the newly fallen snow. There were moments when, almost at the end of their strength, they were about to turn back, but the power of will and the mutual support of the group helped them to go forward to the summit.

Thus, often changing leaders, this combined team went steadily up to the established goal. The success of the French and Italian climbers on the final stage of the ascent was made possible by the activities of the Italian Piero Dennuso and of the lady translator and master of sport M. Garf. In the course of a whole day at about 7,000 meters, they prepared the route for the team through deep snow and with no visibility. Motivation, tenacity, endurance, faith in the team and friendship conquered. Other teams acted the same way in the struggle to reach the top.

There is a saying among climbers that "mountains don't joke." They don't forgive even very minimal carelessness. It is enough sometimes just to place one's foot the wrong way, to slip or to imperceptibly lower one's guard, while hurrying to pass an apparently simple and safe place on the route, for the situation to suddenly becomes injurious.

To avoid such danger, on one steep and icy section of the route, rope railings had been fixed in advance. All those who made use of them passed there safely and without delay. When the Bulgarian team approached this spot, nothing foreshadowed disaster. In the opinion of the trainers, this was a strong group with outstanding team spirit and skill in organizing ascents. Its members were experienced in high-altitude climbing and were not discouraged by rough weather conditions. But, while passing the place with the railings, one of the climbers in the team, Tchetin Ismailov, suddenly slipped and fell. Apparently he let go of the railing and slid down the rough firn surface. After falling about 100 meters, he hit his head against a rock protruding through the snow and suffered a severe trauma.

The doctor, G. Zaharenko, was quickly at the side of the injured man and began to give him medical treatment. But he was unable to prevent the sad outcome: after a few hours, the injured man died without recovering consciousness.

What caused this misfortune? Was it being tired at the end of a hard day that blunted his awareness, so that Tchetin did not make use of the safety rope? Was it being near the next bivouac stage, in the expectation of finding tents, warm sleeping bags and a hot supper, that induced him to be hasty and less careful?

It was a heavy, irretrievable loss. Once again it showed the absolute necessity of unflagging attention to the surrounding conditions of the route of ascent and of appropriate care at every step.

In the process of managing the assembly, the Trainers' Council carefully observed the climbing style of the foreign climbers. On that basis the council accepted the rationale of their respective climbing aims and decisions. But on the question of allowing inadequately prepared alpinists to start out on a climb, for which the rules of Soviet mountaineering permit the solution of such a problem, the activities of foreign climbers include a strange anomaly. Among them it is accepted that each climber may decide for himself whether to start out with his group on a given ascent or not. Often this occurs in spite of contrary opinions by other members of his team.

A representative instance of this occurred within the team of Austrian climbers. After the acclimatizing practice climbs and medical checkups, we came to the conclusion that not all members of this team would be capable of reaching the summit. The members of the team understood this well themselves. Joseph Fuchs took it upon himself to decide whether to go with his group to the top or not, even though the opinion of the doctors and trainers was negative. Fuchs decided to go, thereby putting in doubt the chances of the entire team to reach the top. The Austrians set out, but at 6,000 meters they had to turn back because some members of their team were obviously losing strength. Later they made another attempt. This time they reached a height of 6,900 meters, where most of the team members had neither the strength nor the will to go on. They decided to go down. Fuchs disagreed. He joined a group of Soviet climbers from Krasnoyar and reached the summit. At that point, however, he fell into complete exhaustion, having no strength left either physically or morally. If he had been there alone, a tragic outcome would have been unavoidable. During the following days, the Krasnoyartsy had to transport the helpless climber down, struggling to keep him alive. And the Austrian team did not achieve success. Their two attempts (to 6,000 and 6,900 m) were both futile.

Some difficulty developed with the climbers from West Germany, of whom there were two [Schneider and Hiebeler]. Both were experienced in high-altitude ascents. The route they chose had never been climbed before. It would begin on the Sauk-Dar glacier [south of the peak] and would ascend steep projections of snow and ice on the east face of the mountain. To undertake this route with only two climbers obviously would be risky. Wishing to satisfy the desire of the guests, the directors of the camp organized a joint Soviet-German team, which included two young but experienced high-altitude trainers, Y. Ustinov and O. Borisenok.

The joint Soviet-German team, making the climb from the south, also became a source of anxiety. Bad weather created difficulty for this team. Overcoming the steep, icy pitches, case hardened by low temperatures, required of this group exceptional effort, the ability to use virtually artistic techniques of climbing and special attention to the choice of the route. During the first three days, the climbers successfully ascended the difficult route, often changing leaders and overcoming one obstacle after another. It appeared to them that they were approaching the summit because the slope was becoming less steep. But at that point the reserves of strength of the German climbers proved to be exhausted by the intensity of effort and cold of the previous days. Only 50 meters from the top, Hiebeler fell. Schneider felt himself, to put it mildly, not in brilliant condition. They were both unable to go on, neither up nor down. The Soviet pair, unable to bring down with their own strength two men at the same time, left them warm clothing and all their food supplies and began a rapid descent. They reached the 4,200-meter camp at 11 P.M.

The following morning, a Soviet foursome started out for the rescue: A. Ovtchinnikov, V. Ivanov, Y. Ustinov and O. Borisenok. The last two in this group were the same two trainers who had just come down from the top. With maximum speed, they reached the sick men in two days. The condition of Hiebeler had improved, and he was able to move with the help of two other climbers. The next day they were back at the 4,200-meter camp. There a helicopter was called up. The sick men were rapidly transported to the hospital at Osh, where they were given the needed treatment.

The program of the assembly was coming to an end. In spite of the happenings mentioned above, it took place, in the opinion of our own and foreign climbers, in an interesting, satisfying and gainful way. As they did after 1967, the leaders and members of the various groups spoke favorably about the assembly and expressed a desire to have it become a regular event. That is what we now plan to do.

As a result of this assembly, 86 more climbers reached the summit of the Peak of Lenin, 30 of whom were guests from foreign countries. Including other Soviet climbers who were not connected with the international assembly, a total of 175 persons climbed the peak in 1969, on the centenary of V. I. Lenin's birth, marking it with a significant sporting achievement. This brings the total to date to more than 1,000 climbers of the peak—more than for any other mountain over 7,000 meters high. It also demonstrated the high qualifications of the Soviet climbers, fully at the level of their international colleagues, with whom their friendship and mutual assistance is a bright spot on the record of Soviet mountaineering.

In addition, at the end of the program but not as a normal part of it, the brothers Konstantin and Boris Kletsko fulfilled their long-held dream and descended the Peak of Lenin on skis. All those present congratulated them for this virtuoso achievement.

Upon leaving the Alai Valley, the international climbers expressed their desire to return to these austere but majestic places and to climb other great peaks of the Pamir.

CHAPTER 18

The Peak of Korzhenevskaya

Anatoly Ovtchinnikov, 1967

*In the northwestern Pamir of Tajikistan, the Peaks of Eugenia
Korzhenevskaya and Communism are separated by the junction of the
Traube, Walter and Moskvin glaciers, named for the men who first
reached this icy region in 1932. They are also jointly honored in the
nearby Peak of the Four, the fourth man being a Russian alpinist, Boris
Fried. The Moskvin glacier is the site of the highest of the three international mountaineering camps in the Pamir. Korzhenevskaya,[1] a beautiful
but difficult mountain of 7,105 meters (23,310 ft.), was first climbed in
1953. An expedition of twenty-five Soviet climbers assembled on the
Moskvin glacier in 1966 to establish three new routes on that mountain.
As described in this chapter, Ovtchinnikov's group forced a way up the
formidable south buttress of the peak, an achievement that convinced
both them and the Soviet Mountaineering Federation that they were ready
to tackle the Peak of Communism's vast, overhanging, south face, the
most challenging ascent that still remained to be done in the USSR. The
men in the group included Ovtchinnikov, Myslovsky, Ivanov and
Glukhov—names that are linked in two other major mountaineering
achievements that are described in the following chapters.*

Mountaineers of the Soviet Union organize each year expeditions to the
distant and not easily accessible regions of the Pamir and Tien Shan. The
main difficulties of these expeditions are the altitude of the summits,
which exceed 6,000 meters, and the unknown, unclimbed routes. Members of these expeditions are highly qualified alpinists who have already
achieved grade 5 ascents in the Caucasus. In 1966, the Peak of Eugenia

Korzhenevskaya (7,105 m), the fourth highest in the Soviet Union, attracted several groups of mountaineering sportsmen.

Climbers had visited this sector only on three previous years: 1937, 1953 (under the direction of Ugarov) and 1961 (under that of Romanov). The impossibility of crossing the Muksu and Fortambek Rivers with overland caravans prevented them from reaching the basin on the Fortambek glacier. That is why climbers had so rarely come to this interesting region.

The gorges of Fortambek are deservedly called "the heart of the Pamir." Upstream of these gorges lie the Fortambek, Walter and Moskvin glaciers, coming down at the feet of the summit ridges of the Peter the Great range. Here are found the highest summits of the Pamir: the Peaks of Communism, Korzhenevskaya, Moscow, Leningrad and others, which offer challenging itineraries to climbing expeditions. One of these is the east buttress and ridge of Korzhenevskaya.

Airplanes and helicopters now provide rapid access to the upper parts of the Fortambek glacier. When organizing our expedition, we therefore made use of them to bring its participants and their supplies to the base camp. The climbers in this 1966 group, who were members of the "Burevestnik" student club, set themselves the objective of climbing Korzhenevskaya by three previously unclimbed routes: the south ridge, the buttress of the south ridge, and the east ridge. In addition, they had planned a continuous traverse of the Peaks of Communism and Korzhenevskaya. However, this traverse could not take place because of a helicopter delay of twelve days at the Liakheh airport.

The expedition included twenty-five climbers, of whom twelve had no previous experience with climbs above 6,000 meters. On the other hand, Kuzmin, a first-class climber, and also Shatayev, Sevastianov, Smitt and Buzhukov, had completed major ascents in the Pamir and Tien Shan. I was chosen as leader of the expedition, with Shatayev as assistant leader and Kuzmin as head of the Trainers' Council. A cook, a medical doctor and a radio-telegraph operator made up the auxiliary personnel.

According to the expedition plan, the climbers were divided into three teams of eight, with Dobrovolsky, Tsetlin, and Buzhukov as their respective leaders. Each group was joined by a monitor-trainer with much experience in high-altitude climbing. The first group was made up entirely of alpinists from the sporting club of the Moscow Institute of Technology, none of whom had high-altitude experience. I served as their monitor. The second group was composed of members of the sporting club of the Academy of Sciences of the USSR, most of whom were experienced at high altitudes, with Kuzmin as their monitor. The third group, also inexperienced at high altitude, had Gatkin as its monitor.

The tactic of Soviet high-altitude climbers differs from that of Himalayan expeditions. In the Himalayas, the climbers "lay siege" to the summit, with intermediate camps abundantly provided with food and equipment for bad weather and rest. Sherpa porters bring up the loads, and the final assault of the summit includes only a few expedition members. Our tactic, on the other hand, which is similar to that employed for ascents in the Caucasus [known in the West as the alpine style], provides for all members of the sporting group to make the complete ascent without installing permanent intermediate camps.

This method requires an advanced degree of physical preparation and technique by members of the expedition, since each one has to carry his food, cooking and bivouac equipment in addition to his climbing gear. The weights of their backpacks at the time of leaving base camp often reach 35 kilograms [77 lbs.]. Some climbers for one reason or another (sickness, insufficient acclimatization or physical preparation) remain in base camp. At the moment, we do not have the necessary criteria to judge, at the moment of departure, the capability of a climber who has never reached an altitude between 6,000 and 7,000 meters.

July 13: Liakheh airport. It is not until July 25 that all members of the expedition are reunited at base camp, at the foot of the Peak of Korzhenevskaya on the moraine of the Walter glacier.

Until August 5, the participants familiarize themselves with the region, making practice ascents and acclimatizing on the summits of around 6,000 meters. It is during these excursions that one judges the climbers. Some of our young colleagues suffer visibly from mountain sickness. When the time comes to confirm the makeup of the groups for the main ascents, the opinions of the Trainers' Council members diverge. Most of the trainers, who are accustomed to high altitude, consider that those subject to mountain sickness should not be included in the assault teams. However, from medical examinations of these "doubtful" climbers at the base camp (altitude 3,900 m), the results are declared to be satisfactory. [Thus, the base camp is 2,200 m, or 7,300 ft., below the summit.]

The direction of the expedition, taking into account the medical results and the great desire of these climbers, who have already completed difficult wall ascents in the Caucasus, allows the leaders of each group to decide this thorny question for themselves. The members of the second [most-experienced] sporting group refuse to include any "doubtful" climbers on their team. They unanimously decide that these should actively continue their acclimatization. The first and third groups are more accommodating, and each agrees to include two "doubtful" climbers on its team. It is decided that, if the mountain sickness becomes aggravated, they will return to camp.

Our group, led by Leon Dobrovolsky, leaves base camp on August 6 to ascend the south ridge buttress of the Peak of Korzhenevskaya. We install the first bivouac at 5,100 meters. On the second day, we cross a snow and ice slope and reach the buttress at an altitude of 5,600 meters. On the third day, we begin to climb the buttress. Since the rocks are fairly easy but friable, the group of eight climbers moves rather slowly. We prepare to bivouac at 6,100 meters. However, being unable to find a place where we can make a platform to pitch our tents, we sit up all night with our tents used as blankets. It is cold. At dawn we continue. Edik [Edward] Myslovsky and I had reconnoitered here the previous day and put in the needed pitons. But the actual ascent with rucksacks proves to be much harder, and the climb of a 40-meter overhanging wall consumes much time.

The route above it, over snow-covered rocks, is easier. At about two o'clock, we reach a projection of the buttress that leads to the south ridge. The altitude is about 6,500 meters. Here we make a suitable platform for our tents. Afterward we will have no such place until the exit from the ridge. After a discussion, Edik and I decide to stop. The other three ropes are still far below. The preparation of the platforms takes up the rest of the day. At about six o'clock, everyone is reunited, the platforms are ready and the tents are put up. In comparison with the previous night, we are well installed, and everyone is able to stretch out.

The next morning, Edik and I leave early to open up the route. The others take their time. The preparations of the second tent seem especially long. This doesn't worry us because we know that the first rope has been moving slower. Now we have trouble climbing over sharp, pointed rocks, which are covered in places with snow. At about noon, we have climbed our fourth rope length.

To our surprise, the other members of the group have not yet left. Now we begin to worry. We call to them: "Why are you taking so much time to get started?" They call back: "Arutyunyan is sick, probably mountain sickness." We decide to go down and investigate. To reach the exit from the ridge, we later will have to climb another 300 meters. After that, the way will be easy: a snow ridge leading to the summit and back down.

The condition of Arutyunyan was unmistakably high-altitude sickness. He can't continue climbing because it would get worse. We have to go down; there is no other solution. Arutyunyan doesn't understand. He believes it is possible to continue the ascent.

The next day, August 11, I go up a rope length and invite Arutyunyan to follow. He can't do it. The question is settled. I come back down. Leaving part of our equipment and fuel, we begin the descent. Rope length after rope length, we descend. By evening, we reach the bottom of the buttress (5,600 m). The day after that, Arutyunyan feels better, as generally happens with mountain sickness. He descends with more assurance, which enables us to reach base camp that evening.

The second group, led by Tsetlin, had returned the previous evening after making the first ascent of the south ridge of the Peak of Korzhenevskaya. We had seen them during our descent. We congratulate them. For them, all went well. In the group of Buzhukov, it was necessary to bring down Danilov, who was stricken with pulmonary edema. The second group helped them bring down the sick man to the base camp of the army climbers, situated lower in the Fortambek Gorge. From there, a helicopter took him to the Liakheh airport and on to the hospital at Dushanbe.

After a day of rest at base camp, our group, now composed of only six climbers, starts out again on August 14. This time, the backpacks are lighter and we move faster, since we left an important part of our loads above, which saves us one day. The weather turns bad, and we are enveloped in clouds.

On August 17, we attack the most difficult part of the route, the exit from the ridge. The passage of those 300 meters takes up a whole day, even though we had prepared a considerable part of the route already. The wall of vertical and in some places overhanging rocks alternates with steep slabs deeply buried in fresh snow. When we make our exit to the wide snow ridge at the top, we put up our tent. Now the hard part is behind us, and the summit is not far.

The only problem is the deep snow. It had snowed all night and erased the tracks of the second group. On the morning of the eighteenth, there is practically no visibility, and the wind is strong. The climb to the summit now requires two hours of major effort through the deep snow. At the summit, we have trouble finding the cairn containing a note from the group that had just climbed the east ridge: it is the group of Buzhukov. The note informs us that one of the group, Skurlatov, had fallen sick. All members of our group reached the summit. They were: Dobrovolsky, the group leader, Glukhov, Ivanov, Massyukov, Myslovsky and Ovtchinnikov, the monitor.

Because of the bad weather, we don't delay starting the descent by the south ridge. The biggest problem on the descent in bad visibility is to avoid falling into an avalanche couloir. At an altitude of 6,000 meters, we suddenly see Gatkin, of Buzhukov's group, which is also coming down the south ridge. We learn the details of their ascent and help them to transport Skurlatov. It is the members of Tsetlin's group, who had climbed back up the previous day, who make the transport. To bring the sick man down takes two more days.

The ascents are completed and the members of all the sporting groups are reunited at base camp on August 20. Our expedition had succeeded in making three first ascents of the Peak of Korzhenevskaya: by the buttress of the south ridge, by the south ridge, and by the east ridge. At the same time, a group from the "Spartak" sporting society, led by Budanov, made a first ascent of the peak by the southeast face, while the group of army mountaineers, led by Snegiryov, repeated the ascent by the central southeast buttress first climbed by the Romanov group in 1961.

CHAPTER 19

The Peak of Communism: South Wall

Anatoly Ovtchinnikov, 1972a

The Pamir's lofty ranges run mostly east and west with names such as Trans-Alai, Peter the First (the Great), Yazgulem, Rushan and Shugnan, the latter two having also been the names, in the 1890s, of the Turkestan governor-general's dogs. Hidden within this world of ice, an exceptional range runs north and south, the range of the Academy of Sciences. It intersects the Peter the First range at the former USSR's highest point, the Peak of Communism, at 7,495 meters (24,590 ft.). Today there are sixteen established routes to its summit (Ratzek 1975), all of which are difficult.[1] The hardest one by far, which is rated European grade 6, is by way of the partly overhanging south wall, which is 2,500 meters (8,000 ft.) high. This wall is about twice as tall and technically far more difficult than the Eiger north face. This chapter tells how it was first climbed in 1968 by four of the same men who had mastered the south buttress of the Peak of Eugenia Korzhenevskaya.

The year is 1928. The Soviet-German expedition is working in the Pamir Mountains. For the first time they had measured a height of 7,495 meters and assigned to it the name Peak of Garmo, the most popular name among local Tajiks. But a 1932 expedition, with climbers led by N. V. Krylenko, topographers led by I. G. Dorofeyev and geologists led by A. V. Moskvin, established that the 7,495-meter peak rises 18 kilometers north of the Peak of Garmo. As proposed by N. V. Krylenko, the 7,495-meter peak was named the Peak of Stalin, but in 1960 it was renamed the Peak of Communism [the highest in the USSR].

The 1933 Tajik-Pamir expedition included a section whose purpose was to climb the 7,495-meter peak. This section was headed up by N. P. Gorbunov. After long preparation and working up the route on the mountain's east ridge, twenty-five-year-old Eugene Abalakov reached the top alone, while Gorbunov waited for him 100 meters below on the mountain's east summit. The other members of the assault team had for various reasons stopped climbing above 7,000 meters. Abalakov had climbed the 7,495-meter peak by a very difficult route. Up to that time, the only 7,000-meter climbs were of the 7,123-meter Trisul, the 7,756-meter Kamet, the 7,587-meter Minya Konka and a spur of Kanchenjunga. Abalakov had made the fourth-highest climb in the world.

It is located at the intersection of the Academy of Sciences and Peter the First ranges. To the northeast, it feeds the mighty Bivouac glacier—a tributary of the Fedchenko, which is one of the largest valley glaciers in the world. Northwest from the summit, at an altitude of 5,700 to 6,000 meters, the Pamir Firn Plateau extends for 10 kilometers, an almost level snowfield. To the north, the plateau breaks off into steep walls, at the feet of which the mighty Turamys, Fortambek and Walter glaciers originate, fed by constantly roaring avalanches and falling blocks of ice and snow. The first ascent to the summit from the Fortambek glacier over the Pamir Firn Plateau was completed in 1967 by an expedition led by A. Ovtchinnikov. This route was considered impossible as late as 1961 by climbers of the Trud Society who ascended the Peak of Korzhenevskaya.

To the south, the plateau breaks off into the numerous cirques of the Garmo glacier, the largest of which forms the Belaev glacier at an altitude of 4,600 to 5,000 meters. It lies at the foot of the Peak of Communism's dark south wall, which is 2,500 meters high, vertical and overhanging in places and overpowering in its grandeur and inaccessibility. This is the heart of the high Pamir, the region of its highest summits, deepest valleys, steepest walls and longest glaciers.

In 1955, the Georgian Alpine Club established a camp on the Belaev glacier and climbed the peak from there via the east ridge. In 1959, the first "wall" of a seven-thousander was climbed. The group, whose members were V. Danilov, K. Kuzmin (leader), A. Ovtchinnikov, V. Potanov and A. Sevastianov, went up a steep spur of the south wall to the west shoulder and from there to the summit, after which they descended to the Belaev glacier by the "Georgian" east-ridge route. The summit of the peak is a platform of stratified rock that includes cubes of pyrite. Some of the pyrite had been burned out by electric storms, which had also destroyed all metal objects left on the summit by Abalakov and the Georgians.

In 1962, the Peak of Communism became international. A British expedition led by John Hunt, who had led the first ascent of Everest in 1953, arrived near the Garmo glacier. To join them (in the role of "sparring partner") the Mountaineering Federation of the USSR organized a group of climbers led by A. Ovtchinnikov. The British and Soviet climbers made several ascents in the area, including an ascent of the Peak of Communism. [This is described in the book *Red Peak*, by Malcolm Slesser, who became the leader of the British group when John Hunt returned to London after the tragic deaths of Wilfrid Noyce and Robin Smith in a fall from Peak Garmo. The British intended to climb the south wall of the Peak of Communism, but, after losing their strongest climbers, they went up via the "Georgian" route instead.]

In the spring of 1965, at a special meeting of the Alpine Section of Burevestnik [an honorary Moscow sporting society whose name means "harbinger of storms"], it was decided to prepare a team to ascend the south wall. The successful ascent of the Peak of Korzhenevskaya in 1966, by the crest of its south rib, showed that the south wall of the Peak of Communism was climbable. For this the expedition included V. Glukhov, V. Ivanov, E. Myslovsky and A. Ovtchinnikov, who had climbed Korzhenevskaya by the south rib crest, and also G. Karlov, I. Roshtchy, V. Shataev and N. Altukhov. On July 19, 1968, all the members of the expedition arrived at the upper step of the Belaev glacier.

The start of the attack was not encouraging. Approaching the indicated part of the cliff, the technical leader of the team, A. Ovtchinnikov, and the expedition leader, E. Myslovsky, saw numerous tracks in the snow made by rocks falling from above. They successfully got through this unpleasant zone, took shelter beneath the wall and began to discuss what to do. They decided that it would be possible to go straight up because there the falling rocks would not threaten: it was under the overhanging part of the wall. But they were thinking: "What's higher up?" They climbed several rope lengths. The rock was rather crumbly. A group of four would have trouble working up the route and carrying the needed loads, so that they thought they would need all eight climbers to do it. Late in the evening, they returned to the glacier, where a hot supper awaited them.

The next morning, July 20, while the fog was clearing, Myslovsky and Ovtchinnikov walked over to the second group of four. They gave an account of everything they had found on the wall and proposed that they all take part in the ascent. The proposal was enticing. But in the end the second foursome stated forthrightly that they were not morally prepared for such a route, thanked their friends for their confidence and refused.

By July 23, 600 meters of the wall were already worked up. Along the way, the team had inserted pitons and, on the most difficult parts, they had hung fixed ropes. Concluding that the first stage of the route was prepared, on the twenty-fourth all climbers returned to base camp, where they rested four days, during which time the precise tactics for the ascent were agreed upon. The second team, led by V. Shataev, would climb the peak by the 1959 Kuzmin route. They would provide emergency support for the team on the wall, which would prepare a route up to the large snow shelf and only then begin the final ascent.

On July 29, the "wall" team, made up of E. Myslovsky, A. Ovtchin-nikov, V. Glukhov and V. Ivanov, left base camp, and on the thirty-first they were already on the wall. They discovered that the rockfall had intensified. But that which seemed so frightening before was now accepted calmly. A person gradually gets used to everything. In due course, they bivouacked on the rocky shoulder of the ridge. Apparently the climbers completely forgot that above them rose 2 kilometers of the wall.

During the night they heard rocks falling. Ovtchinnikov and Myslovsky, spending the night in the tent, were confident that they were in a safe place. On August 1, they continued pushing the route higher. It was about 9 o'clock. With the wall facing south, the sun reaches it late, and it is too cold to start out early. They climbed up to a ledge where, on the first stage of climbing, they had left their loads and a tent. They widened the platform as much as they could but were unable to set up the tent.

They continued working farther up and hung four more fixed ropes. Finally, they reached the snow shelf where the tent could be set up. But, because of the late hour, they were unable to get back up with their rucksacks. Myslovsky and Ovtchinnikov again spent the night in the tent on the crest of the ridge below. In the evening, they exchanged a firing of green rockets with the other team to report that all was well. Then, suddenly, high in the sky, a red rocket appeared.

It was the morning of August 2. After hoisting their rucksacks, the pair had begun the ascent. But soon Ovtchinnikov and Myslovsky noticed two climbers coming toward them from base camp. Soon they stopped and shouted something. Finally, it was possible to make out the words: a team on Peak Patriot had had an accident. The two friends looked at each other. They had to go down to the aid of a man in distress.

The injured climber, V. Fedorov, had broken his leg, and it took a week to get him down. During those days, the burden on the climbers was enormous. They had to race up to the site of the accident and carry the wounded man by a difficult route that involved much exertion, worry and stress. At base camp, a doctor brought up by helicopter was waiting, and Fedorov had an operation. It seemed that all worries were over, but clouds had come down so low that it was no longer flying weather. The helicopter got off the ground, but, instead of going up, it moved down through a gap in the moraine. At the bottom of the gap, it began to gain altitude and disappeared around a turn in the gorge. Everyone sighed with relief. Only then did the climbers notice that it was raining hard.

Four climbers (Myslovsky, Ovtchinnikov, Ivanov and Glukhov) got back up to the "Georgian" camp on August 8. The next morning they started out early. Here they were at the foot of the menacing wall. Its lower part was black with fallen rocks. They were falling over a wide channel. When the climbers reached the tent at the crest of the ridge, they saw that it had been perforated by rocks. Myslovsky and Ovtchinnikov examined the inhospitable wall. Rocks were falling left and right. Often they had to take shelter under projections in the cliff. The ascent is discontinued. The climbers decide to wait out the rockfall.

After nineteen hours, the rockfall diminishes. But there is still a long way to go. They know the way, but the rucksacks are heavy. The climbers decide to get up to the next ledge as fast as possible. They would take with them only bare essentials—food and tent. The Primus stove would be left behind. From the ledge they had three fixed ropes to go, although one could not rely on them too much: they might have been damaged by falling rocks. Myslovsky was in the lead the whole time. It was already dark when they came out at the top of a ridge and pitched their tent. Looking around, they decided that the place was protected from falling rocks, at least at night. They agreed that in the morning they would start as early as possible to get past the rockfall zone before noon.

The morning looked good. The climbers got up early. They now had to ascend a snow and ice slope that was not too steep. They decided to put on their crampons and start. But, because of confusion during the rescue, Myslovsky's crampons turned out to be too small. There was no time to beat them out to fit the boots. The only consolation was that the crampon work should be finished today. The foursome moved up with two on each rope, climbing simultaneously or with alternate belays. Always higher and higher. Soon the slope becomes much steeper. The progress slows: it is necessary to belay each climber at each pitch. Rocks begin to fall. When his turn comes, Myslovsky leads slowly. Now he reaches an overhang in the cliff. He tries to put in an ice piton but without success.

At that moment Ovtchinnikov sees a rock falling straight at him. He cannot jump to one side: this might dislodge Myslovsky. Ovtchinnikov bends down, with his helmet pointing at the falling rock. The rock flies by a few inches from his face, sprinkling it with slivers of ice and snow. Finally, Myslovsky inserts the ice piton. Then they climb simultaneously, leaving the rope in place for the next pair of climbers, who are still in the danger zone.

Now Ivanov comes up and after him Glukhov. It is only 2 o'clock in the afternoon, but the rockfall stops. The previous night they had stayed up late, and today they had got up very early, so they were quite tired. They continued only on the part of the wall that was familiar to them. It was essential to get some rest, look around and choose the direction for the rest of the climb.

In front of them was more overhanging wall and above it a rock barrier. They decided to prepare a platform for the tent. Then Ivanov and Glukhov prepared dinner, which, as is customary when climbing, also served as supper. So as not to lose time, Ovtchinnikov and Myslovsky climbed two rope lengths up. There they saw how, some 200 or 300 meters above them, the rockfalls originate. At first the rocks fall individually. But they reach a level where they form into groups, come closer together and, as in a chain reaction, form a continuous stream, rushing down with a frightening roar. Above 6,000 meters, practically no rocks were falling.

Finally, Ovtchinnikov and Myslovsky return to their comrades. An exchange of opinions takes place. They decide to devote the following day to preparing the route through the rock barrier. The night passes calmly. The tents stand up well. In the morning, intensive climbing starts. Seven rope lengths are climbed that day, and the barrier appears to be passed. The climbers leave all their metal equipment here and quickly return to the tents. In the evening, it starts to snow.

The next day, the climbing is much harder because of the newly fallen snow. It becomes necessary to clean off the pitons. Crampons are also needed, as the Vibram soles do not hold at all. By three in the afternoon, they have climbed the section that they had established the day before.

They traverse to the right and come out on the shelf above. Here they are finally convinced that the barrier has not been passed. It begins to get dark, but there is no place to set up the tent. At last, in full darkness, they come out on a projecting rock. They have to put up the tent where it is partly overhanging. Everything is tied down for insurance: the climbers, the tent and the rucksacks. Uncomfortable. Luckily, the night is not so cold.

Morning. Three rope lengths of a sufficiently complex route and the climbers come out on a good platform. After a brief discussion, they decide to put up the tent. Looking around and considering where to go, they come back to the original plan. This requires roping down to the big ice-snow shelf and climbing along it to the left. At that time, through an opening in the clouds, they see Volodya Shataev's group on the shoulder of the peak.

The next day, August 14, the team climbs up the ice-snow shelf under the overhanging barrier; they stop for the night early, at three in the afternoon. During the remaining part of the day, the climbers prepare a platform for the tent. Unfortunately, they pick a bad place, right next to the wall. In the evening it starts to snow, and a continuous stream of snow, like a waterfall, sweeps down from the wall. Sleep is often interrupted, for it is necessary to shake the growing layer of snow from the tent.

In the morning, the tent is buried in snow. It is very cold. Hands and feet freeze painfully. Nevertheless, they decide to start climbing. The sun reaches them at 11 o'clock, and it gets warm. The mood improves immediately. They stop for breakfast. Then they are again on their way along the shelf toward the base of a snow triangle that they see in the distance. They will attack the overhanging barrier from there.

In the second half of the day, an unfortunate thing happens. Myslovsky, having climbed half a rope length on an upward traverse, stops to put in a piton. While moving it from one hand to the other, he slips and falls. Ovtchinnikov jumps down to a small shelf. Even if the lower piton does not hold, it will take up part of the kinetic energy. If the next one doesn't hold, they will both be on the Belaev glacier below in a few minutes. The rope tightens and slackens for about 2 meters. The fall is checked.

Ovtchinnikov calls to Myslovsky: "How is it?" For a long time there is no reply, then some kind of inarticulate muttering. Finally comes the message: "I'm OK." Myslovsky climbs back up to Ovtchinnikov. A short stop, and then again they are on the move. Now Slava Glukhov, from the second pair, takes the lead, and Myslovsky brings up the rear: he needs a rest, at least for his morale. After another three rope lengths, the team stops for the night.

On the morning of August 16, again difficult climbing. Only a few rope lengths are put up that day. The climbers stop for the night in a large rock niche. No one is without things to do. While Ivanov and Glukhov prepare a platform and set up the tent, the other pair hang a fixed rope on the wall. From here, they can see that they have already climbed high—the Peaks of Pravda and Leningrad, and even the Peaks of Russia and Moscow are all below them.

Hard climbing continues the next day too. First straight up, then a traverse to the left. The route now becomes simpler. It seems that at any time the climbers will come out on the crest. Myslovsky, in his turn, climbs up a whole rope length and reports that the rest is just a walk up.

Everyone has had his fill of climbing and wants to get to the summit fast. The next pitch is an overhang. Ovtchinnikov climbs it with difficulty and gladly lies down on a rock to rest. One more rope length and the team is on the crest below the summit. From there they see climbers on the top and another group below it. The next day, the "wall" team reaches its goal.

Now they don't hurry and spend about two hours on the summit. The only things that make them descend are their control deadline and the diminishing supply of food. When they get down to the plateau of the Peak of Pravda, the Spartak climbers meet them with a radio contact to base camp. The "wall" team sends a request—to extend the deadline until noon on August 21. But that is overinsurance. Myslovsky's team is back at base camp on August 20.

Thus, they completed the ascent of the peak by a more difficult route than any had climbed before—perhaps one of the most difficult climbs in general. The members of the south wall team were given the rank of masters of sport of the international class and were awarded medals by the Committee for Physical Culture and Sport "for outstanding sporting achievement."

From 1933 to 1969, the Peak of Communism was climbed by 218 sportsmen, by different routes with different degrees of difficulty, the easiest of which is rated 5B (very difficult). Among them were two women—Lucy Agranovskaya and Galya Rozhalskaya. In addition, 17 climbers ascended the peak by grade 6 routes. These numbers testify to the skill of our country's high-altitude sportsmen, confirming that Soviet mountaineers have the ability to climb the difficult routes on our planet's 8,000-meter peaks.

It remains to be said that the sporting potential of the Peak of Communism is not yet exhausted. There is a whole series of possible new routes. An especially difficult one is on the wall from the Belaev glacier directly to the mountain's highest point. This is still only a dream for the strongest mountaineers.

CHAPTER 20

Traverse of Peak Pobeda

Anatoly Ovtchinnikov, 1973

Of all the world's mountains that rise above 7,000 meters (23,000 ft.), the northernmost, at forty-two degrees north latitude, is Peak Pobeda, the second-highest summit of what was once the USSR.[1] It is the apex of the Kokshaltau range, whose crest, running east and west, marks a segment of the frontier between Kyrghyzstan and China. South of it lies the Takla Makan Desert of the Tarim Basin. On the north slope of the Kokshaltau, where the cold air meets the hot air from the south in frequent violent storms, the snowfall is massive, and both the glaciers and the avalanches are enormous. That is why it has been so murderous to Soviet climbers (see chap. 8). On either side of Pobeda, along 25 kilometers (15 mi.) of the Kokshaltau, its entire crest is higher than 6,000 meters (20,000 ft.). The first complete lengthwise traverse of this ridge, beginning with the first ascent of the Peak of Nehru and including an ascent of Pobeda itself, was successfully achieved by Ovtchinnikov's group in 1970. He thereby earned the rank of "snow leopard," having climbed all four Soviet 7,000-meter peaks. It was, however, the only time in his life when he was in danger, having contracted acute high-altitude sickness. Later he returned and led a joint Soviet-American ascent of Pobeda (Garner 1986; Starrett 1986), which produced the first "snow leopards" outside the USSR.

At the heart of Central Asia, within the boundaries of Kazakhstan, Kyrghyzstan and China, rises the most grandiose of the high summits in the Tien Shan mountain range: the Peak of Victory, or Peak Pobeda. At an altitude of 7,435 meters, it is the second highest in the USSR, after the 7,495-meter Peak of Communism in the Pamir. But at its latitude of forty-

169

two degrees north, Peak Pobeda has the distinction of being the northernmost 7,000-meter peak on earth.

It is mainly for that reason that one encounters there such severe climatic conditions, which compare with those of the Andes in Patagonia. The weather changes with incredible speed; a beautiful day can suddenly change to one of frightful wind and snowstorms. But, if one has to endure such conditions on Fitz Roy at 3,000 meters, at Pobeda they occur at more than twice the altitude, adding polar conditions to those of the storms.

Thus, Pobeda is among the most dangerous mountains on earth. Technically, it looks relatively easy, for the most part consisting of snow slopes that appear to be tranquil, without the vertical or overhanging sections that one encounters on the Peak of Communism's south face. But the appearances are deceiving. During storms, these seemingly friendly slopes become deadly traps on which avalanches may be released from the most moderate inclines. Almost everywhere, and especially on the steeper slopes, the poor consistency and lack of homogeneity of the snow and ice present problems worse than those that one finds, for example, in the Pamir.

All this explains why the conquest of Pobeda has taken a heavy toll. The first ascent was achieved in 1938 by Gutman, Sidorenko and Ivanov. At that time, the peak was still poorly identified, and its actual altitude was not even known. One had to wait until 1942 to find out that these three mountaineers had climbed a great 7,000-meter peak! Afterward, the mountain was ascended several more times by either the east or the north ridge—but the disasters multiplied, often for reasons that were poorly understood. Unforgiving of the smallest errors, Pobeda offers the most draconian conditions to those who aspire to its conquest.

In 1970, mountaineers from several sporting societies decided to vanquish the mountain by attacking its summit from all the routes lying within the USSR. They came from all parts of the Soviet Union, even from the Extreme Orient, the Urals and Kyrghyzstan [within which the mountain mostly lies]. Among them were two women, Ludmila Agranovskaya and Galina Rozhalskaya, who were to achieve the first feminine ascents of the summit.

All of them took part in the Soviet climbing championship within the framework of their respective societies or clubs. This is a true competition, which leads to the awarding of a prize. In 1970, this prize was won by the team from the sporting club of the Moscow Institute of Technology, to which we belong. It was given for completing the continuous traverse of Peak Pobeda from west to east, with an initial first ascent of the completely virgin, unnamed peak of 6,742 meters. At first, our team consisted of ten members, as required in the rules for high-altitude ascents in the USSR. One must know that participation in the championship presupposes rather strict conformity to the rules, both for the composition of the team and for carrying out the ascent at very high altitudes.

Thus, before undertaking a 7,000-meter ascent, the climbers must complete two preliminary ascents: first at 5,000 meters, with a bivouac at that altitude; and, second, at 6,000 meters, with immediate return to the point of departure. These ascents were each monitored by medical examinations and by observing the performance of the climbers during the ascent. Furthermore, the obligatory size of the team is ten in the high-altitude category and eight in the category of traverses. This point in the rules would present us with a problem that was especially difficult to resolve. In effect, instead of the ten climbers prescribed for our enterprise, we were only nine, since one of our members had departed to investigate the mountains of France. This departure from the rules was not an obstacle in the stage of the preliminary ascent and acclimatization. But that is what it became at the moment of launching the definitive ascent because we were then obliged to observe the norms strictly.

The objective that we had set for ourselves was to make a continuous traverse, from west to east, of the immense ridge between China and Kyrghyzstan, which includes a whole series of summits between 6,700 and 7,500 meters in altitude. One part of this route, between the Peak of Vazha Pshavela (6,918 meters) and over Peak Pobeda to the Peak of the Soviet Army at 7,050 meters and the east peak at 7,039 meters, was already known. On the other hand, the unknown part was concentrated mainly at the beginning of the route, especially the access to Peak 6,742 meters, which first had to be discovered.

This, to be sure, was the objective during the days devoted to acclimatization. The adventure began on July 15, 1970. The approach was facilitated by using a helicopter. The base camp was established at approximately 4,200 meters altitude, on the vast glacier that lies between the spurs of Peak 6,742 and Vazha Pshavela, which is called the Diki ("Wild") glacier.

On the first day, all our efforts were directed toward the north ridge of Vazha Pshavela, which provided invaluable observation points from which to study Peak 6,742. In addition, it was possible to make on this ridge the two preliminary acclimatization ascents prescribed by the rules and at the same time use them for establishing a supply of food near its summit, which we would find when making the actual traverse. That is what we did. We reached the north ridge of Vazha Pshavela on July 18, after a load had been brought up by helicopter to 5,200 meters.

This initial contact allowed us to appreciate the problems that are specific to the Pobeda. We first had to plow our way through a surface layer of snow 30 to 40 centimeters thick, lying on top of a layer of wet snow, which was extremely unstable. And, when we turned our eyes toward Peak 6,742, it was to discover innumerable avalanche tracks. Thus, the first observation left us puzzled. We had to go there and see.

The team was then provisionally divided into two groups. The first one, consisting of Galkin, Dobrovolsky, Putrin, Bobrov and Maximov, left on July 21 for the summit of Vazha Pshavela for the purpose of completing their acclimatization and establishing the depot of food at the summit. The second group, with Ivanov, Myslovsky, Glukhov and Ovtchinnikov, was assigned to reconnoiter the access route between the Diki glacier and the north spur of Peak 6,742. It was an affair of two days, during which time it was possible to equip 500 meters of rock pitches and afterward climb over a series of snowy projections that almost abutted the ridge. Now we were sure of success.

However, the main assault could not commence immediately. It was necessary, before that, to complete the acclimatization of the second group, which took its turn on the route of the Vazha Pshavela. Moreover, we had to resolve the unpleasant problem of eliminating the ninth member, to the great consternation of Glukhov, who was the unlucky one in drawing lots. Finally, the whole team had the right to rest in the valley for a whole week—a week with frequent bathing in the immense Lake Issyk-Kul, interspersed with gastronomic experiences and, it is true, a false alert about three climbers carried away by a huge avalanche on a nearby peak. Luckily, these climbers got off with only a bad scare, and our rescue effort was confined to a hair-raising night trip by helicopter to the base camp.

The day to really begin the traverse finally arrived. It was August 7, 1970. Conditions for climbing were not ideal. There had been recent snowfalls, and a violent wind came up, which made us wonder if we had missed the best moment to get started. It took us three days to reach the huge plateau of snow at the beginning of the north ridge of Peak 6,742. Our progress was painful. On the glacier, we sank in snow up to the waist. To climb back up the 500 meters of rock pitches, even though they were now equipped with pitons, was a real battle. Finally, near the top, the snow changed and became so powdery that we had to pack it down and virtually crawl through it. Under these conditions, no one had much desire to be the leader.

But a first reward was about to crown our efforts. After a huge and difficult *bergschrund* [large crevasse], which defended the access to the plateau, it became evident that Peak 6,742 would in the end surrender its arms. On the tenth, Ivanov and Myslovsky took on the attack of the great cornice dominating the plateau. It was then that a storm announced itself. Very rapidly, the team found itself divided, and the two lead men had no recourse but to bivouac in a snow hole without food. On the eleventh, the storm continued, but it was necessary to climb nevertheless. It was a real race between the two leaders and the six others in the midst of an unleashed wind, violent snow in explosive gusts and ice sticking to one's face in a labyrinth of cornices with dangerous crevasses. In the evening, finally, the team was brought together again.

On the twelfth, the sun made a return appearance, but the strong wind continued. We arrived in the zone of 6,000 meters, and the effects of the altitude made themselves felt. Fatigue weighed upon us, and our pace became slower. After a sheer wall of ice that Ivanov and Myslovsky took three hours to climb, the terrain became easier, with alternating passages of steep but convenient rock. We were approaching the rocky section of the ridge. Then began the most painful stage of the entire ascent. The bad weather did not let up, while the technical difficulty increased to a good grade 4, which at 6,600 meters on a wall battered by icy wind has little resemblance to the usual climb of the crack on the Grepon. Besides that, the bivouac locations were remarkable mainly for their narrowness and lack of comfort. In spite of the snow shovels and duralumin saws that we had brought with us, it was not possible to dig comfortable caves. How miserable were the two nights that we spent in this manner, dehydrated, packed against each other and immobilized with cramps.

Nevertheless, as always, our reward came at last: on the fourteenth, the big, beautiful, weather system finally greeted us on our arrival at the first of our summits. Peak 6,742 was vanquished! Eight days had already passed since our departure from base camp, 2,500 meters below. Another whole week separated us from our return to where we had started, but it would not be the same. We had survived the storm and the cold, and now these were behind us. No new unpleasant incidents (Galkin lost his gloves on the ridge of Vazha Pshavela and Ovtchinnikov fell sick at 7,000 meters) would be allowed to stop us now. We arrived on known terrain, found our food depot, established during the acclimatization climbs, and also found the traces of those who had preceded us on Vazha Pshavela and Pobeda. Some of these traces were bitter: a note on Vazha Pshavela informed us that Tchelyabinsky had expired on the summit.

Three days after our victory on Peak 6,742, Peak Pobeda was finally ours on August 17, 1970. Dobrovolsky, Maximov, and Ovtchinnikov (sick) descended from there by way of the north ridge of the peak to the Zvezdotchka ["Little Star"] glacier, which they reached on the evening of the nineteenth. The five others—Ivanov, Myslovsky, Galkin, Putrin and Bobrov—made the further traverse of the Peak of the Soviet Army and the East Peak, on the eighteenth and nineteenth, before reaching the Pass of Tchontaren and the Zvezdotchka glacier. On August 20, the entire team reconvened at base camp. In total, the great circular voyage on the Pobeda had lasted fourteen days.

CHAPTER 21

Realized Dreams on Everest

Anatoly Ovtchinnikov, 1984

In 1982, on the first Soviet expedition to Mount Everest, of which Ovtchinnikov was the technical leader, a prospective climber, through negligence, fell into a crevasse on the Khumbu icefall. He was rescued without major injury. The Sports Committee in Moscow, being advised of this, ordered the climbing stopped. However, taking advantage of delayed communications and with the tacit approval of the leaders (Ovtchinnikov and Tamm), the last three climbers went on to the top as planned. Thus, eleven men reached the summit of Everest in five separate ascents, by a new direct route up the immense southwest face of rock and ice, with minimum use of porters and oxygen.[1] It was a major triumph. In this chapter, Ovtchinnikov explains how the expedition's members were selected and physically prepared, which contributed basically to their success. He also describes the actual climbs, with an exceptionally gripping narrative of the ascent by the first pair: Myslovsky, age forty-four, and Balyberdin, who together forced the formidable new route through to the top. Both of these men later became presidents of the Soviet, now Russian, Mountaineering Federation.

Dreams of Everest—the highest peak in the world—came to us from older mountaineers. As early as 1958, a Soviet-Chinese expedition planned to climb Everest the following May by the Mallory-Irvine route from the north, but by March the situation in Tibet was unfavorable. Three Chinese climbers—former members of our combined group—reached the top of Everest in 1959. For a long time after that, our dreams about climbing it were futile.

A Himalayan expedition became possible after 1974 when the international mountaineering camps in the Pamir and elsewhere in the USSR provided the needed financial backing. Leading Soviet climbers then took on the negative attitude of the Sports Committee toward Himalayan expeditions and obtained a positive decision to organize such a project.

We considered that climbing Everest would be a sporting achievement if it contributed to world-class mountaineering. This would require a more difficult route than those previously used. We decided on a route up the southwest face, with continuous, steep, rock climbing from 6,500 meters to 8,500 meters, where it would exit to the west ridge. Inspection of Everest in 1980 convinced us that, with adequate preparation, this route would be feasible for Soviet climbers and would be highly regarded by international mountaineers.

We then had to select and prepare the participants for this physical, technical and moral challenge; provide equipment, clothing, oxygen, radio equipment, food and fuel for extreme oxygen deficiency, low temperatures and powerful winds; and work up a calendar with adequate time for acclimatizing, setting up the route and upper camps and carrying up supplies.

Out of 150 candidates nominated by ten Soviet climbing clubs, preliminary trials in January 1980 picked 39, including 1 woman, for the second round in August 1980 at the international mountaineering camp in the Pamir. Final selections were based on achievements in USSR championships of high-altitude and technical classes; on the number of high-altitude ascents of the highest category of difficulty from 1978 to 1980; on the number of 7,000-meter ascents in 1980 (minimum three); on comparative technical performance in selected rock and ice climbs and exposed grass traverses at 35 degrees of slope between 3,600 to 4,000 meters; and on the number of horizontal-bar pullups a candidate could do. In addition, results of the "Hamburg test" and the testimony of local clubs were taken into account. In the end, 26 candidates were selected, including Ivanov, Ilyinsky, and Myslovsky, who were appointed as group leaders without competition.

Winter and summer outings in 1981 included trials of Himalayan tactics for route preparation, hanging ropes as required for carrying loads and setting up camps at intervals of one day's daylight climb. One would not think such tactics would hinder an ascent, but they can if exhausted climbers reach an upper camp that is not in good shape or if needed supplies are missing or buried under snow. This differs from the situation of a team of climbers that, as is customary for us in the Pamir or Tien Shan, carries everything it needs for a major ascent. The use of Himalayan tactics can help to assure the success of a climb, but with poor organization it can cause friction among the climbers, which has happened more than once on Himalayan expeditions.

It was important to evaluate individual capacities for work above 8,000 meters at low temperatures with varying usage of oxygen or none at all. Participants were tested in the laboratory at the Institute for Biomedical Problems, from which we obtained recommendations on the most effective use of oxygen at different altitudes, up to 2 liters per minute rather than the widely used 4 liters per minute. The efficacy of this was confirmed during the expedition. Other training questions, however, had to be answered from experience obtained during climbs in the Pamir and Tien Shan, where altitudes are significantly below those of the Himalayas. In the period between outings, the candidates trained on individual programs recommended by the expedition trainers under the supervision of their own club trainers.

The experience of our mountaineers under unfavorable weather conditions in the Tien Shan was useful in the Himalayas. As it turned out, the Himalayan bad weather, which causes most foreign climbers to remain in their camps, did not prevent work by our mountaineers. This astonished the Sherpas, who refused to go out in the bad weather of the expedition's first few days.

Our acquaintance with the Sherpas during our reconnaissance on Everest in 1980 had convinced us that most high-altitude porters have insufficient technical ability even on established rock-face routes. This meant that loads to the upper camps would have to be carried by expedition members. Instead of six auxiliary participants, including high-altitude porters for each intended peak climber, which was typical of Himalayan expeditions, our expedition would have only five auxiliary Soviet mountaineers and ten high-altitude porters for twelve climbers of the peak, with the porters carrying only up to Camp 2 at 7,350 meters.

Our plan was to make three acclimatizing ascents to set up the route and upper camps and carry up the loads. These climbs would go up successively to 6,500, 7,500 and 8,500 meters, each followed by rests at base camp for four to six days. We arrived at base camp on March 21. The acclimatizing ascents were completed by Myslovsky's group on April 15, by the Ivanov and Ilyinsky (Valyev) groups on April 19 and by the Onitsenko (Homutov) group on April 24. Medical examinations showed that the climbers had acclimatized normally, except for Tchorny, Shopin, Ilyinsky and Herghiani, whose prospects for a summit climb became doubtful.

However, setting up the route and carrying loads were behind schedule. The route was put up to 8,250 meters, and four upper camps were established, but the higher ones were not fully supplied. Only Camp 2 was supplied with oxygen, but it was also needed at Camp 3; otherwise climbers would have to carry too much weight on their final ascent. The delay was caused by heavy snow and strong winds; by the inability of climbers to carry planned loads of 16 to 18 kilograms before acclimatization; by the high-altitude sickness of Efimov, Ilyinsky, Onitsenko, Tchorny and Shopin, sometimes requiring their early descent; by the low work capacity of the porters; and by loss of several bales of rope, carabiners and pitons en route from Katmandu, so that, instead of carrying up loads, some porters returned to Namche Bazaar to buy the missing supplies.

On the eve of their third ascent, the Homutov group promised to make up for lost time and put the route up to 8,500 meters, setting up a Camp 5 tent there. However, a fall (without injury) by Golodov destroyed their morale, and they did not go above 8,250 meters, where the route and Camp 4 were already set up.

After that, we had to review the program for the expedition. To set up Camp 5 and carry planned loads to the higher camps would now require at least ten more days. This additional work after acclimatization would drain the physical and psychological strength of the climbers and threaten the final ascent. We decided to avoid such a delay.

Our best chance was for Tchorny, Shopin and Hergiani, with Sherpa porters, to climb twice from Camp 2 to Camp 3, bringing up the needed oxygen. Meanwhile, Ivanov's group, which had the largest number in fit condition after their rest below at Thyangboche, would extend the route to 8,500 meters, set up Camp 5 and complete the ascent.

On April 22, without a full rest period, Tchorny, Shopin, Hergiani and the Sherpas started up from base camp. They carried the needed oxygen up to Camp 3, though only two Sherpas got up that high. However, Efimov, speaking for the Ivanov group, said they would not be fully rested until April 25 and could not accept their assignment. The Valyev group also refused, perhaps being weary or feeling that we did not appreciate their work so far, which was not true.

Our last hope was pinned on Myslovsky and Balyberdin, who up to now had not refused any extra work. But for two men to do what the groups of four refused to do would be very hard indeed. We could only rely on their enthusiasm and goodwill for this major task. When they returned from Thyangboche on April 22, they agreed to take it on, only requesting that the departure be delayed by one day. They would have to work at the limit of human capacity and sometimes beyond that. Sherpa Navang, a strong and congenial porter, volunteered to help them carry loads, also hoping to climb the peak.

Myslovsky, at forty-four, was far from his top physical form, but his willpower, assurance and desire for the fabled goal were good companions in this very hard task. As a further handicap, apparently from exhaustion, he lost his rucksack with its vital supplies on the final climb.

Balyberdin had not only enormous motivation to reach the top but also exceptional work capacity even at great heights. The rapid passage of the Khumbu icefall under this year's bad conditions had been due to Balyberdin and Shopin, who were the first to reach Camp 1 and carry loads to Camp 2 and higher. Setting up the route on steep rock up to Camp 4 was also done by Balyberdin during his acclimatization without oxygen, and he put up the route to Camp 5 partly solo. Without disparaging the others, he was clearly the most valuable member of the expedition and deservedly reached the top of Everest first. We were proud that this talented mountaineer, previously little known, had been chosen for the expedition.

On that day, May 4, when Balyberdin and Myslovsky reached the summit, an unfortunate thing happened on the icefall. Before crossing a wide crevasse, Moskaltsov did not check the security of the safety rope piton and didn't attach a carabiner. When he stepped on the ladder, it began to swing and he lost his balance. He grabbed the rope, whose partly melted piton came loose, though it did slow him down. Luckily, after falling 10 to 12 meters, he hit the sloping wall of the crevasse and held on to a ledge. Golodov radioed base camp, and immediately a rescue party went out, headed by the Dr. Orlovsky. Though he was only 400 meters up on the icefall, the transport of the injured man took a whole day.

While doing this, at 14:35, we heard Balyberdin on the radio, saying that he had no higher to go and was apparently on the summit. He was peppered with questions. Could he see the Chinese tripod? How did he feel? Where was Myslovsky? At 15:05, we heard that Myslovsky had also reached the highest point on our planet. After many congratulations, we were still in a guarded mood. Evening was approaching. We hoped that Balyberdin and Myslovsky would recover enough strength to return to Camp 5 and the Ivanov group, which was already there. We, too, had to get back to base camp by daylight and turned off the radio while carrying Moskaltsov down.

Meanwhile, at 17:00, Ivanov sent out Bershov and Turkevitch with oxygen and warm canned fruit to meet Balyberdin and Myslovsky, who were exhausted and coming down very slowly. They met at 21:30. After making sure Balyberdin and Myslovsky could continue on their own, the others hurried on, having obtained permission from expedition leader Tamm to make the climb at night. When I learned of this, I agreed, because the next morning they would have less chance for the climb, having used more oxygen when they went back to Camp 5. At 22:25, Bershov and Turkevich were already on the summit. Such speed at that height by moonlight could be achieved only by outstanding mountaineers. On the descent, they overtook Balyberdin and Myslovsky, and the four got back to Camp 5 at 5:30 A.M.

Sometimes we are asked whether it was too risky to allow the climb by Myslovsky and Balyberdin. It appears to me that risk occurs when a decision is not based on confidence in the reality of completing the undertaking. In this case, we (actually I) were convinced of its reality, through the physical and moral strength of these men, who do not panic when tested severely.

Others also got to the top. Ivanov and Efimov reached the summit at 13:20 on May 5. The Valyev-Hristchaty pair made the climb under unusually bad conditions. Daytime weather on May 7 prevented their ascent, but they climbed that night in hurricane winds up to 40 meters per second [90 mph]. Their hands got stiff from the cold, and their radio froze, cutting them off from base camp. Nevertheless, they reached the top at 1:47 A.M. on May 8 and descended without aid to Camp 5. This was possible only for climbers who were technically and physically excellent, also having the highest morale and willpower.

Ilyinsky reported that Valyev and Hristchaty had frozen hands. At that moment, in front of us stood Myslovsky with frostbitten hands. Ilyinsky and Tcheptchev were also exhausted, and we had no choice but to instruct them to accompany Valyev and Hristchaty the rest of the way down.

It seemed that nothing would hinder the climb by Homutov, Golodov

Ala Archa valley, Kyrghyz Tien Shan, leading up to the Peak of Manas. (*Photograph by N. and N. Shoumatoff.*)

Scythian burial mounds on Kazakh steppe on the route of Genghis Khan's hordes. (*Photograph by N. and N. Shoumatoff.*)

Sher Dar medressa, Samarkand, named for its tigers which were Tamerlane's emblem. (*Photograph by N. and N. Shoumatoff.*)

Uzbek women in Sher Dar medressa, showing loggias used as religious classrooms. (*Photograph by N. and N. Shoumatoff.*)

Uzbek trio on a street in Tashkent. In the foreground is an *arik* irrigation ditch. (*Photograph by N. and N. Shoumatoff.*)

Uzbek men at Shakhi Zinda, Samarkand, leaving a tomb of Tamerlane's family. (*Photograph by N. and N. Shoumatoff.*)

View of steppes from Bolshoi Chimgan. (*Photograph by N. and N. Shoumatoff.*)

Red granite boulders, Bolshoi Chimgan, like those used to build Tashkent. (*Photograph by N. and N. Shoumatoff.*)

Bolshoi Chimgan peak, Uzbek Tien Shan. In the foreground is *Achillea filipendulina*. (*Photograph by N. and N. Shoumatoff.*)

Towering Hissar crags flank Varsob Gorge upstream from junction with Siama River. (*Photograph by N. and N. Shoumatoff.*)

Arid Hissar mountains above Siama River. (*Photograph by N. and N. Shoumatoff.*)

Tajik oasis in Varsob River Gorge. (*Photograph by N. and N. Shoumatoff.*)

Impromptu gymkhana at Ala Archa. (*Photograph by N. and N. Shoumatoff.*)

Herd of horses in Lake Issyk, Kazakhstan, in typical northern Tien Shan landscape. (*Photograph by N. and N. Shoumatoff.*)

Kyrghyz nomad camp on bank of Achik Tash River, Trans-Alai mountains, Pamir. (*Photograph by N. and N. Shoumatoff.*)

Alai Valley hamlet of Darautkurgan, with reception from dwellers of mud brick huts. (*Photograph by N. and N. Shoumatoff.*)

Piraev family setting up Achik-Tash yurt using wood pole frame and felt cover. (*Photograph by N. and N. Shoumatoff.*)

Kyrghyz Abdul Piraev and Uzbek wife Nasiba. (*Photograph by N. and N. Shoumatoff.*)

Abdul Piraev beneath Trans-Alai peaks with his horse and dogs. (*Photograph by N. and N. Shoumatoff.*)

Hawk and edelweiss in Trans-Alai panorama, with immense bird-like shadow on the snows. (*Photograph by N. and N. Shoumatoff.*)

Flags at Achik-Tash international camp, welcoming climbers from fourteen nations. (*Photograph by N. and N. Shoumatoff.*)

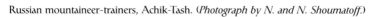

Russian mountaineer-trainers, Achik-Tash. (*Photograph by N. and N. Shoumatoff.*)

The Peak of Communism and one of its climbers, an Austrian in his sixties. *(Photograph by N. and N. Shoumatoff.)*

Peak of Eugenia Korzhenevskaya's southeast buttress with *Ajonia tibetica* flowers. *(Photograph by N. and N. Shoumatoff.)*

Peak of Eugenia Korzhenevskaya's summit, soaring above its forbidding north flanks. (*Photograph by N. and N. Shoumatoff.*)

An avalanche from the Pamir Firn Plateau, coming down its 6,000 foot high north wall. (*Photograph by N. and N. Shoumatoff.*)

The Peak of Moscow and the Fortambek camp, with Peaks of Krupskaya and Shatayeva. (*Photograph by N. and N. Shoumatoff.*)

The Peak of Moscow and the Fortambek Glacier, with protruding medial strip of white ice. (*Photograph by N. and N. Shoumatoff.*)

Moskvin Glacier, Peak of the Four and small glacier from Peak of Korzhenevaskaya. (*Photograph by N. and N. Shoumatoff.*)

Moskvin base camp for Peak of Communism, via north wall of Pamir Firn Plateau, across Walter and Traube Glaciers. (*Photograph by N. and N. Shoumatoff.*)

Nina Shoumatoff and Moskvin ice towers, with a view of the Peter the Great range. (*Photograph by N. Shoumatoff.*)

Walter Glacier below Moskvin base camp with protruding medial white ice towers. (*Photograph by N. and N. Shoumatoff.*)

Five *Colias erate* arriving one by one on sandy shore of Lake Issyk, Kazakhstan. (*Photographs by N. and N. Shoumatoff.*)

A poisonous snake related to the vipers, *Agkistrodon halys*, near Medeo, Kazakhstan. (*Photograph by N. and N. Shoumatoff.*)

and Putchkov. They had everything: oxygen, food, a positive mood and strong performance on the way up. According to plan, they would reach Camp 4 on May 8, Camp 5 on the ninth, and the top only on the tenth. However, a different kind of obstacle arose. Evidently because of Moskaltsov's accident, the Sports Committee radioed the following order via Katmandu: "Discontinue all climbing at whatever stage, and bring all climbers down." This reached us on the eve of May 8. Evgeny Igorevitch [Tamm] asked me what I thought.

To carry out the order seemed impossible to do, though I understood it expressed concern for a successful end to the expedition. I had full confidence in the planned ascent by the Homutov trio, now expecting to reach the summit on May 9. Up to that time I had not been one to force ascents to the summit, but now I had to do the opposite. I replied to Evgeny Igorevitch: "If the group can reach Camp 5 today, May 8, and the summit before noon on May 9, it makes no sense to prevent it. We will have only one contact with Katmandu during the day on May 9, when we can report on the successful completion of the ascent. I am for their going ahead. There is no other way!"

Evgeny Igorevitch agreed, and we so informed Homutov. But the trainer Romanov wanted to obey the Sports Committee's order and proposed a general discussion. It appeared to me that our decision was consistent with the spirit of mountaineering and that all true mountaineers would support it. I was wrong. After a long discussion, Kononov and Voskoboinikov supported us decisively, but Myslovsky, to our disappointment, advised that Homutov's group should give up the summit climb, ostensibly because it had no support from below. His view prevailed, and the decision was made to forbid the ascent. Homutov was informed by radio, but he understood the real viewpoint of the expedition leaders and continued the ascent. He and his group reached the summit at 11:35 A.M. on May 9.

Thus, the ascent of Everest by eleven Soviet climbers, starting May 4, was completed on May 9. A resounding victory! With the exceptionally difficult route, excellent preparation of the climbers and minimal supporting personnel, it was recognized in the foreign press as an outstanding achievement.

We also proved the possibility of climbing Everest without oxygen. Balyberdin used it only while sleeping (.5 liters per minute), and Hristchaty got up to 8,500 meters without oxygen, after which time he used it on the summit ridge in hurricane winds at night. The others used not more than 2 liters per minute while climbing, and .5 liters per minute while asleep.

The expedition members showed high morale, motivation, friendship and a willingness to help their companions even at sacrifice to themselves. As a result, they reached their goal.

CHAPTER 22

Walks in a World of Grandeur and Legend

Nicholas and Nina Shoumatoff

In the northern Pamir, sixteen flags of different nations are flying, their citizens having been invited to climb and walk in the beauty of mountains over 6,000 meters (20,000 ft.), with fields looking like carpets full of flowers and rushing streams. You can feel Asia at every step, and see *yurts* and yaks, mountains and glaciers and, they say, snow leopards, eagles and ibex. We had a wonderful visit with a nomad family in its portable, dome-shaped yurt and actually saw it being put up. It belonged to the Kyrghyz shepherd Abdul Piraev, his Uzbek wife Nasiba and their small sons, Udasha and Alexis. We looked longingly at dozens of beautiful rugs piled against the walls of the yurt, some to sleep on and others for the serving of tea and entertaining. We were greeted with great warmth, and for most of these nomads we were the first Americans they had ever met. This place, known as Achik-Tash, or informally as Edelweiss Valley, had belonged to them and their ancestors for more than a thousand years. They were our real hosts, and the Kyrghyz flag flew over our camp next to the red banner of the USSR.

That was in 1982, a year in which the Soviet Union had organized three international mountaineering camps in the Pamir, near its three 7,000-meter (23,000 ft.) peaks. The main camp was in Edelweiss Valley at 3,800 meters (12,700 ft.), while the other two were among the glaciers across the Trans-Alai in Tajikistan. The fourteen flags of the non-Soviet delegates were lined up in Russian alphabetical order: Austria, Bulgaria, Hungary, East Germany, Spain, Italy, Norway, the United States, France, West Germany, Czechoslovakia, Switzerland, Yugoslavia and Japan, with

183

rows of tents on either side of the line of flags. Among the three hundred people at the three camps were eighty Austrians and sixty Swiss, but we two plus a pair of leading climbers from Virginia, William Garner and Randy Starrett, represented the United States.

Being then well into our sixties, we did not attempt the major ascents but did much walking and climbing on the approaches to the peaks, over glaciers, moraines, snowfields, boulders, screes, meadows, riverbeds, ridges and adjacent valleys, seeking flowers, butterflies, rocks and the grandeur of the mountains. At dusk in Edelweiss Valley, we were often still high above the camp. Deep shade covered the valley, down the middle of which a winding stream reflected the fading light like a fluorescent orange snake. The fire of the setting sun had turned the great peaks crimson against a darkening sky. Deep blue shadows etched the avalanche trails and the wavy contours of the snow-draped slopes. This panorama of the Pamir Mountains, once only a dream, is permanently etched in our minds.

One day, near the camp, we came across a large bird of prey, tethered to a stake. It was an immature hawk of the Central Asian species *Buteo rufinus,* which Oleg Galkin, assistant to chief trainer Anatoly Ovtchinnikov, had found in the valley and was trying to keep alive, even with its own tent, until it could hunt and fend for itself. As we approached the hawk, it was quietly strolling through the edelweiss with a backdrop of soaring snow peaks, which at the moment were partly darkened by a shadow literally in the shape of an immense flying bird. The shadow must have come from one of the wispy clouds hovering close the mountains in an otherwise cloudless sky. But could it have been the shadow of a roc, that enormous bird of Asiatic legend that was believed to carry off elephants? That evening Oleg sadly reported that his "eagle," as he called it, was missing. Next morning, farther up the valley, we found its scattered feathers and bones. It had been eaten by a real eagle or a snow leopard—or a roc.

All of Central Asia is a land of legend. For generations, the Kyrghyz have handed down their greatest treasure orally, a saga of the mountain hero Manas, who rode from peak to peak on a wingless flying horse, punishing all those who attempted to harm his people. In the 1920s, the epic of Manas was finally written down. In the Kyrghyz range of the north Tien Shan, two peaks are named for him. We tried to reach one of them in 1978, during a series of walking trips through the Caucasus and four republics of Central Asia, when we carried the Explorers Club flag no.

179. The Peak of Manas dominates the upper end of the long and lovely valley of Ala Archa, whose outlet overlooks the Great Steppes.

Walking far beyond a climbers' camp, just the two of us alone, we met only one person, a young herdsman who greeted us briefly and hurried on down the valley. Later we learned that we should have done the same, but instead we walked blissfully upward. Coming back, in the middle of a milewide glacial delta, we were horrified to see that a rivulet we had easily crossed in the morning was now a wide raging torrent blocking our way, swollen with snow that had melted in the mountains during the day. By grasping widely spaced willow saplings and holding each other, we crossed without being swept away into the roaring river below, but our legs were lacerated by melon-sized stones carried in the torrent, which clanked against each other loudly. Pilgrimages to the Peak of Manas should not be undertaken casually.

Returning to the lower part of the valley, we visited a Kyrghyz nomad camp and watched four teenaged boys riding bareback, two on each of two horses. At full gallop, they crossed in front of each other in hair-raising encounters, in a wild demonstration of horsemanship that had been in their genes for generations. That year in southeast Kazakhstan at little Lake Issyk, we spent a quiet day with two herds of lovely horses and their foals, which grazed on partly submerged grass while wading in the shallow end of the lake. In that part of the world, these descendants of the wild horses of Tibet are the core of nomadic pastoral life and also the main source of milk. The lake nestled among the slopes of partly wooded mountains, with patches of bare rock that were said to be a favorite haunt of snow leopards. The landscapes were typical of the northern Tien Shan, with seemingly diagonal strips of forest descending the slopes where coniferous trees grew in narrow, shaded ravines. When the shadows of the mountains moved over the lake and signaled the approaching end of the day, the horses waded out of the water and walked toward the exit road, where they waited until the herdsmen came to lead them home.

In 1893, when General Nicholas Avinoff was in command of a brigade of sharpshooters at the Russian headquarters in Tashkent, he had his family with him for two years. Included was his son Andrey Avinoff, who was coauthor Nicholas's uncle. Unlike the Soviets, the prerevolutionary Russians, who had recently conquered Turkestan, respected the ancient Islamic taboos, including those against the consumption of pork and alcohol. To satisfy their craving for pork, they once smuggled in a sedated pig in a darkened carriage, disguised in a general's uniform. On one occasion, when the daughter of the governor-general had been afflicted by a tape-worm and the worm duly emerged after treatment by a specialist who had come all the way from St. Petersburg, an artillery officer celebrated with an excess of smuggled vodka and, deciding that the victory over the worm was an important affair of state, fired off a strictly unauthorized, twenty-one-gun salute. That summer, the heat in Tashkent was so intense that men sat in barrels of water while playing cards at the *tchaikhana* (tea-houses), and the Avinoff family slept in tents at a military encampment at 2,100 meters (7,000 ft.) at Chimgan on a spur of the Tien Shan.

Eighty-five years later, we climbed the north slope of Big Chimgan to 2,700 meters (9,000 ft.) through red granite pinnacles overlooking the pasture where the Avinoff family had camped. Beneath us, on the sweep-ing curve of a snowfield, two summer skiers practiced their maneuvers. At our feet, through a layer of barren gravel, three tulip plants had pushed up their bright yellow flowers. The view opened below us on a wide expanse of rolling hills receding to a far horizon. In the shadow of the mountain, the flowering meadows were green with patches of bare red earth, but on the sun-baked hills beyond the grass had turned brown. With the effect of increasing distance, it progressed in a rich sequence of apparent color changes from sepia to mauve to cerulean blue. Several herdsmen's yurts dotted the distant pastures. From the meadows full of *artemisia* (worm-wood), there was a special pungent smell in the air that for us will be an eternal remembrance of Central Asia.

In 1966, one-third of Tashkent was leveled by a powerful earth-quake, with its epicenter in the middle of the city, directly above the Karzhantau fault. When the newly homeless but undaunted residents were asked where they were going, they would jokingly reply, "To the epicenter." The next day at the local stadium, with intermissions during the aftershocks, the local soccer team defeated the team from Minsk. The center of town was rebuilt with earthquake-resistant structures in tasteful modern versions of the Samarkand style. On a cool summer night, while we walked through the new part of Tashkent with the great mountaineer Vladimir Ratzek, that part of the town was a symphony of pleasing sights and sounds. The gurgling waterfalls, reflecting pools and gushing foun-tains were illuminated in changing colors, all of which was impressive in that arid land.

In Samarkand, at the western tip of the Tien Shan mountain system between the Turkestan and Zerafshan ranges, we walked as in a dream for two glorious days in that legendary city. In the evening, while dining on a tenth-floor roof, we saw all the famous domes from Tamerlane's time—those at the great universities of the Registan, at the tomb of Muhammad's cousin Shakhi Zinda and at the Gur Emir, which contained Tamerlane's tomb between those of his astronomer-grandson Ulugh Beg and his spiritual tutor Mir Sayed Barak. The domes were encrusted with tiles of Tamerlane's favorite turquoise and lapis lazuli, which reminded him of the blue of the rivers, the blue of the glaciers and the blue of the sky. In the glow of the setting sun, Samarkand in its stupendous entirety was spread out before us, between the two chains of golden-red mountains. Its past and present became a reality for us before receding into memory like a mirage of the mind.

Bibi Khanym, who was Tamerlane's favorite wife, had built a dome in the great mosque of Samarkand while her husband was off on a conquering expedition in India. Meanwhile, she was also having an affair with the young Persian architect. When Tamerlane returned, he did not believe the rumors of her infidelity until he stumbled upon fateful evidence: a secret room in the mosque fitted with cushions and a table on which there were two glasses half full of red wine. In one version of the legend, Tamerlane, in spite of his lameness, chased the architect to the top of the structure and was about to decapitate him with a sword when the young man simply spread his arms and soared off into space, never to be seen again. Bibi Khanym, it is said, was entombed in a wall of the mosque. Tamerlane had foretold that if his own tomb should ever be opened it would bring on a terrible catastrophe. When the Soviet archaeologist Michael Gerasimov did so, he found the tall skeleton of Tamerlane in the fragments of a shroud of his favorite blue, with one leg shorter than the other and his large, thin head facing Mecca. Gerasimov then learned that on that very day—June 22, 1941—the German armies had unexpectedly invaded Russia.

Before a walk up the beautiful Siama River valley in the arid Hissar Mountains of western Tajikistan, we visited a botanical station beside a unique primeval grove of huge wild apple trees, where we sampled the cool shade of trails that were said to be infested with cobras. This interaction between trees and snakes suggested that "garden eastward in Eden" with "the tree of life also in the midst of the garden and the tree of knowledge of good and evil" (Gen. 2:8). The fruit of both trees provided divinely classified information, which was forbidden to ordinary mortals like ourselves. We found the apples to be tasty, but, being already afflicted with Original Sin and fully clothed, we suffered no ill effects. Afterward, during lunch with the prominent botanists Akram Ahmedovitch Ashurov and Anatoly Konnov, we nibbled on large wafers of Arab bread. It was lubricated with a rich red wine named "Omar Khayyam" after the poet of twelfth-century Nishapur, the capital of eastern Persia, whose domain at that time included the place where we sat. He wrote much about the futility of life, not forgetting the snake:

> O Thou, who Man of baser Earth didst make,
> And who with Eden didst devise the Snake,
> For all the Sin wherewith the Face of Man
> Is blacken'd, Man's Forgiveness give—and take.

Mostly, however, he wrote about love and wine, especially the latter, and his best-known quatrain seemed most appropriate to the moment:

> Here with a Loaf of Bread beneath the Bough,
> A Flask of Wine, a Book of Verse—and Thou,
> Beside me singing in the Wilderness—
> And Wilderness is Paradise enow.

In our walks throughout Central Asia, we were always under its spell, but nowhere more so than in the Pamir. A helicopter of the military type brought us from Edelweiss Valley to the two higher base camps in Tajikistan, 120 kilometers (75 mi.) farther west. For mile after mile, we flew about halfway up the north slopes of the snow peaks and across many lateral upper valleys, each dotted with the yurts of nomadic herdsmen nestled among rocky outcrops in varying shades of red, ochre and green. At the high pasture of Altyn Mazar, we flew through a break in the Trans-Alai, the towering northern front range of the Pamir. This brought us to the so-called Mazarsky Alps, from whose 6,300-meter (20,700 ft.) summit a nearly vertical wall, one of the great north faces of the world, plunges 4,000 meters (13,000 ft.) to the torrential Muksu River draining the vast Fedchenko glacier, which is 77 kilometers (48 mi.) long. This was our entrance into the icy heart of the Pamir, a region not frequented by the nomads since neither they not their flocks could cope with the Muksu River.

We stayed several days at the Moskvin glacier camp at 4,500 meters (15,000 ft.), beneath the Peak of Eugenia Korzhenevskaya and facing the Range of Peter the Great below the 7,495-meter (24,590 ft.) Peak of

Communism, the Soviets' highest. We walked up the glacier to 5,100 meters (17,000 ft.), and, after we descended, we crossed the moraine to a large, round tent about a mile from our camp. It was the shelter of a group of Russian soldiers on vacation—eleven men and one woman, all from Leningrad and all of them attractive. We accepted the offer of their commanding officer, Col. Lukyanov, to join them for a drink of cognac, which they poured from a metal flask. During banter back and forth, with numerous personal questions, it turned out that they all knew the name, Elaghin, of coauthor Nina's mother, it being the name of the large island in St. Petersburg that contains the Elaghin Palace built by Catherine the Great and the city's main stadium, and also being the name of Natasha's uncle in the wolf hunt in *War and Peace*. Afterward, the colonel accompanied us on our walk, during which, with a sweep of his hand toward the soaring peaks, he said, "This is a Godly place." We were startled by this remark from a Red Army officer presumably well versed in Soviet atheism. This hidden, hard-to-reach cirque among the glaciers was unknown to the nomads and not included in their legends, but it was an immense cathedral in which we felt the presence of God, and we thanked Him for the grandeur we had seen.

CHAPTER 23

The Spell of the Mountain World

Nicholas and Nina Shoumatoff

For many who live or travel among the mountains of Central Asia, the frontiers between the natural and the numinous domains often seem to overlap or even vanish. Reactions to such phenomena vary from credulity or skepticism through curiosity and amusement to wonder, reverence and awe.

One of the solid skeptics was the indomitable New Englander Fanny Bullock Workman, fellow of the Royal Geographical Society and honorary member of the American Alpine Club and numerous other prestigious geographical and mountaineering organizations. On her last expedition with her husband to the immense Karakoram "ice wilds," she noted (Workman and Workman 1917) that their Muslim porters wore "magic amulets, hanging by bits of cord from the coolies' necks. They were said to contain petitions to the gods to bring storms or other calamities, that might limit our stay in the snows" (126). Wryly, she remarked: "Whatever the more erudite mullahs may know of the tenets of the Prophet, or however much they may bow in the direction of Mecca, in no way interferes with their exercise of priestcraft in fostering belief in the power of magic and gods in the simple minds of the villagers" (127), especially those to whom glaciers are even more terrifying than mountain storms.

The Parisienne Alexandra David-Neel, who devoutly practiced and studied Buddhism but disdained its shamanistic aberrations, and who walked 2,000 forbidden miles to Lhasa disguised as a pilgrim, observed a curious ritual during that remarkable journey (1927): "The Tibetans believe that certain lamas, expert in magic, have the power to transfer upon the head of the willing victim all the spiritual failings, all the moral and religious transgressions of the people, to which is attributed the anger of

190

the divinities made manifest by destructive rebellions, epidemics and other calamities. Thus, each year, a man called Lud Kong kyi Gyalpo is, in the course of a special rite, blamed for all the iniquities of the sovereign and his subjects, and chased into the sands of Samyé" (313). Omar Khayyam even ascribed to God himself some of the blame for the sins of mankind (see chap. 22).

Heinrich Harrer, after his years among the Tibetans (see chap. 5), concluded that they "do not recognize any physical explanation—for them all is magic and spells and the sport of the gods. Our behavior, which remained uninfluenced by any of their superstitions, must have given the Tibetans something to think about. We used to go by night into the forests without being molested by demons; we climbed mountains without lighting sacrificial fires, and still nothing happened to us. I think they must have credited us with supernatural powers." However, he assimilated important practical benefits from the Tibetan faith: "Though I learned, while in Asia, how to meditate, the final answer to the riddle of life has not been vouchsafed to me. But I have at least learned to contemplate the events of life with tranquility and not let myself be flung to and fro by circumstances in a world of doubt."

Lama Anagarika Govinda (a German) disliked mountaineering because of his Buddhist respect for mountains: "While the modern man is driven by ambition and the glorification of his own ego to climb an outstanding mountain and to be the first on top of it, the devotee is more interested in his spiritual uplift than in the physical feat of climbing. To him the mountain is a divine symbol, and as little as he would put his foot upon a sacred image, so little would he dare to put his foot on the summit of a sacred mountain" (1970, 197). Some modern mountaineers have respected such feelings. When George Band and Joe Brown made the first ascent of Kanchenjunga, the world's third-highest mountain, in 1955, they stopped a few feet below its summit, as they had promised the maharajah of Sikkim, and later climbers did the same.

Significantly, Lama Govinda (1970) chose the physical milieu in describing the power of a major peak—the sacred Mount Kailas of Tibet's Trans-Himalaya.

> To see the greatness of a mountain, one must keep one's distance; to understand its form, one must move around it; to experience its moods, one must see it at sunrise and sunset, at noon and at midnight, in sun and in rain, in summer and in winter and in all other

seasons. He who can see the mountain like this comes near to the life of the mountain, a life that is as intense and varied as that of a human being. Mountains grow and decay, they breathe and pulsate with life. They attract and collect invisible energies from their surroundings; the forces of air, of the water, of electricity and magnetism; they create winds, clouds, thunderstorms, rains, waterfalls and rivers. They fill their surroundings with active life and give shelter and food to innumerable beings. Such is the greatness of mighty mountains. (198)

The great mountaineer George Leigh-Mallory wanted to reach the world's highest summit "because it is there." But, with inhibitions like those of Lama Govinda, Leigh-Mallory wrote: "Mount Everest, therefore, apart from its pre-eminence in bulk and height, is great and beautiful, marvelously built, majestic, terrible, a mountain made for reverence; and beneath its shining sides one must stand in awe and wonder . . . how can I help rejoicing in the yet undimmed splendour, the undiminished glory, the unconquered supremacy of Mount Everest? . . . Surely Chomolungmo should remain inviolate" (1923, 126, 124, 123).

For others, mountaineering has a more positive spiritual impact. When Mallory and Andrew Irvine vanished in a cloud near the summit of Everest in 1924, the last person to see them alive was Noel Odell. That evening, alone at Camp 5, before his solo climb the next day beyond Camp 6 in a vain attempt to find them, he had an almost mystical experience of the sunset in the mountain panorama, as described by Younghusband: "Odell had climbed many peaks alone, and witnessed sunsets from not a few, but this, he says, was the crowning experience of all. We may well believe it. He was in the very midst of the most awe-inspiring region on this earth. He was in the near presence of God. Revealed to him now were the might and majesty, and the purity, the calm, and the sublimity of the Great World-Spirit" (1926, 282).

Saint Paul reported that on the hill of Mars in Athens, "I found an altar with this inscription, To the Unknown God" (Acts 17:23). Wilfrid Noyce alludes to this in the title of his book, *To the Unknown Mountain* (1962), about the first ascent of Trivor (7,733 m, 25,370 ft.) in the Karakorams near Hunza. In his final paragraph, he wrote: "The mountain remains unknown as before. But perhaps those who climbed it know themselves a little better, for the climbing."

Edwin Bernbaum (1988), a scholar of the world's sacred mountains who climbed the perilous Ama Dablam, likewise found that mountaineering can yield a personal insight.

> Despite the hardship and suffering, even the fear encountered in mountains, people return to them again and again, seeking something they cannot put into words. . . . Climbers knowingly risk their lives for the sense of exultation they get in climbing a high and dangerous peak—or just being in its presence . . . a reality that has the power to transform our lives. (12)

Most westerners look to Tibet as the ultimate land of mystery, but the Tibetans themselves look for that elsewhere. As Bernbaum wrote in *The Way to Shambala* (1980), this mythical kingdom, lying somewhere beyond the great Kun Lun range, was thought to be the home of the powerful Lord of the World, who at the proper time will defeat the forces of evil in a great battle and establish a golden age of peace. Ossendowski (1922) describes it from a Mongol Buddhist viewpoint, with lurid details reminiscent of the Apocalypse of Saint John.

Bernbaum (1980) also gives an account of his search for the valley of Khembalung, which was perhaps the original Shangri-La of James Hilton's *Lost Horizon* (1933). In local tradition, it is one of several hidden valleys that Padma Sambhava had prepared for Tibetans as a refuge from external attack, but one had to have the right karma to find it, see its treasures and return alive. Bernbaum heard from a lama and a local woman that Khembalung was surrounded by sheer snow mountains, its entrance guarded by a giant snake. It was ruled by a majestic king whose palace had smoke rising from a chimney and who possessed a treasure of innumerable diamonds in the heart of a lovely valley where one could hear the singing of beautiful voices and drink from a magical spring with aphrodisiac powers.

Accompanied by his wife, Bernbaum (1980) found and described Khembalung in a remote region between Ama Dablam and Lhotse.

> Thousands of feet up a wall of granite dripping with glaciers, a band of metamorphic rock twisted into the shape of a cobra with its head drawn back ready to strike. . . . We descended in mist to the valley floor and camped in a meadow beside a quiet stream. . . . We heard the clear voices of birds singing to one another and saw golden mist

rising like smoke off the treetops. . . . In the woods around us, drops of bluish water gleamed like diamonds on necklaces of hanging moss . . . [and] we glimpsed and felt the presence of a majestic snow peak that seemed to rule over the valley. . . . When we came to a glade with a spring welling out of the base of a mossy rock, I knelt to drink the water out of my hands, and felt the peace and beauty of the valley flow into my body. (58ff)

Thus, the Bernbaums found the legendary signs and treasures of Khembalung, or Shangri-La, which were no less magical for being the work of nature in a place that was never inhabited by man. After drinking from the enchanted spring, they produced their first child.

In his description of Shangri-La, James Hilton (1933) mentioned its "gradual revelation of elegance . . . touched by the mystery which lies at the core of all loveliness" and its "vast encircling massif" whose "superb and exquisite peril . . . could only enhance the total loveliness of the present" while "avoiding excess of all kinds—even of virtue itself" (94, 101, 107, 74). In this sophisticated version of the Central Asian myth, as in Bernbaum's experience of it, the humor is subtle. One is tempted to express it in the idiom of Lao Tse, that the way to Shangri-La "is not the way that can be told."

In the real world of the Tibetans, on the other hand, humor is more earthy and explicit, as underscored by Baker (1993) and Schulteis (1991): "This lightness of heart permeates the Tibetan attitude toward Buddhism itself. They are people of deep and abiding religious faith—during the Chinese invasion, hundreds died refusing to renounce Buddhism—but at the same time they can laugh about it. Humorous folk tales about lecherous, dishonest and fraudulent lamas abound, and respect for spiritual leaders and tenets is tempered with jocularity." At Lamayuru (see chap. 2), Avinoff observed that this was so even when it verged on the macabre: "Strange looking masks of fantastic birds, skulls and infernal beings, festooned with beads fashioned out of human bones, seemed to provide for our obliging hosts a source of undisguised and contagious merriment." But this did not obscure his appropriate sense of reverence: "I am inclined equally to treasure the calligraphic refinement of a court painter of Shah Tahmasp or Shah Jehan, or the devout pictorial prayer of a nameless monk in a forgotten monastery."

The marvelously human fourteenth Dalai Lama, who has written profoundly about the sacred foundations of his Buddhist faith (1984), also clearly loves the amusing side of its Tibetan traditions (1990): "Of all the festivals, the one that I most enjoyed was the week-long opera festival. . . . People dedicated themselves to having fun—something that Tibetans are naturally good at. . . . Even a few members of the monastic community joined in, though illegally and therefore in disguise. It was such a happy time! . . . The only time you could be sure of everyone's complete attention was when satires were performed. Then the actors appeared dressed as monks and nuns, high officials and even the state oracles to lampoon public figures" (46ff). He also wrote: "Since we human beings come from Nature, there is no point in our going against Nature, which is why I say the environment is not a matter of religion or ethics or morality. These are luxuries, since we can survive without them. But we will not survive if we continue to go against Nature . . . we need to cultivate a universal responsibility for one another and for the planet we share" (1990, 269).

Omar Khayyam, the astronomer, perhaps shared this planetary view when he wrote that "wilderness is paradise enow." If so, we would now call it environmentalism. For us, as for him, however, this line meant something more immediate than a global abstraction in its context of "a book of verse and thou, beside me singing in the wilderness." Our book of verse was with us throughout Central Asia and inspired us often. At a fairly large, often frozen pond on the Pamir's Moskvin glacial moraine, we recalled a phrase of Rupert Brooke: "There are waters blown by changing winds to laughter . . . and after, frost, with a gesture, stays the waves that dance" (1943, 104). This mentions laughter but is too exquisite to be a kind of humor. Its message is the same frailty of life that pervades the *Rubaiyat*.

In another part of the Himalayas, John Clark (see chap. 6) tells of a climb with one of his Ismaili students: "Together we crept out on the rim of a great mountain buttress, like flies on the shoulder of God. We rounded a curve, and there suddenly was the whole sweep of the Hunza Valley, tiny below us, and the great rock peaks above. Sherin Beg sat down. 'What are you doing?' I asked. 'Looking at my mountains,' he murmured. He showed me then the meaning of worship, which is a quietly deep emotion that our bustling analytical minds must relearn."

In his book *On the Pamir* (1975), Okmir Agakhanyantz departs from his usual, slightly sardonic tone in describing how, when he first saw that region, he "understood that everything else had been a mere prelude" and how it left him "breathless, literally and figuratively—from the altitude and from being enraptured by its beauty. In time the height became habitual, but the spiritual jolt remained forever. Literally everything was astounding: the grandiose structure of the mountains, the combination of great height and monstrous dryness, the pastel tones of the landscapes, the madly changing altitudes in the Western Pamir, the insane cascades of the rivers, the glaciers hanging above the deserts, the blue and purple sky, the slopes of fallen boulders, the vegetation unlike anything seen before, with no room for forests or meadows on the mountain slopes. From all this something inside was torn apart and sang. . . . Then the memory was filled with something new, which suddenly appeared around a turn in the road" (12). The enigmatic touch at the end is typical of Agakhanyantz, relieving the emotion of his paean to the Pamir.

Within our own Asian experience, the grandeur of the Pamir's icy wilds is the apex of both physical and spiritual altitude, while Samarakand is the ultimate in human aesthetic achievement; and beyond that the entire mountain world of Central Asia is, for us, an immense numinous shrine to its creator. After we had camped high on the Roof of the World, coauthor Nina wrote in her notebook: "In spite of very high altitude, one feels the peace born of the faith of Buddhists, Christians and Mohammedans whose feet have walked for centuries on these pastures and mountains. How many millions of eyes have looked up, always up, not down, at the highest mountains on earth, searching for many things, perhaps the most important, to find themselves. . . . In all this beauty was the spell of Asia, which will remain with us and in us forever."

Notes

Chapter 2

1. After leaving the university, Avinoff served as assistant secretary general of the Senate (Supreme Court) at St. Petersburg, as gentleman-in-waiting and member of the Department of Ceremonies at the Imperial Court and as marshall of nobility and district judge in the province of Poltava. In 1915, and again in 1917, he was sent to the United States by the All-Russian Zemsky Union, a council of local self-governing bodies. In 1919, he attended the peace conference at Versailles and witnessed how the "tiger" Clemenceau, in an argument with President Wilson, shook him by the neck. In 1924, Avinoff joined the Carnegie Museum in Pittsburgh, Pennsylvania, as assistant curator of entomology, and two years later he was appointed its director. In that capacity, he was elected twice as chairman of the International Committee on Museums of Science under the League of Nations in Geneva. When he retired as director emeritus in 1945, he was vice president of the American Association of Museums and was made a trustee of the American Museum of Natural History in New York.

2. On his Pamir expedition in 1908, Avinoff crossed the 15,275-foot (4656 m) Ak-baital (White Mare) Pass and reached the high encampment of Kyrghyz nomads at Subaty on a westward extension of the Tibetan Plateau. His major interest in lepidoptera was in their "distribution in Central Asia where . . . the Tibetan fauna wedges into the typical Turkestan faunistic region, forming an irregular indented line which had to be carefully investigated" (Shoumatoff 1995). An important early result of this work was his discovery "that two races of one and the same species can exist side by side as . . . diametrically opposite variations, linked by uninterrupted transitions at other locations, but flying together without merging like two independent species. . . . Such species in the process of formation are observed in just those that develop a large number of geographical races, in which their adaptation to surrounding conditions has not yet been concluded" (Avinoff 1912; see also Avinoff 1928, and Avinoff and Sweadner 1951). The evolution-

197

ist Ernst Mayr (1942) stressed this "overlap of terminal links of the same species. The perfect demonstration of speciation" (180). In 1978, a bronze tablet in memory of Avinoff was mounted at the high altitude research station of the eastern Pamir, where he traveled in 1908. A prolific artist, Avinoff was a master of traditional, modern and original styles. John Walker, director of the National Gallery in Washington, pronounced him to be "the finest flower painter of this century" (Alberts 1986, 233). His paintings and drawings of landscapes, portraits and fantasies, including those of Central Asia, have been reproduced and exhibited widely (Lewis 1953). He was also a professor of the history of art at the University of Pittsburgh.

Avinoff's friend, the entomologist Walter Rothschild (the founder of the Tring Museum and the "Dear Lord Rothschild" of the Balfour Declaration supporting the future state of Israel) had a celebrated collection of fleas featuring individual magnifying glasses for each specimen. When he heard that Avinoff was going to Western Tibet, he asked him to capture a certain kind of mouse from which fleas had never been collected and which therefore might yield a new species. Avinoff did capture such a mouse and tried to collect its fleas according to detailed instructions from the great entomologist Dr. Karl Jordan, director of Tring. To the great disappointment of Rothschild, Jordan and Avinoff, that particular mouse did not have a single flea. Later, in 1928, when Jordan visited Pittsburgh, Avinoff took him to the posh fox-hunting Rolling Rock Club, which Jordan pronounced to be one of the greatest flea-collecting places he had ever found.

3. Experience with foreigners at the Russian Imperial Court, combined with a sure instinct and quick wit, enabled Avinoff to meet an extraordinary challenge of "Chinese ceremony" in Central Asia during his 1912 expedition (Hellman 1948).

> At a sixty-course banquet given in his honor by the governor general of Kashgar, a district of Chinese Turkestan, he asked his host for permission to take a picture of him and was surprised, but not stymied, when the governor replied, "I am afraid I am so ugly that the lens of your camera will crack." "On the contrary, your Excellency," said Avinoff, "I shall make a thousand copies and paste them all over my room." The governor beamed and asked how old he was. Dr. Avinoff knew that the Chinese regard age as a virtue. "A sparrow like myself is in his teens," he replied, "but you must be well over a hundred." The governor blushed with pleasure. "My head may be bald, but it is completely empty," he said. "Nothing of the sort," Dr. Avinoff assured him, "It is only transparent, like a beautiful crystal." The governor, realizing that he was dealing with a man of parts, presented Dr. Avinoff with a document investing him with the rank of a mandarin, third class, and this facilitated his penetrating regions of Chinese Turkestan where the natives are highly suspicious of foreigners.

Chapter 3

1. We quote from Birnbaum 1946: "While Europe was on fire, he [Iacovleff] had crossed Mongolia on horseback. . . . The Chinese critics declared that the drawings and paintings of the then thirty-year-old Russian were the first pictures by a European which interpreted their race with acute understanding, and were worthy of comparison with works by native masters" (5, 8).

2. After "La Croisière Noire," the expedition from Algiers to Mozambique in 1924, Iacovleff's heroic-size portraits of native men and women caused a "*furore*" of African styles in the world of Parisian fashion and "the phenomenal popularity of American Negresses, dancers both of them, Josephine Baker and Florence Mills" (Whitney 1935).

3. Because the USSR refused to allow passage north of the Hindu Kush, the first set of vehicles had to be left at Srinagar, but two of them crossed the Himalayas to Gilgit and one went on for 207 miles where no wheels had ever been before. After a pleasant visit with the mir of Hunza at Baltit, the group crossed the Karakoram into the Chinese Pamir, inhabited by Kyrghyz: "At Beyik, we were met by Iacovleff, Sivel and our caravan of [sixty] fine-looking camels and [eighty] ponies from Kashgar" (Williams 1932a). In October, at Urumchi, the capital of Sinkiang, they made contact with a second set of vehicles that had come from Peking, but there and at Suchow they were detained for agonizing winter weeks by local Chinese commanders who were at war with each other and who coveted the expedition's supplies and even its vehicles. After complex negotiations materially assisted by Iacovleff's pastel of the local ruler (Birnbaum 1946), they escaped across the Takla Makan and Gobi Deserts and arrived in triumph at Peking and Tientsin (Haardt 1931; Williams 1931, 1932a, 1932b).

4. We became acquainted with Iacovleff separately: in Paris in the 1920s and Boston in the 1930s. In 1937, he left his teaching post at the Museum School in Boston and returned to Paris to develop a more daring approach to his art. One year later, when this effort was in full bloom, he died from an attack of cancer. His close friend and ours, the American sculptress Malvina Hofmann (1965) tells that three days after his death she received a letter from him at her studio in New York in which he wrote: "My wings will carry me to higher mountains than I have been able to reach before. It is wonderful to feel this new power and happiness in my work" (206). She was in Peking at the time of the Trans-Asia Expedition and waited there to meet two of her friends who were among its members, Iacovleff and the paleontologist F. Pierre Teilhard de Chardin. Because there was neither word from the long-delayed expedition nor any idea of its whereabouts, she had to leave to continue her great work on the Hall of Man for the Field Museum in Chicago.

Chapter 4

1. When Murray returned to the United States after his Kyrghyz summer, he enrolled at the State University of Iowa Medical School where he earned his M.D. degree in 1938. Thereafter he served in various capacities at the Montreal General Hospital, in the U.S. Army Medical Corps during World War II, and in the Johns Hopkins School of Public Health and the Harvard School of Public Health, also teaching internal medicine at the Harvard Medical School. He became a specialist in research on infectious diseases, mainly those of China, Siberia and Central Asia, to which he made repeated trips to obtain specimens for analysis. The Russian language became increasingly useful to him, so that while at Johns Hopkins he took lessons in it from coauthor Nina's mother, Mrs. N. M. Adamovitch, who was a teacher at the Bryn Mawr School. Through this connection, we developed a close friendship with him, in the course of which he visited our home at Bedford, New York, several times. In 1947, his mother, Janette, née Stevenson, who was a resident of Cedar Rapids, was named "Mother of the Year" in recognition of her two outstanding sons.

Chapter 5

1. The fourteenth Dalai Lama wrote (1990, 196): "In 1973 I made my first trip to Europe. It was especially good to see Heinrich Harrer once more. He was his usual jovial self, and his sense of humour was as earthy as ever." He further wrote (1992, 17): "Now, as we both grow older, we remember the happy days we spent together in a happy country. It is a sign of genuine friendship that it doesn't change, come what may. . . . Harrer has always been such a friend to Tibet. . . . Still today, he is active in the struggle for Tibetan people's freedom and rights, and we are grateful to him for it." After returning from Tibet, Harrer extended his mountaineering exploration with ten major first ascents: one in Peru (1953), two in Alaska (1954) and seven in New Guinea (1962) (Neate 1978). In 1969, he received us kindly at what was then his home in Kitzbuhel, Austria, and showed us his impressive Tibetan library. He had just come down from his daily workout of cragsmanship on the Wilde Kaiser wall, which dominated the view from his house. Two years earlier, he had inspected the large Tibetan and Central Asian library at our home in Bedford, New York, where he was pleased to see major works by men he especially admired: Charles Bell and Sven Hedin. All three of our children— Nicholas, Alexander and Antonia—have met Harrer at various times. In 1991, Harrer was awarded the Explorers Club Medal and attended the congressional ceremony at the Capitol Rotunda in Washington for the Dalai Lama, who had received the Nobel peace prize.

Chapter 6

1. When Clark appealed to the U.S. State Department for assistance in establishing a demonstration project in Central Asia, he was informed that the State Department consults civilians only on its own initiative and, besides, the department was interested in large, expensive projects only. He then organized the Central Asiatic Research Foundation with private donations. He returned to Sinkiang in 1948, hoping to work with the Kyrghyz, but the Chinese situation was unfavorable and he retreated to Pakistan, where the newly independent government was more receptive. He then visited eight mountain tribes and chose Hunza as the most suitable place for his experiment. From this scouting trip, Clark returned to the United States to raise more money. We helped by arranging a successful fundraising lecture for him at Bedford Hills, New York, and became closely acquainted with him. U.S. Supreme Court Justice William O. Douglas also visited Hunza and wrote of Clark's work there (1952, 312): "He spoke the language of the people and lived with them as they lived. He became part of the community life. He developed craft schools . . . specialized in the crafts they already knew—wood carving, leathercraft, weaving and spinning. He taught them how to make waterwheels that generate power . . . convinced that a hundred-dollar project at the village level is worth more than a million-dollar project that tries to bring a new civilization." Afterward, Clark worked for many years, until his retirement, at the Field Museum in Chicago, specializing in the geology of the Dakotas.

Chapter 7

1. We first learned of Ratzek's legendary reputation among Soviet mountaineers during a visit to their oldest climbers' camp, at Tsey in the North Caucasus in 1978. That year in Tashkent, after we presented a letter from his close friend Dr. Agakhanyantz, Ratzek gave us a memorable evening tour on foot through the tastefully rebuilt center of the city, which had been annihilated by an earthquake in 1966. Of all the master explorers of Central Asia whom we knew, Ratzek was the only one who lived there all his life except for a few childhood years.

Chapter 8

1. In 1955, a Kazakh and an Uzbek group competed to climb Pik Pobedy. They were caught in a violent blizzard near the top in which eleven Kazakhs perished and fourteen Uzbeks were swept away in an avalanche. As the leader of the Uzbeks, and in the absence of witnesses, Ratzek was blamed for the disaster instead of the politicians who had ordered the race on one of the world's most murderous mountains. He was stripped of all his mountaineering titles, which was

the extreme punishment for a sportsman. Undaunted, though no longer a young-ster, he started all over from the bottom and worked his way up through the five stages of achievement until he regained his title of distinguished master of sport, probably the only person who ever did it twice. Publicly, the government covered up the disaster with almost ludicrous lies because its officials were ashamed or afraid to admit that such an accident had happened. However, in 1989, the Kazakh newspaper in Alma Ata reported that a small notebook had been found frozen in the ice near the top of Pik Pobedy, which proved to be the diary of a climber who had perished there during the ill-fated expedition of 1955. It docu-mented Ratzek's heroic role in the accident, unfortunately after his death in 1980. Throughout his life, Ratzek continued to study the beguiling mountain citadel of the central Tien Shan and to report his findings in scientific and popular media. His writings include the story of a lake that rises each summer from the meltwater on the surface of the Inylchek glacier until it breaks through its ice barrier with a roar and ceases to exist for the balance of its annual cycle (Ratzek 1984) and his analysis of lumpy streaks of "firlike" snow on the slopes of the Tengri Tag, which he explained in terms of warm air coming through the passes from the Takla Makan Desert in China (Ratzek 1976). The only other place where we have identified similar snow formations is on a photo of Lhotse, adjacent to Everest (Bishop 1962).

Chapter 9

1. As reported to us by Okmir Agakhanyantz: In 1964, Ratzek was in com-mand of a group of climbers on the Peak of Garmo in the Pamir and was in contact with them by radio from base camp, when they ran into bad weather about 90 percent of the way up, with some 500 meters of a wall left to climb. He proposed that they come down, but they pleaded with him for permission to wait out the bad weather. Knowing how they felt, he allowed them to stay suspended on the wall, provided it cleared up within two days. It actually cleared within twenty-four hours, and the group completed the climb. This was a courageous decision on Ratzek's part, with his career on the line after the tragedy on Victory Peak (see chap. 8), but it showed how, as a true leader, he took responsibility (a risky thing to do in the USSR) after a considered judgment in the spirit of mountaineering.

2. Also from Agakhanyantz: "In 1970, at the University of Moscow, Vladimir defended his dissertation on 'Distinctive Characteristics of the Orography and Glaciation of the High Mountain Zones of Central Asia,' and was awarded the academic degree of Master of Geographical Sciences. I attended that defense, which was tempestuous with polemics, but his defense was unanimously accepted. Nearly all of his hypotheses were afterward confirmed. However, in 1978 all of the Pamir was excitedly following the outcome of a famous wager between Ratzek and Professor L. Dolgushin, a glaciologist. Ratzek maintained that after the surge

of the Medvezhy ("Bear") glacier in 1968 it would remain calm for fifty years, while Dolgushin predicted that it would surge again in 1978, which it did. Ratzek lost. The wager consisted of a case of cognac (twenty bottles). He bought a case of the best Armenian cognac and brought it by air to the Glaciology Department of the Institute of Geography in Moscow, where there was a wild party to celebrate the wager. Ratzek acknowledged Dolgushin as the winner, and the entire case was consumed by the glaciologists with great gusto."

Chapter 10

1. Through his fieldwork, Agakhanyantz became the author of the following official geobotanical maps for the Pamir: Bartang (1955 and 1961), Shugnan (1956–57), Sarez (1957), Western Pamir (1958), Yazgulem (1958–59), Shakhdara (1960), Kara-Kul (1964) and Tokhtamysh (1966–67). He has, indeed, authored more than two hundred publications in four languages: educational texts, popular books and scientific monographs, including the Eurasian volume of a German treatise on the ecology of the world (1994). Demonstrating his personal brand of wit and drama, he also wrote of a close encounter alone with a snow leopard at the top of a glaciated ridge and of three dangerous days without food or water on an intensely hot, arid plateau (1987).

In the snow leopard incident, in the course of his West Pamir botanical survey, Agakhanyantz scrambled up the steep slope of a ridge and sat down for a rest on a patch of snow, where his altimeter read 5,400 meters. There he began to feel strangely uncomfortable, possibly from the altitude. Soon, it was time to go back down. He stood up, looked around, and froze. About ten meters away, a snow leopard—a female—was crouched at the top of the ridge and looking at him intently. Her long tail was curling and uncurling while slowly moving from side to side. Carefully and without losing eye-contact, he picked up his ice-ax, his only weapon. After some hesitation, he stamped his foot for a firmer stance in the precarious snow, then resolutely pointed the tip of the ax at the leopard. Only then he noticed that something had happened. She had simply and silently vanished, as though she had never been there. Looking down the slope, he caught a fleeting glimpse of her spotted gray shape disappearing around some rocks. He lost no time going down the less steep side of the ridge. There he saw the remains of a mountain goat that had evidently been the leopard's most recent meal. This explained why she had not attacked him, since she was not hungry. In his haste, he forgot his camera at the top. The next day, one of the village men, armed with a rifle, climbed up and retrieved the camera, where he saw the leopard's tracks in the snow (Agakhanyantz 1987, 76).

2. Using computerized and genetic concepts applied to botanical survey data, Agakhanyantz developed two theoretical models of florogenesis, that is, the origins of plant species. The first one is for isolated mountains in the process of uplift,

whose vegetation is being raised to higher altitudes where it must adapt to more severe environments, thus forming belts of different plant types at varying heights. In his more general, second model, uplift is still the basic process, but migration of plants is introduced and the mountains are connected in ranges. This model predicts that the maximum number of species will occur at the middle altitudes, while in the isolated mountain model the maximum occurs at the bottom. He verified both predictions through actual data (1981a).

Chapter 11

1. In its typically colorful Asian bazaar, Agakhanyantz listened to the music of the *zurna*—a long, straight horn, almost identical to the type used by the lamas in Tibet, used in folk music throughout Central Asia (Belaiev 1975). Maybe that is why that region is thought to have been the source of the alpenhorn, which has a curved outlet in Switzerland but a straight one in the eastern Alps, the Carpathians and Scandinavia.

Chapter 12

1. In his scientific work, Agakhanyantz was attracted to the study of plants adapting to extreme conditions: the Arctic, high altitudes, crags, loose gravel slopes and deserts. After years as a plant-hunting explorer, identifying and mapping the geographical distribution of mountain plants, in which the Pamir is exceptionally rich, with more than four thousand species, he applied this information to larger problems such as the natural ecological boundaries of different areas (1965–66) and the chronology of plant evolution (1981a). The western Pamir is deeply cut not only by large rivers but by smaller streams, producing a rugged terrain with adjacent slopes facing in different directions. Since the direction of a slope and its exposure to the sun affects its vegetation, the roughly horizontal boundaries between different types of mountain plants are highly irregular there, in what Agakhanyantz calls mosaic patterns (Agakhanyantz and Lopatin 1978). He also showed how the plateau plants of the eastern Pamir retreated into the ravines of the western Pamir during the ice ages, when the plateau was completely covered with ice but the deep valleys were not, and how when the ice receded these plants moved back to the east.

Chapter 13

1. Agakhanyantz (1975) also tells of Maria Pavlovna, a tiny Ukrainian woman in her sixties who also was attracted by Lake Sarez but with a sad ending. For five years, on a small pension, she had walked several hundred miles alone each summer in the Carpathian, Caucasus and Tien Shan Mountains and now in the Pamir.

When he first overtook her on a dusty road near Khorog, she resembled a huge rucksack on thin little legs. Her pack contained a sleeping bag, a Primus stove for making tea and her rations for the whole summer, consisting of a large jar into which she had poured molten lard over croutons (for which the good English word is *sippets*). After spending the night at the research station, she continued her trek and was last seen by a border guard as she climbed the gorge in the direction of Lake Sarez. She may have perished in a torrent across the trail, or at the landslide, where boulders are still falling, or perhaps in the steep-sided lake itself.

2. In his book *Sarez* (1989), Agakhanyantz gives a detailed geographic description and historical account of the subsequent scientific explorations, investigations and debates, of the powerful and colorful personalities involved, of the once-feared danger of the natural earth dam giving way, of its effect on local flora and of the lake's ecological and aesthetic uniqueness, which is being threatened by the current proposals of hydrologists from Tashkent for developing its water resource potential.

Chapter 14

1. Between the Imperial Russian and Soviet regimes, a curious reversal of colonial policies prevailed. The czarist Russians gave full respect to the Islamic religion and its taboos but placed their own people at the top of the various official organizations. The Soviets, apparently, did just the opposite. Nominally, they tolerated religion, and even the education of clerics, but drastically limited its freedom by allowing only a small percentage of working mosques and fostering secular education generally. Meanwhile, for the sake of form, they placed indigenous people in the top positions of each official organization. But resident Russians held the number two and many staff positions and were thus the real powers. Both systems seemed to work fairly smoothly but were not immune to jurisdictional problems such as the one that Agakhanyantz encountered (in 1978, we did, too, between Intourist and the Academy of Sciences). The winter months at Dushanbe were the time for Agakhanyantz to work up his field data. It was also there that he met and married his charming wife Lydia. The couple now lives in Minsk, where we were their guests. We also met Agakhanyantz on four other occasions in Moscow, the Caucasus and Central Asia.

2. From Agakhanyantz's letter of October 30, 1995: "*Exochodra albertii*, a shrub in the rose family, originated in China and spread widely throughout Central Asia as far as Iran. *Bunium persicum* [hawk-nut] belongs to the parsley family (*Umbelliferae*). *Prangos pabularia*, also in the parsley family, is a gigantic grassy plant, 2 meters or more in height, with soft, feathery and seemingly harmless leaves, which cause terrible burns on one's skin, not noticeably at first but becoming intensely painful in two or three hours. But when these leaves are cut and dried they lose their poisonous essence. They are then stored in heaps on the

flat roofs of the Asiatic houses and are used in winter as fodder for the flocks. It is a rough fodder, but in winter they are glad to have even that."

3. We met some American and Russian earthquake experts who came to Nurek because the dam, spanning a tectonic fault, has actually caused and intensified earthquakes because the lateral hydrostatic pressure pushes the sides of the fault apart.

Chapter 15

1. The words of one Kyrghyz love song are lyrical but with an oddly philosophical (Platonic?) anticlimax: "At the height of summer on a mountain slope, I remember how you plucked the most beautiful flowers for me. When dawn gilded the mountain tops, and you put out the stars, do you remember those pure, frank smiles, which you exchanged with me? I wanted to give you my whole self. I wanted to gather the flowers of life. But my darling was busy with thoughts, trying to discover the secrets of life" (Belaiev 1975, 10).

Chapter 16

1. From Ovtchinnikov's articles for which he had distinguished coauthors who did not share or witness the particular events that are the subjects of our chapters, we have extracted his narratives and ascribed them in our headings to him alone, while giving the full authorship of the source in our bibliography. While still a student at Moscow Technical University, Ovtchinnikov climbed many major peaks in the Caucasus and later in the Pamir, Tien Shan, France, North Wales, Scotland, Japan and the Himalayas. In 1965, in bad weather, he ascended the notorious Bonatti Route on the Petit Dru in Chamonix, after which he was elected a member of the elite French Groupe de Haute Montagne, from which he obtains the transliteration of his name. In the USSR, he received every formal award in mountaineering, including its highest rank as a distinguished master of sport. He is well known to hundreds of mountaineers throughout the world who, including ourselves, have attended the international mountaineering camps in the Pamir, of which he was the technical leader for many years. We later became closely acquainted with him and his family as guests at their Moscow apartment.

2. Slesser (1964b, 195) referred to Ovtchinnikov, a bit ruefully, as "that iron man of Soviet mountaineering," who ironically is a metallurgist specializing in the behavior of ferrous metals under stress. As Slesser wrote, when the British wanted a day's rest on the final approach to the Peak of Communism, "Tolya [Ovtchinnikov] declined to wait. His party would press on to the col and fill in the intervening day climbing the 6,878 meter peak, formerly Molotov. Talk about Lifeman gambits! Were they truly so fit that they could knock off a 22,000 foot peak in a spare day? Feeling for the moment rather humbled, I retired to my sleeping bag,

and left them to the chill wind of the morning" (188). The British were inconvenienced by the lack of bearers, and Noyce's dispatch to the *Daily Telegraph* was printed under the headline "Each His Own Porter!" When the Russian Gippenreiter mentioned being an honorary member of the Association of Sherpa Mountaineers, Slesser joyfully exclaimed, "Well then—this is the one who will carry our loads" (Ovtchinnikov 1966, 68). Because of the accident, the remaining climbers changed their planned route from the unclimbed south wall of the Peak of Communism to the established and somewhat easier "Georgian" route to the top. There McNaught-Davis lit a cigarette, which prompted Vladimir Malachov's memorable remark, "How is it, Mac, that you are so decadent yet climb so well?" (Slesser 1964a).

Chapter 17

1. At the end of our month in the Pamir in 1982, after all the climbers were back at the main Achik-Tash base camp, Ovtchinnikov, at age fifty-five, together with his assistant Oleg Galkin and Galkin's wife, who were also not youngsters, gave a demonstration of the "alpine style" of rapid, lightweight climbing. One day, after a 4-mile truck ride to the upper end of the valley, they crossed the Pass of the Travelers, walked up the Lenin glacier and climbed more than halfway up the Peak of Lenin before spending the night. The next morning they finished the ascent and walked all the way back to base camp in time for supper, thus achieving in two days what most successful climbers, carrying supplies to four intermediate camps, took more than a week to do. Two days later, it now being the latter part of August, the first snowfall submerged the previously verdant landscape of Edelweiss Valley, including foothills, flowers and butterflies, under a solid blanket of white, hinting that the time for us to go had come. Our small buses bounced over the roadless lower pastures where a few hungry wild dogs were now the only signs of life.

Chapter 18

1. Most mountains in Europe have ancient local names such as Eiger, Pilatus, Vesuvius, Parnassus and Olympus. Likewise, we find Ararat, Elbrus and Kazbek in the Caucasus; Kanchenjunga, Annapurna and Makalu in the Himalayas; and Aconcagua, Chimborazo and Huascaran in the Andes. However, following the age of exploration, it became customary in both the Old and New Worlds to name peaks for individuals such as Everest, Cook, Bolivar, Washington, Rainier and McKinley. This was also the custom in the USSR, but with changes reflecting political tides. With the fall of the USSR, further changes may occur but have so far been eclipsed by more pressing problems. It is touching, therefore, that the only 7,000-meter Soviet peak that retained its prerevolutionary name is the Peak of

Eugenia Korzhenevskaya. It was christened in 1910 simply as the Peak of Eugenia for the lovely young wife of explorer Nicholas Korzhenevsky, who discovered it, but in the 1930s her married surname was added to the name of the peak. Some Russian mountaineers affectionately call it Korzheneva. Eugenia died in 1969. Her older brother, Captain D. Topornin, was a cartographer for the Anglo-Russian Border Commission of 1895. We mention this because the Topornin family, which still resides in Tashkent, has been trying to locate a branch of its family that emigrated to America some years ago.

Chapter 19

1. The first ascent of the Peak of Communism was from the east, but its most popular approaches are now from the north, along the crest of the Peter the First range on a flat, elevated glacier called the Pamir Firn Plateau, which is about 10,000 meters (6 mi.) long and 1,000 meters wide, with an altitude of 6,000 meters (20,000 ft.), and nearly vertical walls 1,800 meters (6,000 ft.) high on both the north and the south (Ratzek 1975, 1980). A notch in its north wall, with a view of the Peak of Communism, is the outlet from the plateau through which the emergence of large blocks of ice is almost as regular as the Old Faithful geyser. After falling 3,000 feet, they shatter on a rocky ledge and bounce the remaining 3,000 feet in a shower of pulverized ice. Because of the bounce, this unique phenomenon is called the Trampoline glacier. The plateau was first reached from the south via the Belaev glacier in 1965 and from the north via the Fortambek glacier in 1967, both by expeditions led by Ovtchinnikov. An international mountaineering base camp at the Fortambek glacier, and a higher one farther east at the Moskvin glacier, give access to the plateau from the north. The "lady's room" of the Fortambek camp is directly below the Trampoline glacier, a rather unnerving location. While we were there, women were relatively few, partly because of a Soviet rule that, after the loss of the eight on the summit of Lenin Peak (Craig 1977), there should be no more than one per climbing group, which by coincidence seemed to apply to the foreigners too. An exception was a group of seven Yugoslav girls who successfully climbed the Peak of Communism. However, on their way back along the firn plateau, the last one fell into a crevasse unnoticed by the others. When they met a Soviet trainer who told them that one was missing, they counted themselves twice before admitting they were only six. They then walked back an hour and luckily found the seventh, whom they extracted from the crevasse unhurt but badly shaken. When they reached base camp, she hid in her tent so that she would not have to be taken to a hospital for observation.

Chapter 20

1. In Russian, the name of the peak is Pobeda, which is in the nominative case, but it often is called Pik Pobedy (Peak of Victory). Thus, it is improper in English

to use the word Pobedy by itself as its name, since that is in the genitive case. The usual approach is an ascent of the large South Inylchek glacier, which flows west along the northern foot of Pobeda, between it and Khan Tengri, the graceful, cone-shaped mountain of the Tengri Tag range. The name Tengri Tag is Turkic for "celestial mountains" and is therefore synonymous with the Chinese term Tien Shan, though the region described by the latter, in current usage, is geographically much larger. The region of Pobeda and the Tengri Tag forms the soaring center of the Tien Shan system, which stretches 1,700 kilometers (1,060 mi.) from the Timurid treasures of Samarkand (chap. 1) to the Buddhist murals of Turfan (chap. 3). The central Tien Shan, a remote place whose exploration has been relatively recent, is the site of interesting occurrences, both cultural (chap. 4) and physical (chap. 8). It also appears to be a locus of biological stress in the form of zoo-geographical discontinuities and anomalies whereby new species are in the process of formation (Avinoff 1912, 1922a).

Chapter 21

1. According to a legend of the Tibetans (S. Noel 1931), the drama of Mount Everest, which they call Chomolungma ("Mother Goddess"), began in the eighth century A.D. That was when the Indian tantric master Padma Sambhava walked across the formidable Himalayas, bringing Buddhist teachings to Tibet. He was challenged by Pombo Lama, the preeminent teacher of the local Bon religion, to a race for the summit of Chomolungma, which was also known then as Turquoise Peak. According to the legend, after the challenger began floating up the slope on a magical drum, Padma Sambhava overtook him by sailing to the top on a sunbeam and thereby became the founder of Tibetan Buddhism. It is said that at the summit he sat on a jeweled throne, which many twentieth-century Tibetans believed was the objective of the mountaineering expeditions. The actual climbing of Everest began in 1921 when George Leigh-Mallory and two companions reached the North Col at 6,990 meters (22,930 ft.). The following year Mallory was back, but he and a large party were swept away in an avalanche that killed seven porters. In 1924, he and Andrew Irvine disappeared in a cloud near the summit, which they may or may not have reached. That year Norton and Somervell climbed to 8,530 meters (28,000 ft.) without oxygen, pointing the way to the eventual oxygen-free ascents. These were the first three of ten British expeditions, which culminated in the first ascent of the 8,848-meter (29,028 ft.) peak by Edmund Hillary and Tenzing Norgay in 1953. Ten years later, five Americans and one Sherpa made the fourth, fifth and sixth ascents, which included the first ascent by the west ridge and the first traverse of the peak. On an expedition of fifteen Japanese women in 1975, Mrs. J. Tabei made the first ascent by a woman. That year eight Tibetans and one Chinese, including a Tibetan woman named Phanthog, made the seventeenth ascent of the mountain. In 1978, the Tiroleans Peter Habeler and Reinhold

Messner made the first ascent without oxygen. Three years later, Messner did the same entirely alone, supported only by the Canadian Nena Holguin, who remained at base camp. After the 1982 expedition, when we talked with Ovtchinnikov in the Pamir, he told us how the use of oxygen on Everest, even in small quantities, had helped prevent frostbite. Leigh-Mallory (1923) also referred to its "warming" effect, which otherwise is rarely mentioned in the literature.

Bibliography

Titles of items published in Russian are shown in English only.

Agakhanyantz, O. E. 1965–66. *Physical Geography of the Pamir.* 2 vols. Dushanbe: Acad. Sci. Tajik SSR.

Agakhanyantz, O. E. 1975. *On the Pamir.* Moscow: Mysl. German translation, 1980. Leipzig: Brockhaus.

Agakhanyantz [Agachanjanc], O. E. 1979. "Besonderheiten in der Natur der ariden Gebirge der UdSSR." *Petermanns Geographische Mitteilungen* 2:73–77.

Agakhanyantz [Agachanjanc], O. E. 1980. "Die geographischen Ursachen fur die Lückenhaftigkeit der Flora in den Gebirgen Mittelasiens." *Petermanns Geographische Mitteilungen* 1:47–52.

Agakhanyantz, O. E. 1981a. *Arid Mountains of USSR.* Moscow: Mysl.

Agakhanyantz, O. E. 1981b. "Problems of Lake Sarez." *Priroda* (Acad. Sci. USSR), 7:41–47.

Agakhanyantz, O. E. 1986. *Botanical Geography of The USSR.* Minsk: Vysheyshaya Shkola.

Agakhanyantz, O. E. 1987. *One Pamir Year: The Year of the Snake.* Moscow: Mysl.

Agakhanyantz [Agachanjanc], O. E. 1988. "Wasserbilanz und wasserwirtschaftliche Probleme der mittleren Region der UdSSR (Mittelasiens und Westsibirien). "*Petermanns Geographische Mitteilungen* 2, no. 132:109–15.

Agakhanyantz, O. E. 1989. *Sarez.* Leningrad: Gidrometeoizdat.

Agakhanyantz [Agachanjanz], O. E. 1994. In *Ökologie der Erde—Band 3: Spezielle Ökologie der Gemassigten und Arktischen Zonen Euro-Nordasiens.* edited by H. Walter, W. Breckle and O. Agachanjanz. Stuttgart: G. Fischer.

Agakhanyantz, O. E., et al. 1981. "Ancient Glaciation of the Pamir." *Seria Geographicheskaya* (Acad. Sci. USSR), 4:123–34.

Agakhanyantz, O. E., and I. K. Lopatin. 1978. "Main Characteristics of the Ecosystems of the Pamirs, USSR." *Arctic and Alpine Research* 10:397–407.

Agakhanyantz, O. E., and K. Y. Yusufbekov. 1975. *Vegetation of Pamir and an Experiment on Its Reconstruction.* Dushanbe: Donish.

Alberts, R. C. 1986. *Pitt: The Story of the University of Pittsburgh, 1787–1987.* Pittsburgh: University of Pittsburgh Press.

Antipina, K. I. 1977. *Folk Art of the Kyrghyz.* Frunze: Kyrghyzstan.

Avinoff [Avinov], A. N. 1910a. "Contributions to the Fauna of *Rhopalocera* of the East Pamir." *Horae Societatis Entomologicae Rossicae* 39:225–46.

Avinoff [Avinov], A. N. 1910b. "New Forms of *Rhopalocera* from Ferghana." *Horae Societatis Entomologicae Rossicae* 39:247–50.

Avinoff [Avinov], A. 1912. "Some New Forms of the Genus *Parnassius* Latr." *Horae Societatis Entomologicae Rossicae* 40:1–21.

Avinoff [Avinov], A. N. 1913. "Zoogeographical Subdivision of Palearctic Regions of British India Based on Distribution and Grouping of *Rhopalocera.* *Bulletin of The Imperial Russian Geographical Society* 49:1–41.

Avinoff, A. 1916. "Some New Forms of *Parnassius.*" *Trans. Ent. Soc. London* 1915:351–60.

Avinoff, A. 1920. "Notice sur la Collection de Lepidoptères formée par A. Avinoff." *Études de Lépidoptérologie Comparée* 17:71–84.

Avinoff, A. 1922a. "Considerations sur les Parnassiens d'Asie Centrale." *Études de Lépidoptérologie Comparée* 19:41–70.

Avinoff, A. 1922b. "Tibetan Drawings." *Century* 103:371–76.

Avinoff, A. 1928. "A Variable Palearctic Satyrid." *Fourth International Congress of Entomology* (Ithaca) 2:290–93.

Avinoff, A. 1931. "The Roof of the World." *Pittsburgh Record* 5, no. 4:39–47.

Avinoff, A. 1936. "In Honor of A. Semenov Tian-Shansky." *Ann. Ent. Soc. Am.* 29:557–60.

Avinoff, A. 1937. "An Elusive Butterfly [*Parnassius Przewalskii* Alph.]" *Carnegie Magazine* 11:103–6.

Avinoff, A., and W. R. Sweadner. 1951. "The *Karanasa* Butterflies: A Study in Evolution." *Annals of The Carnegie Museum* 32:1–251.

Azatian, A. A., et al. 1969. *History of The Discovery and Exploration of Soviet Asia.* Moscow: Mysl.

Baker, I. 1993. In Dunham and Baker 1993. Baker wrote chapters 6 through 9.

Baume, L. C. 1978. *Sivalaya: Explorations of the 8,000-meter Peaks of the Himalayas.* Seattle: Mountaineers.

Belaiev, V. M. 1975. *Central Asian Music.* Middletown, Conn.: Wesleyan University Press.

Bell, C. 1924. *Tibet Past and Present.* Oxford: Clarendon.

Bell, C. 1928. *People of Tibet.* Oxford: Clarendon.

Bernbaum, E. 1980. *The Way to Shambala.* Garden City: Anchor.

Bernbaum, E. 1988. "Sacred Mountains." *Parabola* 13:12–18.

Birnbaum, M. 1946. *Jacovleff and Other Artists*. New York: Paul A. Struck.

Bishop, B. C. 1962. "Wintering in the High Himalayas." *National Geographic* 122:503–47.

Bishop, B. C. 1978. "Changing Geoecology of Karnali Zone, W. Nepal Himalaya." *Arctic and Alpine Research* 10:531–43.

Bishop, I. B. 1894. *Among the Tibetans*. New York: F. H. Revell.

Bishop, L. M., and B. C. Bishop. 1971. "Karnali, Roadless World of Western Nepal." *National Geographic* 140:656–90.

Bonvalot, G. 1888–89. *Du Caucase aux Indes a Travers le Pamir*. 2 vols. Paris: E. Plon, Nourrit.

Bonvalot, G. 1889. *Through the Heart of Asia*. 2 vols. London: Chapman and Hall.

Bourliere, F. 1964. *The Land and Wildlife of Eurasia*. New York: Time.

Brooke, R. 1943. *The Collected Poems of Rupert Brooke*. New York: Dodd, Mead.

Bruce, C. G. 1923. *The Assault on Mount Everest, 1922*. New York: Longmans, Green.

Bryk, F. 1935. "*Parnassiinae*." *Das Tierreich* 64:1–788. Berlin: W. deGruyter.

Bychkova, E. A., ed. 1988. *Paths into an Enigmatic World*. Alma Ata: Kazakhstan.

Cammann, S. 1951. *Trade through the Himalayas*. Westport, Conn.: Greenwood.

Clark, J. 1956. *Hunza: Lost Kingdom of the Himalayas*. New York: Funk and Wagnalls.

Clench, H. K., and Nicholas Shoumatoff. 1956. "Lepidoptera *Rhopalocera* (Insects) from Afghanistan: Third Danish Expedition to Central Asia (Zoological Results 21)." *Vidensk. Medd. fra Dansk naturh. Foren.* 118:141–92.

Coales, O. 1919. "Eastern Tibet." *Geographical Journal* 53:228–52.

Craig, R. W. 1977. *Storm and Sorrow in the High Pamirs*. Seattle: Mountaineers.

Crosby, O. T. 1905. *Tibet and Turkestan*. New York: G. P. Putnam.

Dainelli, G. 1934. *Buddhists and Glaciers of Western Tibet*. New York: E. P. Dutton.

Dalai Lama XIV. 1984. *Kindness, Clarity and Insight*. Ithaca: Snow Lion.

Dalai Lama XIV. 1990. *Freedom in Exile: The Autobiography of His Holiness the Dalai Lama of Tibet*. London: Hodder and Stoughton.

Das, S. C. 1902. *Journey to Lhasa and Central Tibet*. London: J. Murray.

David-Neel, A. 1927. *Voyage d'Une Parisienne à Lhasa*. Paris: Plon.

Director, L. B. 1990. *High Mountain Passes*. Moscow: Profizdat.

DiRusso, L., and J. M. Gilbert. 1992. "Heinrich Harrer: Medalist '92, Explorer/Photographer." *Explorers Journal* 70:29.

Dolgushin, L. D., and G. B. Osipova. 1989. *Glaciers*. Moscow: Mysl.

Dorofeev, I. G. 1976. *On Heights above the Clouds*. Moscow: Mysl.

Douglas, W. O. 1952. *Beyond the High Himalayas.* Garden City: Doubleday.

Dunham, C., and I. Baker. 1993. *Tibet: Reflections from the Wheel of Life.* New York: Abbeville.

Faegre, T. 1979. *Tents: Architecture of the Nomads.* Garden City: Anchor.

Fedchenko, A. P. 1875. *Journey in Turkestan.* Vol. 1, *In the Kokan Khanate.* St. Petersburg: Stasyulevich.

Fedchencko, A. P. 1950. *Journeys in Turkestan.* Moscow: Geographicheskaya Literatura.

Fedchencko, B. A. 1912–15. *Flora of Asiatic Russia.* St. Petersburg: Y. N. Erlich.

Field, W. O., ed. 1975. *Mountain Glaciers of the Northern Hemisphere.* 3 vols. Hanover N.H.: Army Corps of Engineers.

Fitzgerald, E. 1859. *The Rubaiyat of Omar Kayyam.* London: N.P. Pamphlet.

Flint, V. E., et al. 1968. *Birds of the USSR.* Moscow: Mysl.

Garner, W. 1986. "High Road to 'Victory.'" *National Geographic* 170:256–71.

Gavrilyuk, A., and V. Yaroshenko. 1987. *Pamir.* Moscow: Planeta.

George, G. S. 1974. *Soviet Deserts and Mountains.* Amsterdam: Time-Life.

Geyer, G. A. 1994. *Waiting for Winter to End: Extraordinary Journey through Soviet Central Asia.* Washington, D.C.: Brassey's.

Golstein, M., and C. Beall. 1989. "The Remote World of Tibet's Nomads." *National Geographic* 1989:752–82.

Govinda, Lama A. 1970. *The Way of the White Cloud.* Boulder: Shambala.

Grousset, R. 1970. *The Empire of the Steppes.* New Brunswick: Rutgers University Press.

Gvozdetsky, N. A., et al. 1964. *Russian Geographical Exploration of Caucasus and Central Asia.* Moscow: Nauka.

Gvozdetsky, N. A., and Y. N. Golubnikov. 1987. *Mountains.* Moscow: Mysl.

Haardt, G. M. 1931. "The Trans-Asiatic Expedition Starts." *National Geographic* 59:776–82.

Hambly, G., ed. 1969. *Central Asia.* New York: Delacorte.

Harrer, H. 1954. *Seven Years in Tibet.* New York: E. P. Dutton.

Harrer, H. 1965. *The White Spider.* London: Rupert Hart-Davis.

Harrer, H. 1984. *Return to Tibet.* London: Weidenfeld and Nicolson.

Harrer, H. 1992. *Lost Lhasa.* New York: H. N. Abrams.

Hedin, S. 1899. *In the Heart of Asia.* 2 vols. St. Petersburg: A. F. Devrien.

Hedin, S. 1910a. *Trans-Himalaya.* 3 vols. London: Macmillan.

Hedin, S. 1910b. *Overland to India.* 2 vols. London: Macmillan.

Heeren, A. H. L. 1846. *Asiatic Nations: Scythians, Indians.* London: H. G. Bohn.

Hellman, G. T. 1948. "Profile of A. Avinoff." *New Yorker,* August 21, 32–47.

Herzog, M., and M. Ichac. 1951. *Regards vers L'Annapurna.* Paris: Arthaud.

Higgins, L. G. 1941. "Palearctic *Melitaea* (*Lep. Rhopalocera*)." *Trans. Ent. Soc. London* 91:175–365.

Hilton, J. 1933. *Lost Horizon.* New York: Morrow.

Hofmann, M. 1965. *Yesterday is Tomorrow.* New York: Crown.

Howard-Bury, C. K. 1922. *Mount Everest: The Reconnaissance, 1921.* New York: Longmans, Green.

Howard-Bury, C. K. 1990. *Mountains of Heaven.* London: Hodder and Stoughton.

Huc, M. 1857. *Travels in Tartary, Thibet and China.* London: National Illustrated Library. Includes Lhasa.

Hunt, J. 1978. *Life is Meeting.* London: Hodder and Stoughton.

Iacovleff, A. 1934. *Dessins et Paintures de l'Expedition Citroën Centre-Asia.* Paris: J. Meynal.

Iacovleff, A. 1936. "Faces and Fashions of Asia's Changeless Tribes." *National Geographic* 69:1–16.

Jouguet, P. 1926. *L'Imperialisme Macedonien et L'Hellenisation de L'Orient.* Paris: La Renaissance du Livre.

Kalinin, G. 1983. *Fortambek and Its Summits.* Tashkent: Uzbekistan. Includes Pamir.

Kalinin, G. 1984. "Vladimir Ratzek: His Summits and Routes." In Ratzek 1984.

Keller, B. 1988. "Developers Turn Aral Sea into a Catastrophe." *New York Times,* December 20, sec. C, 1, 6.

Korzhenevsky, N. L. 1979. *Geomorphology and Glaciation of The Pamir-Alai.* Tashkent: Fan.

Kozlov, P. K. 1905. *Mongolia and Kam, 1899–1901.* 2 vols. St. Petersburg: Gerold.

Krader, L. 1971. *Peoples of Central Asia.* Bloomington: Indiana University Press.

Krylenko, N. B. 1929. *On the Unexplored Pamir.* Moscow: Gosudarstvennoe Izdatelstvo.

Lamb, H. 1927. *Genghis Khan: Emperor of All Men.* New York: R. M. McBride.

Lamb, H. 1928. *Tamerlane: The Earth Shaker.* New York: R. M. McBride.

Leigh-Mallory, G. H. 1923. "The First Attempt." In Bruce 1923.

Lemercier-Quelquejay, C. 1969. "The Kazakhs and the Kirghiz." In Hambly (1969).

Lewis, V. E. 1953. *An Exhibition of Andrey Avinoff.* Pittsburgh: Carnegie Institute, Department of Fine Arts.

Liddell-Hart, B. H. 1963. "Mongol Campaigns." Chicago: *Encyclopedia Britannica,* 15:706–8.

Mallory. See Leigh-Mallory.

Mani, M. S. 1968. *Ecology and Biogeography of High Altitude Insects.* The Hague: W. Junk.

Maillart, E. K. 1934. *Turkestan Solo.* New York: G. P. Putnam.

Maraini, F. 1964. *Where Four Worlds Meet: Hindu Kush.* London: H. Hamilton.

Michaud, R., and S. Michaud. 1977. *Caravans to Tartary.* New York: Viking.

Michaud, R., and S. Michaud. 1980. *Afghanistan: Paradise Lost.* New York: Vendome.

Michaud, S., and R. Michaud. 1975. "Trek to Lofty Hunza and Beyond." *National Geographic* 148:644–70.

Miller, L. 1976. *On Top of the World: Five Women Explorers of Tibet.* New York: Paddington.

Mirsky, J. 1977. *Sir Aurel Stein.* Chicago: University of Chicago Press.

Molnar, P. 1986. "Geologic History and Structure of the Himalaya." *American Scientist* 74:144–54.

Molnar, P. 1989. "Geological Evolution of the Tibetan Plateau." *American Scientist* 77:350–60.

Molnar, P., et al. 1987. "Geologic Evolution of Northern Tibet." *Science* 235:299–304.

Murray, E. 1936. "With the Nomads of Central Asia." *National Geographic* 69:1–57.

Neate, W. R. 1978. *Mountaineering and Its Literature.* Seattle: The Mountaineers.

Nicolson, N. 1975. *The Himalayas.* Amsterdam: Time-Life.

Noel, J. 1928. *The Story of Everest.* Boston: Little, Brown.

Noel, S. 1931. *The Magic Bird of Chomo-Lungma.* Garden City: Doubleday, Doran. Illustrated by A. Avinoff.

Noyce, W. 1962. *To the Unknown Mountain.* London: Heinemann.

Olsufiev, A. A., and V. P. Panaiev. 1899. *On the Trans-Caspian Military Railroad.* St. Petersburg: M. O. Wolf.

Olufsen, O. 1904. *Through the Unknown Pamirs: The Second Danish Expedition to Central Asia, 1898–99.* London: Heinemann.

Olufsen, O. 1920. *The Second Danish Pamir Expedition: Studies of the Vegetation.* Copenhagen: Gyldendalske.

Ossendowski, F. 1922. *Beasts, Men and Gods.* New York: E. P. Dutton.

Ovtchinnikov, A. G. 1966. "Flags of Two Countries above the Pamir." In *Pobezhdennye Vershiny,* by E. B. Gippenreiter and A. G. Ovtchinnikov. 1961–64:58–84. Moscow: Mysl.

Ovtchinnikov, A. G. 1967. "Expedition Sovietique 1966 au Pamir." *La Montagne et Alpinisme* 5:173–77.

Ovtchinnikov, A. G. 1972a. "The Peak of Communism," by K. Kuzmin and A. G. Ovtchinnikov. *Pobezhdennye Vershiny* 1968–69:5–22. Moscow: Mysl.

Ovtchinnikov, A. G. 1972b. In *The Summit Named for Lenin,* edited by A. Polyakov and A. G. Ovtchinnikov. *Pobezhdennye Vershiny* 1968–69:242–60. Moscow: Mysl.

Ovtchinnikov, A. G. 1984. "Realized Dreams." In *Everest 1982,* edited by P. P. Zakharov. Moscow: Fizkultura i Sport.

Ovtchinnikov, A. G., and B. Garf. 1973. "La Traversée du Pic Pobeda." *La Montagne et Alpinisme* 3:104–7.

Pollis, M. 1939. *Peaks and Lamas.* London: Longmans, Green.

Polo, M. 1926. *Travels of Marco Polo.* New York: Boni and Liveright.

Polunin, O., and A. Stainton. 1984. *Flowers of the Himalaya.* Delhi: Oxford University Press.

Pratt, A. E. 1892. *The Snows of Tibet.* London: Longmans, Green.

Ratzek, V. I. 1972. *On the Roads of Central Asia.* Tashkent: Uzbekistan.

Ratzek, V. I. 1975. *The Five Highest Summits of The USSR.* Tashkent: Uzbekistan.

Ratzek, V. I. 1976. "Firlike snow forms on the Tengri Tag." *Pobezhdennye Vershiny* 1973–74:59–64. Moscow: Mysl.

Ratzek, V. I. 1977. *N. L. Korzhenevsky.* Tashkent: Fan.

Ratzek, V. I. 1980. *The Icy Heart of the Pamir.* Tashkent: Uzbekistan.

Ratzek, V. I. 1984. *Off the Beaten Path.* Tashkent: Uzbekistan.

Rayfield, D. 1976. *The Dream of Lhasa.* London: Elek.

Rickmers, W. R., et al. 1929. *The Alai-Pamir Expedition, 1928.* Berlin: K. Siegismund.

Rogers, R., and J. Harlin. 1991. "Heinrich Harrer." *Summit* 37, no. 3:48–63.

Rowell, G. 1977. *In the Throne Room of the Mountain Gods.* San Francisco: Sierra Club.

Royal Geographical Society. 1987. *The Mountains of Central Asia.* London: Macmillan.

Sadmuradov, K. M., and K. V. Stanyukovich. 1982. *Tajikistan: Nature and Natural Resources.* Dushanbe: Donish.

Schaller, G. B. 1977. *Mountain Monarchs: Wild Sheep and Goats of the Himalaya.* Chicago: University of Chicago Press.

Schaller, G. B. 1980. *Stones of Silence.* New York: Viking.

Schulteis, R. 1991. "The Tiger and the Buddha." *Summit* 37, no. 3:38–46.

Schultz, A. 1916. *Landeskundliche Forschungen im Pamir.* Hamburg: L. Friederichsen.

Schuyler, E. 1876. *Turkistan.* 2 vols. New York: Scribner, Armstrong.

Shipton, D. 1950. *The Antique Land.* London: Hodder and Stoughton.

Shipton, E. 1950. *Mountains of Tartary.* London: Hodder and Stoughton.

Shoumatoff, Nicholas. 1956. In Clench and Shoumatoff 1956.

Shoumatoff, Nicholas. 1979. "Caucasus Mountain Expedition." *Explorers Journal* 57:52–57. Includes Central Asia.

Shoumatoff, Nicholas. 1995. "Andrey Avinoff Remembered." *Carnegie Magazine* 62, no. 8 (March & April):24–29.

Shroder, J. F. 1989. "Hazards of the Himalaya." *American Scientist* 77:564–73.

Slesser, M. 1964a. "Peak of Communism." Swiss Foundation for Alpine Research: *Mountain World* 1962/63:133–43. London: Allen and Unwin.

Slesser, M. 1964b. *Red Peak*. New York: Coward-McCann.

Snellgrove, D. L., and H. Richardson. 1968. *A Cultural History of Tibet*. London: Weidenfeld and Nicolson.

Snellgrove, D. L., and T. Skorupski. 1977. *The Cultural Heritage of Ladakh*. 2 vols. Boulder: Prajna.

Stanyukovich, K. V., et al. 1968. *Atlas of the Tajik SSR*. Dushanbe: Academy of Sciences of the Tajik SSR.

Starrett, R. M. 1986. "Snow Leopards on Pik Pobedy." *American Alpine Journal* 28:21–26.

Stein, M. A. 1902. "A Journey of Geographical and Archaeological Exploration in Chinese Turkestan." *Geographical Journal* 20:575–610.

Stein, M. A. 1912. *Ruins of Desert Cathay*. 3 vols. New York: Benjamin Blom.

Suslov, S. F. 1961. *Physical Geography of Asiatic Russia*. San Francisco: W. H. Freeman.

Swan, L. W. 1961. "The Ecology of the High Himalayas." *Scientific American* 205:68–89.

Sweadner, W. R. 1942. "Three Miles Up: The Avinoff Collection of Butterflies from Central Asia." *Carnegie Magazine* 16:163–67.

Tagore, R. 1916. *Sadhana: The Realization of Life*. New York: Macmillan.

Thubron, C. 1994. *The Lost Heart of Asia*. New York: HarperCollins.

Tolstoy, I. 1946. "Across Tibet from India to China." *National Geographic* 90:169–222.

Trevor, J. C. 1963. "Afghanistan: The People." Chicago: *Encyclopedia Brittanica*, 1:237–38.

Tsibikoff, G. T. 1903. "Lhasa and Central Tibet." *Smithsonian Report* 47:727–46.

Tucci, G., and E. Ghersi. 1936. *Shrines of a Thousand Buddhas*. New York: R. M. McBride.

Valla, F., and J-P. Zuanon. 1976. *Pamir: Escalade d'un 7,000 au Pays des Kirghizes*. Domène: Zogirep.

Vanis, E. 1970. "Austrian Pamir Expedition to Pik Lenin." Swiss Foundation for Alpine Research: *Mountain World* 69:86–93. London: Allen and Unwin.

Verity, R. 1905–11. *Rhopalocera Palearctica*. Florence: R. Verity.

Vitkovich, V. 1967. "When the Ground is Rocking." *Sputnik* 67, no. 6:16–27. Deals with the Tashkent earthquake.

Von Le Coq, A. 1929. *Buried Treasures of Chinese Turkestan*. New York: Longmans, Green.

Waddell, L. A. 1905. *Lhasa and Its Mysteries*. London: Methuen.

Warren, B. C. S. 1936. *The Genus Erebia [Rhopalocera]*. London: British Museum of Natural History.

Wheeler, G. E. 1963. "Turks or Turkic Peoples." Chicago: *Encyclopaedia Britannica*, 22:622–624.

Wheeler, G. E. 1964. *The Modern History of Soviet Central Asia.* London: Weidenfeld and Nicolson.

Whitney, I. 1935. "A. Iacovleff: New Art Teacher at the Museum." *Sunday Herald* (Boston), April 7.

Wilby, S. 1987. "Nomads' Land: A Journey Through Tibet." *National Geographic* 172:764–85.

Williams, M. O. 1931. "The Citroën-Haardt Expedition Reaches Kashmir." *National Geographic* 60:387–444.

Williams, M. O. 1932a. "First over the Roof of the World by Motor." *National Geographic* 61:321–63.

Williams, M. O. 1932b. "From the Mediterranean to the Yellow Sea by Motor." *National Geographic* 62:513–80.

Wilson, A. 1875. *The Abode of Snow.* London: Blackwood.

Workman, F. B., and W. H. Workman. 1917. *Two Summers in the Ice-Wilds of Eastern Karakoram.* New York: E. P. Dutton.

Younghusband, F. 1896. *The Heart of a Continent.* London: J. Murray.

Younghusband, F. 1905. "Geographical Results of the Tibetan Mission." *Geographical Journal* 25:265–77.

Younghusband, F. 1909. *Kashmir.* London: A. and C. Black.

Younghusband, F. 1926. *The Epic of Mount Everest.* London: Arnold.

Younghusband, F. 1936. *Everest: The Challenge.* London: Nelson.

Yusufbekov, K. Y., and A. A. Konnov, eds. 1973. *Pamir.* Dushanbe: Donish.

Index